YANNIS RITSOS

POEMS

SELECTED BOOKS

YANNIS RITSOS

POEMS

SELECTED BOOKS

Translated by Manolis
Edited by Apryl Leaf

libros libertad

First published by:
Libros Libertad Publishing Ltd.
PO Box 45089
12851 16th Avenue, Surrey BC V4A 9L1
Ph. 604-838-8796
Fax 604-536-6819
www.libroslibertad.ca

Library and Archives Canada Cataloguing in Publication

Ritsos, Giannes, 1909-1990

    Yannis Ritsos, poems : selected books / Yannis Ritsos ;
translated by Manolis ; edited by Apryl Leaf.

Includes bibliographical references and index.
ISBN 978-1-926763-07-1

    1. Ritsos, Giannes, 1909-1990--Translations into English.

I. Manolis, 1947- II. Title.

PA5629.I7A294 2010   889'.132   C2010-904771-0

Design and layout by Susan Mellor
Printed in Canada by Printorium Bookworks

ACKNOWLEDGEMENTS

I would like to express my deepest appreciation to Katya Lembesis of Kedros Editions, Athens Greece, who introduced me to Ery Ritsos, the poet's daughter, who granted me her permission for this effort. I extend my deepest thanks and appreciation to Ery, and I hope my humble effort is accurate, precise and a true reflection on the greatness of her father's works.

My sincere appreciation and gratitude is extended to Apryl Leaf for her dedication and untiring effort in editing and making this book as pleasant to the eye as it is to the mind.

I would also like to express my sincere gratitude and appreciation to the scholars who took time out of their very busy schedule to read through this enormous tome of poetry and enrich it with their positive and insightful comments. They are:

Cathi Shaw, PhD., Communications Instructor,
      Okanagan College, and poet

John Wall Barger, PhD., Lecturer at Saint Mary's University, Halifax,
      Nova Scotia, and poet

Ilya Tourtidis, M. Ed., University of Victoria, retired school
      instructor, and poet.

– Manolis

PRAISE FOR THIS BOOK

One can certainly appreciate Ritso's poetry in terms of the social and cultural referents that weave in and out of his work. I doubt very much if Ritsos believed even for an instant that the archaic struggle of man against the forces that subdue him would end in freedom from illusory attachments and entanglements.

On the contrary, what he skillfully presents in his work are mediating symbols, incarnating out of the depths of his awareness–diligently crafting a literary isthmus to the heart of his personal truth. His is the poetry of waiting, and yearning, and finally projecting the heroic Eros of the Greek psyche: the dominant imperative of an unfettered existence at the zero point of man's subjectivity. Such an assertion I'm sure issued out of the odyssey of his life, a life sustained not only by the ancestral hiss of myth and political rationalism, but also by the differentiating activity of consciousness which works, collectively at least, in favour of the soul that still must survive its harness.

Indeed, his poems lack the compliance of subjugation and the often wounded indulgence of a narcissistic persona. What they do exhibit however, is the very authentic human endeavour of striving, reaching... imagining, and somehow, against all odds, assimilating the dissonance of an encountered self in the midst of upheaval through what he had to intuit as a metaphoric fall from grace despite his religious denouncements. This desire for a unitary reality is the value I see, feel, and admire in his work.

Ritsos was a poet who lived in chaotic but exciting times, and like Odysseus, was fated by the gods to take the scenic way home. I am awed by the integrating expanse of his gaze and by the process of his mind that was able to distinguish between reality and its representation... and also... also by the sense-memory in things he projected–things lost–but still things yet to be gained. He was a poet who survived the enchantment of rival impulses, as well as a poet who celebrated the sacred return of the imagination out of the deep ocean that contained him.

– Ilya Tourtidis, M. Ed., University of Victoria,
retired school instructor, and poet

In this amazing collection, Manolis introduces us to the life work of Greek poet, Yannis Ritsos. This translated collection paints the poetry of a man's life and as such it captures the great magnitude of that life lived. From the sea-soaked childhood through the impatient adventures of a naïve summer youth and shattered innocence. The reader can follow the poet, Ritsos, through the heartache of life to experience the shifting of his voice into a maturity that is cynical and painful but edged with truth. And all is enveloped in the metaphor of nature, upon the backdrop of a Greece, painted in white and pastel and gold, tastes and textures exotic and foreign but beautiful and real.

Ritsos writes of seasons shifting to reflect a coming darkness. The bitter desolation that is war. Hard, sharp, hostile words that paint a time too painful to remember and yet which must be written.

Ritsos writes about life and in this collection, spanning so many years, the reader is gifted with the true sense of a life experienced. One is able to see a poet play with form and style to reflect an abundance of shifting moods and experiences, each poem telling its own story but also echoing the larger story of life. Each poem is a snapshot of a place in time, of a moment in a life, of a story being told. The reader is invited to browse through a truly amazing anthology of observations, both personal and public. This collection reflects a depth and vastness that must be savoured and digested, revisited and reviewed.

– Cathi Shaw, PhD., Communications Instructor,
Okanagan College, and poet

We should be grateful to Manolis for hauling this horn o' plenty to Canada. He doggedly traces the manifold styles and voices of the remarkable Ritsos, who is at times like Rilke, in his sweeping metaphors and comprehension of the human heart; at times Lorca, with his visionary surrealism: hand mirrors, shadows, statues descending their plinths; and at times Kay Ryan, with lyrics so fragile that they might crumble if touched. Yet Ritsos is always Ritsos. He suffered much personal and public violence, in the autocratic Greece of the 20th century, but his poems resist judgment. They flower with the force of humility and pathos. We readers are his brothers and children and comrades, under the hot sun which is and is not a god, beside the "endless sea." Love trumps Death. Every object is awake. "Every hour is our hour."

– John Wall Barger, PhD., Lecturer at Saint Mary's
University, Halifax, Nova Scotia, and poet

CONTENTS

FOREWORD

Yannis Ritsos, quite literally came into my life like a song. In 1958, at home in Greece, at the age of eleven, I heard for the first time the musical composition *Epitaphios*, which combined poetic verses of Ritsos set to music by the internationally celebrated composer, Mikis Theodorakis. Even as a young man, I was moved in an unprecedented way by the songs. Importantly, these songs were a soothing caress over our young and rebellious souls at a time when the Cold War was causing deep divisions between the communist east and capitalist west, and the recent civil war in Greece had seen our country reduced to ruins.

It may be accurately stated that the effects of the civil war would define the continuous dichotomy influencing the lives of Greek citizens until the middle of the nineteen-eighties, and in Yannis Ritsos' life, became emblematic of this struggle.

Throughout our high school years, Ritsos remained prominent, and we felt him walking next to us with every step we took. The new wave of socialism and resistance against outside interests influenced the political life of Greeks, and became the fertile ground for a voice such as Ritsos' to reach and establish itself in our psyche. This growing force brought us to the small secluded bars called '*bouats*' where with a drink of a vermouth at the cost of about 60 cents, we listened to music most Greeks weren't even aware of, and where we recited verses of contemporary poets.

One such poet was our comrade, Yannis Ritsos, whose work resonated with our intense passion for our motherland and also in our veracity and strong-willed quest to find justice for all Greeks. In the mid nineteen-sixties, I identified ever more closely with this poet who was imprisoned, along with thousands of other Greeks branded enemies of the state, to various prison camps in the Greek islands or mainland Greece, like my father, who was imprisoned for one year for no apparent reason; my unfortunate father's crime was likely that he listened to the music of Mikis Theodorakis and to the news from a German radio station, the famous *Dautche Welle*, where all Greeks found refuge and a sense of hope that the world was listening to the Greek cries for justice and freedom.

Thus I learned what it meant to live under censorship and what it meant to be under the iron fist of a dictatorship. In those days Ritsos' poem *Romiosini*, which was set in music by the same Mikis Theodorakis, and banned by the military, truly became our secret national anthem that we all sang on our walks, at our gatherings and our parties. Although the danger of an unfriendly ear hearing us was always around, in a small gesture of our resistance, we took part in the rebirth of freedom for our country in her darker hours.

Even while in the army, performing my duty in the country I was born to, we used to sing all these forbidden songs, though in a low voice or at safe distance from the ears of the officers who couldn't reconcile with our fervour for new things, freedom: the officers who couldn't understand our yearning for change and a new direction toward a democratically-elected government, our vision for a new and free Greece. Years later in the nineteen-seventies, when Ritsos lived in a house in Saint Nikolaos, I was also dwelling in Petroupolis, a suburb of Athens just a kilometre away from the poet's neighbourhood where I walked and roamed. Should I have known his address, it's likely I would have made an effort to go and meet him in person. Since discovering how closely situated we were, I regret this meeting didn't happen.

The 15 books selected for this edition represent a broad view of the poet's career from the mid nineteen-thirties to the nineteen-eighties, and most of them appear for the first time ever in a North America translation. While *Moonlight Sonata*, *Romiosini* and *Helen*, have been published in translation a number of times, we believe that the more intimate treatment we give to these books makes them stand apart from other translations, as though unfolding another petal of the same rose, while having more of the original fragrance.

According to several sources, Ritsos wrote all his life, from as early as eight years old to his eighties. Reportedly, it wasn't uncommon for Ritsos to write 15 to 20 poems in one sitting, and before his death, he was able to enjoy seeing the majority of his work published. We had at our disposal, a total of 46 books (in Greek) written by Yannis Ritsos from his first published book *Tractor*, to the 14th edition of *Yannis Ritsos - Poems XIV*, published by Kedros in 2007. Out of these 46 volumes we selected 15 books for this translation. The books included in this translation are whole instead of selected poems from each and that is because first we had only a certain number of his books available and second it was awkward to separate them to satisfaction. These 15 books range from his earliest publications up to some of his last, since this presents the reader with a broad view as to who this significant poet is and how his poems reflect a contemporary style as much as they did in Greece more than 50 years ago.

In surveying the materials chosen, we witness that a certain transformation occurs from his early days when he was just the unknown defender of a cause, up to the period during his midlife when he finds a variety of admirers from around the world. Here we discover a mature and didactic man reflected in his poems, more laconic and precise, more careful with his words: they have become more and more precious as he uses them with utmost care. Then we witness the end of Ritsos' creative life, where the poems reveal his growing cynicism and utter disillusionment with the human condition; the reasons for this lying solely on the way his world collapsed around him a number of times over the years. Even as he is gazing back, we see primordial truths hovering over his thoughts; the human pettiness that drives some people's lives shadows him with a deep disappointment that he appears to take with him to his grave.

I have tried to remain as close as possible to the original Greek text, to preserve the linguistic charm of Ritsos' style. For this reason the restructuring of sentences from their original settings are implemented only when it seemed too difficult for the reader to follow the poet's true meaning and deep thought. The writer has a lot more freedom in Greek as to how to order a sentence as opposed to English, which is more a positional language, and the sequence of words somewhat more strict. I hope that this translation gives the reader a taste of Ritsos' poetry from the admirer's point of view, and with all due reverence and respect to other translations and to the great Yannis Ritsos himself, whose innermost feelings and thoughts we try to convey to the reader as accurately as possible.

The reader will notice dates under most poems and according to the notes in *Yannis Ritsos – Poems XIV* by Ekaterini Makrinicola they are all the poet's notes and refer to the exact day that he wrote that particular poem. It is important to point out that even if the poet reworked that poem at a future date, and even if the poem was altered in a significant way, the poet insisted in keeping the date of the original composition of each of them. Perhaps this was his way of relating to the reader or to himself, the conditions of that day or days, and the reasons which influenced him to write that as a response to a particular event.

– Manolis

INTRODUCTION

Yannis Ritsos, the most prolific Greek poet of the twentieth century, was born in Monemvasia in the Southern part of Peloponnesos, May 1st 1909, to a noble and wealthy family with extensive land holdings. After a lengthy life of 81 years, after enduring the pain and anguish of the flesh and the spirit, having seen his world collapse in front of his eyes, and after fighting for the purely idealistic concept of freedom beyond any precondition or human border, he died in his sleep in Athens on November 11, 1990.

Ritsos began composing poetry at the rather young age of eight, and since the appearance of his first published poetry book *Tractor* in 1934 he compiled a colossal amount of work consisting of 181 individual collections, sequences, long poems, from as small as sixteen pages, (a 16-page pamphlet, a *decahexaselidon* as it was called in the publishing circles of those days) to long poems and extensive translation books: a body of accomplishments covering some thousands of pages of published material. He wrote short poems, long poems, and prose poems, and he experimented with various formats; early in his poetic adventure he tried the well known form of 15-syllable-verse, or *decapentasyllabus*. He also wrote in rhyming verse early on, before he turned into the free verse which he kept for the rest of his life.

Ritsos' poems have been translated in 45 different languages and the latest tome of his works was published by Kedros in 2007. From his early days to his latest books, his inspiration remains undiminished and his acute eye for detail and exquisite perception is evident throughout his long creative life. Nothing miniscule or great went unnoticed by Yannis Ritsos, and every possibility was exposed and experimented with in his poems. His works incorporate endless infusions of color, melody, jest for catharsis and infinite tenderness. His perspective is infused with wonder about everyday events, drawn with the most eloquent images a poet can reach for when rendering his thoughts with love and compassion even for the simplest person.

His creative materials also included drama, fiction, essays and numerous volumes of translations. He became the voice of Greece in his own lifetime, and was internationally recognized for his endless accomplishments. He was awarded a number of national and international awards, such as the National Prize for Poetry in 1956 for his *Moonlight Sonata*, the Grand International Prize for Poetry of the Bienniale

Knokke-le-Zoute Belgium (1972), the International Dimitrov Prize of Bulgaria, the Alfred de Vigny Award of France (1975), the International Poetry Prize of Etna-Taormina in Sicily, the Lenin Prize of USSR (1977), the Citation and Plaque with the designation 'Poet of the International Peace' by the United Nations Society of Writers, and he was nominated though unsuccessful, nine times for the Nobel Prize for Literature.

Ritsos' poetry evolved in such a way as though reflecting on the poet's life from his youthful enthusiasm, idealism and rebelliousness, to the mature, pragmatic and didactic man who searches for each person's place under the sun, for each hungry man's chair at the table during the most elaborate feast. His poetry stands quite gracefully apart from hatred, as he never resorted to vitriol, not even against a system and a dogma that incarcerated him time and again for his political views. Even his political poems have, "a tone of gentle elliptical complaint; it is a tone that almost commiserates with those who persecuted him," Minas Savvas writes from impressions gleaned while interviewing Ritsos.

And referring to his more or less healthy life, despite of all the physical abuses he endured because of harsh conditions in the concentration camps and prisons, the poet explained: "I learned the art of mental defence, since I found myself in the midst of many ordeals; I learned in the course of time that the mind is a lifebuoy. Work has rejuvenated me and continues to rejuvenate me. I have learned that working defeats hardship and today, if I do not work eight to ten hours, I'll get sick."

"In spite of all injustices against you," Savvas continues, "your poetry is not bitter as Avgeris' or Varnalis' so often is."

"Yes, yes, it's not. I'm proud it is not," Ritsos concurred, "bitterness ages us, Mr. Savvas."

Ritsos managed to stay above demonizing and persecuting his opponents via the power of his medium, being a believer in the strength of human spirit as redeemer of all wrong doings. He held true to his ethics, proving once and again that no matter how often one is forced down or how low by the oppression of others, and no matter from what high position, one's invincible spirit lifts and sets him on firm ground. It reflects, in the manner of a fairytale, the image of a thin thread suddenly appearing from nowhere and linking a person to an immortal, spiritual side of himself, gracing one with the ability to carry on.

Ritsos remained a simple man throughout his days, and the austere manner of his everyday life struck a chord of sorrow to his interviewer, Savvas who commented about Ritsos' apartment being next to a school and having to work daily, amid its clamor.

"Aren't you bothered by the noise?" Savvas asks.

"No, the songs, the mingling of the voices, the fighting, they are all a collective sound of life,' Ritsos explained, 'Then when it's quiet in the afternoons, I taste a much sweeter silence. Goethe said that we must experience the depths if we are to appreciate the heights."

"Do you find your neighbourhood depressing?"

"Not at all. It's an old Athenian section, full of simple folk and color."

"I only asked because a certain American critic called it depressing."

"Some Americans are spoiled; they think lawns and trimmed grass make good neighbourhoods."

During the 1970s in Greece, the country pendulated between the philosophies of east and west, and as powerful external forces influenced the hearts and minds of the populace, Greeks looked to their history and myths for a cultural compass. Ritsos' work reflects this reality, repeatedly making references to the ancient myths and symbols within a setting of contemporary issues and Greek dilemmas. He reached back into ancient tributaries, into myths and symbols for guidance and for meaning while witnessing the injustices of contemporary Greek life. Drawing strength from the ancient heroes, he discovers the other side of things, the eloquent side of words won by chance, the poetic pleat of the ordinary, the serendipitous answer to every difficult or almost unanswerable question; he discovers as though in a form of epiphany, the answer to many difficult questions. Most significantly, Ritsos gains the perspective that nothing happens at random, nothing comes to the life of a person or a populace without a specific reason, and it's the duty of the person or populace to recognize, appreciate and find solace in the opportunities provided by such meanings.

Ritsos resurrects images of heroes such as Philoctetes, Orestes, Ajax, Agamemnon, Persephone, Chrysothemis, Helen, Ismene and Phaedra. And by transposing their plight and anguish into his here and now of Greek life, he not only brings them back to life but also positions them into an expos of how Greeks of his day suffer and need guidance in order to find their path to the light. Under this perspective, the ancient heroes become today's heroes and they take the flesh and blood of the fighters in the mountains of Greece against German invaders, or taking part in the liberation of the ancient spirit suffering under the oppression and the darkness of the time.

For Ritsos, the space created is where myth survives, resonates, embalms, while it rejuvenates and rebirths heroes and ideas; so the soil is not the dead dirt of other poets, but the primeval uterus, the ancient Gaia giving birth to the immortals. This is the role played by the Greek landscape – the same important role it plays in Elytis' poetry where it localizes, and from the localized it turns to the worldly and from there to the eternal. This introduction will touch further on the prominence of location, when it examines Ritsos' poem, *Caretaker's Desk*.

In the same spirit as when referring to classical statues, the mythical images featured throughout his poetry, are not only abundant but they identify the contemporary space with the ancient, they reinforce the power of the resistance and finally when answers are sought from them, when the poet relies upon them seeking resolve, they are used by Ritsos as well as by Elytis in a manner similar to the *deux ex machina*, *Από μηχανής Θεός – (apo michanis theos)* – of the ancient tragedies where the god presents a respite by becoming the solver of any riddle, any dichotomy. Thus the myth preserves historic time and memory as through time it has been the same since ancient days, to the present. And when matters are stretched to the point of no return, to the highest point of tragedy, the god, myth, and the people's perception of current events is re-established, and brings about a new resolve and a renewal for the people.

Myth, in Ritsos' poetry, works and develops on three main levels; it reflects on the mythological-historical background, on personal memory and also on contemporary social problems. The mythological-historical background bestows on the poems, a deeper perspective by extending their dimensions via another concept of time and by means of pure endurance – thus becoming the stability sought by modern Greeks; the personal memories of the poet are anointed by the poet's early childhood and suffering at a tender age, his family, their fate and the image of their house in Monemvasia, he identifies with a historical grandeur that at the same time defines an entrapping medium: resembling both a palace and a prison.

The relative location, in this case is the ancient space where Clytemnestra and Orestes live, and at the same time the house where his sister dies of illness. The space carries sweet memories of tender motherly and fatherly love, and at the same time the grief for his and his family's suffering. It is also the space occupied by the ordinary people, nurses, gardeners, and servants of old days.

On the third level of development, we see the contemporary social problems and injustices predominantly straddling the poems the same way they did for the ancient heroes, whereas the Atreides family's events reflect on modern problems of inequality, and the search for meaning-ful change, for an improvement of everyone's life; these become the duty of the poet to uncover and suggest, thus creating not only a poem or poems but a new life and by extension, a new world.

Due to the symbolic weight that the myth carries, it empowers the psychological truth of the real-life persons that the poet carries within himself to extrude, as if through a sieve and while doing so, he also carries the emotional weight of a childhood destined to crumble under disease, disaster and grief. The poet himself transforms into the new Prometheus bringing about the anticipated release via his creation of a new world beyond the influence of disease, or in this case of the Greek nation's civil war, by leading the people to a new dawn.

There are times that Ritsos' poetry seems flat and somewhat simplistic, or lacking that phantasmagorical poetic embellishment other poets often resort to. But in that simplistic way where platitudes don't exist, he discovers the true meaning of himself. He even becomes a bit simpler in his later works and particularly in his short poems. In the poem *Hercules and Us*, written during the dictatorship years he describes the creative efforts of dissidents like himself in the remote places of interment...

> '...*Our only diplomas, three words: Makronissos, Yiaros,*
> *and Leros*
> *And if our verses*
> *will someday strike you as clumsy, remember*
> *that they were written*
> *under noses of guards and always with the bayonets*
> *ready by our side*
> *not that we need excuses: take the words bare as they are*
> *Dry Thucydides will tell you more than elaborate*
> *Xenophon*'

Along with these locations, certain images are used time and again throughout his poetic landscape and it's imperative that we refer to them as we find their repetition quite interesting and peculiar at the same time.

First and foremost, the *mirror* appears in thousands of instances and one cannot but see themselves in one: the image being used as a means of self-reflection, appreciation of who one is and what one believes, while at the same time a mirror fills an empty spot on the wall as it fills the void of a loss or puts under a spotlight, the new direction a person may take. The poet repeatedly brings a mirror in front of the reader's eyes with the suggestion of turning the reader into a poet and at the same time turning himself into the reader who reflects on the idol of the poet-creator.

A *window* appears in almost all his short poems, always leading the reader to the openness of the horizon where everything is wide and well lit, where the world can be seen at its enormity and its endlessness. This is where the poet basks under the creative and rejuvenating force of the sun and the reader is never enclosed or incarcerated.

Often we see the poet bringing in the midst of a poem, the *third person ...he said...* who speaks for the rest of the conversing partners, thus reflecting on the objective observer of the world who is not of special education or wealth, but the common person from whom the wisest statements come. In this way, the poet suggests that it takes only common sense to arrive at the most profound answers to the question at hand.

A *woman* always exists behind the window or the curtain looking on at things, gazing on life outside the house, which at this time represents her imprisonment, her labour camp, as she walks from room to room preparing a meal, ironing her husband's clothes or sewing socks. Or one may see such images as images of the woman in her realm, the family home, and more particularly the kingdom of every Grecian mother-wife in the nineteen-forties and fifties, which is often her kitchen. It can also be ascertained, that the poet's mother is in his mind.

The *soldier* is also predominant in Ritsos' imagery, perhaps in reference to the duty the poet sees in everyone's life, any common person who must offer something: a poet or a construction worker, a street cleaner, a small flower vendor with his basket. In this case, it is a soldier with his gesture of offering, always standing amid the catastrophe of war, particularly a civil war when a brother may fight against a brother and a father may kill his own child standing on the other side of the fence, the other side of the dividing line based on political views or differences. This handling of the ideal exposes the twisted ethos created for a civil person and their position in society, being asked to contribute something beyond duty, for uncertain benefit or outcomes.

The color *red* is also abundant in many poems, and always referring to the poet's ties to the cause of the Left and communism; we always find a red tree, a red wall or road painted by the poet himself. Red also speaks of life, death and powerful emotions.

Remarkable is the transformation that takes place throughout Ritsos' creative years and his change of attitude from the idealistic and rebellious stance of the nineteen-thirties and forties as he writes *Ocean's March*, *On the Margins of Time*, *Romiosini*, *Skirmish*, and *Smoked Earthen Pot*, moving into more reflective and philosophical views of the nineteen-fifties and sixties in his middle years: books such as *Parentheses*, *Moonlight Sonata*, and *Helen*.

These also stand in contrast to poems of the dictatorship years in Greece with his doubtful and cryptic *Caretaker's Desk* in the nineteen-seventies, and then the mature, didactic man of the nineteen-eighties whose teaching voice we hear in books such as the *Short Admission*, *The World is One*, *Replacements*, as well as *They Left, Furnished Rooms* and *Inhalings*.

The poet himself refers to this transformation, when he comments from his exile in Karlovasi Samos, August of 1972, looking back at his work of nearly forty years:

"As time goes by, I notice clearer everyday that my work in its development, its evolution and its exercise, tends to camouflage (not intentionally) every nightmare and in a more general sense, death into the comical and funny by ridiculing and exploiting it. If there is certain redemption in this, it's based in the liberation from the weight of pain and fear (natural, moral or social) with a selective irony from our historical illusions, in the communion of emotions from a true or imaginary inclusion and involvement – in the community with a common fate.

The dominated seem to acquire the power of a domineering force, amid this vague and unverified space – resulting in the visual pinning down of the nightmare in a transforming way – something like a redemption or liberation. The inescapably tragic transcends into the tragicomic or in other words into the paradoxical, and therefore into the objective. Perhaps this is deeply tragic, though it embraces a certain catharsis and compassion in a willed, final grimaced smile that at times via poetry, arrives at a real smile dipped in emotion: a decisive action and power of a new beginning, a new act. And this is not only the result of the sensual act influencing the reader or listener, but it is exactly the reality of the sensual act. This is verified and witnessed in a lot of my older poems, in such books as 'Testimonies' but also in some newer poems such as 'Tanagra', 'Figurines', 'Exercises','Wall in the Mirror', 'Gestures', 'Corridor' and 'Stairs' and very often in 'The Caretaker's Desk.'

In this reality of the sensual act, the unbearable "rareness" of the individual dissolves in a serene way amid the innocent wholeness that shelters everyone and everything. The lack of communication and inability to understand, transform into a leniency and forgiveness, if not into an acceptance and agreement that presents the achievable, the friendly "joking" even the sarcasm – as though it is something extended beyond the differences and mutual accusations when reaching for grace in the spirit of brotherhood. – It is as though we discuss the morality of aestheticism."

Ritsos continues, "*Only before the truly familiar (or perhaps even before the foreign and unknown) can we disarm ourselves from any defensive or aggressive and apparent seriousness or pretentiousness, and may we joke with them. Only before them may we disguise ourselves, quite openly at that, (like actors of an ancient tragedy or comedy) or we may undress, displaying each piece of garment, hair-pieces, the beads, the hats with feathers, the buskins and masks, the wooden swords of the act – actors of a real unwritten drama; actors who take off his or her makeup in pretence and undress after the performance, leaving the impression that the just-performed drama, live-act was only a theatrical piece that ended, and cannot be repeated though we can re-stage it after we improve it.*

The real (and this real originating in a fantasy or a dream) transforms into the fabulous, and the tyrannical into entertainment in a mocking travesty. Not always, of course. But by the portrayal of the twisted and accompanying images of the nightmare and the inexplicable human condition (along with its poetic transformation, distortion, and transmutation) one has the impression that the result is (not only for its creator) some extreme satisfaction of meaning, perhaps the ability and power of self-control and even the virginal feeling of the inexhaustible, of continuance, and even a sense of accomplishment."

What we find strange is the lack of fanfare for or reference to the church in Ritsos' writings, opposite other poets who devoted plenty of space and attention to organized religion and the church. Perhaps it is this poet's desire to ignore the issue, at least to the level that other poets have paid attention to it and perhaps that is because of his adherence to communist doctrine and its position that the church is a negative influence in the psycho-spiritual development of a person. Perhaps Yannis Ritsos is a true believer of the axiom, "Religion is the sigh of the oppressed creature, the heart of a heartless world, and the soul of a soulless condition," Karl Marx wrote, "Religion is the opium of the masses. The abolition of religion as the illusory happiness of the people, is the demand for their real happiness…" and Ritsos, by ignoring the church, pays them back with the proper coin.

What is most astonishing about Ritsos' work, is its power to render *entelechia* to its reader, to bestow a potency that suddenly pokes through the hard soil like new shoots, and transforms the reader into part of his creative force. One immersed in such potency is often swept by emotions of gratitude and respect for the power of his eloquence springing up to bloom its flowers in an unprecedented way. Also deeply touching to a reader aware of the poet's circumstances, is Ritsos' self-sacrifice, by staying true to his beliefs up to the bitter end, by enduring the worst adversity in order to not be silenced or coerced into hiding his views.

Another respected quality is the attention Ritsos pays to miniscule aspects of life and the potent value he gives to that miniscule. It would be impossible for any reader to miss the attention to detail: the sway of the lower pleat of the curtain, the almost imperceptible movement of the eyelid at sleep or waking, or the slightest fragrance of chamomile, images that render an eloquence and richness to his writings as they reveal the heart and soul of Greece. Had he not been such an expert observer and charismatic creator, it is thinkable that some may have forgotten how to name simple things and feelings he brought to prominence. As the great author, Nikos Kazantzakis once said… "Happiness – and all other things – is a small shrub in your front yard, and you go by it every day without even seeing it…" and as another great poet, Odysseus Elytis put it, "What you save during the lightning will last, cleansed forever."

The Ocean's March, the first book included in this translation, was written between 1939 and 1940 and was published in 1940. At this time, Yannis Ritsos is in Athens, mostly in bed due to illness and he writes prolifically.

The Ocean's March is a stout, 31-page poem that opens with a dark scene of a dark harbor and "faces without memory or continuance" referencing war with slaves tied on anchors while a poet searches for direction via a sea voyage to a far locale, he notes, "A seagull is calling me", highlighting comradeship and brotherhood: this is a book about all of these elements, and not just a single person,

> *'but we don't know anything*
> *about the taste in the ash of the voyage',*

this is also a book about struggle, and the fate of the émigré who will travel with empty pockets to a foreign land seeking a better future for himself but most importantly for his children, since

> *'we heard the song of the sea*
> *and we can't sleep anymore'*

he has knowledge of far away lands that he collects via seamen coming back with stories and experiences

> 'we saw ships bringing mythic lands here
> in the blond sand'

innocence as a true human condition of young age is extolled in the passage

> 'venerable heart
> unsuspecting childish heart
> who never refuses'

drawing from mythology, his references to Odysseus, Laertis and Nausica, who he brings to life in his day and age, with their austere conditions and hunger

> 'from Troy, on the Hellenic clay pitchers
> mother you…salted our supper with tears…
> girls who got engaged to Odysseus sighed'

and here he questions the eternal justice of why and who

> 'who cuts to pieces God's soul
> and our joy?'

and like a new Odysseus, he admits that the voyage is of utmost importance

> 'the voyage always remains with us
> and the endless clamour of the sea'

as the injustices of his time overshadow every shred of goodness in the hearts of the people and in the poet's mind, he feels

> 'tonight we go to sleep with a bitter heart
> like the bread of fishermen in the storm'

and is deeply grieving for his personal situation, being ill with tuberculosis and also bitter and disappointed by the conditions for the majority of Greeks during the war against the Italians in 1940. And as he finds strength from his human spirit, he finds solace from what seems an endlessness of the struggle against the day's enemy and against any future enemy; he declares that his cry will stand next to the undiminished power and endurance of the sea that never sleeps and never lets go – never succumbs

> 'sea sea as you are
> we are
> we shall never succumb

> *to the night and to sleep'*

and his final cry is to his comrades, who he calls for a unified fight against any darkness and against any oppression and it is nothing but an invocation to the sun, to whom the poet is willing to sacrifice his life

> *'Sun – sun that paints the sea with blood*
> *I offer myself naked to your fire*
> *to light the eyes of men*
> *My brothers listen to your voices*
> *to my voice listen*
> *to the song of the sun and the sea'*

Notes on the Margins of Time, the second book in this translation was written between 1938 and 1941, while the poet was still in Athens, yet the book was not published until 1961, as part of the collection, *Yannis Ritsos – Poems I*. This is Ritsos' first book of short poems and from this point he pendulates between the long poem format and the short poem, continuing like this until the end of his life. On this, Kimon Friar says in his commentary, "There is to be a seeming dichotomy in the style of Ritsos, between short poems and those long poems in which he can ruminate at leisure on large themes involving character-ization, motivation, the political scene, or whatever he felt needed long and subtle elaboration."

In *Poems I*, however he follows a laconic and precise format and although he experiments with it for the first time, we find still, his well-known themes, and all Ritsos' heated elements remaining on guard and at attention, ready to strike with brief, powerful jolts to any naive onlooker as equally as to the dear, thoughtful reader.

In *Doxology*, we find the sun giving life to everything, while at the same time burning the tree, the dominant symbolic element for giving life and death;

> *'He stood at the far end of the road*
> *like a leafless dusty tree*
> *like a tree burned by the sun*
> *praising the sun that cannot be burned'*

These poems are the short cries echoing the universal sobs of planets and the microcosm, reflecting the mega-cosmos and the transforma-tion of the marginally important to the utmost serious, evident in lines such as,

> *'Next to the wine jugs*

next to the fruit baskets
we forgot to sing
On the evening of our separation
with the consent of the evening star
alone we sang'

they are short bursts of energy aimed at the defeated energy of the Greek nation under the wrath of war but where,

'memory doesn't feel sorry for you anymore'

but stands vigilant and ready to reignite the soul of his people, who while everything dies around them, they do not, because that fear of death is the breath that keeps them alive,

'and the fear that perhaps you wouldn't die
and the fear of water trickling
the fear the water the breath – life'

they are Zeus' lightning bolts striking the unsuspecting reader with energetic bursts such as,

'Moments – moments
uncounted
tamed by the sun
Countless
Then we counted them
with the palm of a dry grapevine leaf
we secured the summer'

Then they become tender riddles that stay afloat, waiting for the reader's interpretation and response to the emotion stirred by admissions,

'And I have something to tell you
that even I cannot hear'

Romiosini is Ritsos' long narrative poem, consisting of seven parts of various lengths; it was written between 1945 to 1947 when the poet had joined the EAM, (National Liberation Front) the Greek Leftist party, that in conjunction with Republicans became the main arm of resistance against the Axis during WWII. EAM's struggle with Greece's violent right-wing factions and against foreign interference that divided the nation and inflamed into a civil war in 1946, lasting for three years. The events of this time had a lasting effect on Ritsos' works.

He contributed theatrical plays to the People's Theatre of Macedonia that were performed in Thessaloniki and other northern cities, especially Kozani. *Romiosini*, published for the first time as part of the book *Vigilance,* in 1954, is an epic poem in the same format as Odysseus Elytis' *Axion Esti*, in that they both try to unfold the condition of Greece at this junction of her history, though Ritsos focuses primarily on the life of the Leftist army in the mountains, who though living under harsh conditions, still uphold a code of honor and dedication to their cause.

The poem became very popular because of the pride it evoked and because it coincided with the Greek people's persistent search for a guiding symbol during the dark hour of the civil war.

The poem's central them is the resistance against any oppressing force or doctrine; it is the resistance of the free Greek spirit against the subversion of freedom; a resistance to anything working against the needs of the populace with its thousands of years of struggle against external or internal enemies. The landscape in *Romiosini* is described as harsh, but at the same time luminous and gleaming under the merciless sun

> 'This landscape is merciless like silence
> it hugs its fiery rocks tightly in its bosom…
> … there is no water Only light'

suggests the landscape suffers the same as these proud fighters defending it against all odds. The basis of these songs derive from the old 'klephtic' songs of the war for Independence against the Turks and the Cretan 'rizitika' songs, having numerous repetitive stanzas and matching sentences. The dedication of the mountain fighters to their cause extols their commitment and willingness to die instead of betray such a cause

> 'their hands are glued to their rifles
> their rifles are extensions of their souls'

even when the elements themselves stand against it, they never question the validity of their struggle, and they accept death as their companion

> 'sweltering has devoured their fields and salinity has
>   drenched their homes
> wind has pushed down their doors and the few lilac shrubs
>   of the plaza
> death goes in and out the holes of their overcoats
> the rain pounds on their bones'

yet these fighters follow the example of the Byzantine hero, Digenis Akritas, on the same threshing floors where he fought against death for three days, so they stay fixated on their posts and they are,

> 'petrified on their battlements, they smoked
> cow dung and the night
> keeping watch on the furious pelagos where
> the broken mast of the moon sank'

Among the wealth of imagery in *Romiosini*, one element is heard above the rest: the *bell* with its rhythmic peal for death,

> 'Silence any time now the bells will chime
> This soil is theirs and ours
> Under the earth in their crossed hands
> they hold the bell rope – waiting for the hour
> they don't sleep they don't die
> waiting to ring the resurrection'

for celebration, mass, or for a wedding. Bells echo in revolution, and they persevere over the harsh Greek landscape, orchestrating the new beginning after a war that will pass like so many others in history. These people know what perseverance is; they have tasted bitterness, lived on through the anguish of war, and yet they discover a new beginning;

> 'Ah what silky stars will the pine needles
> still need to embroider
> over the scorched fence of summer
> this will also pass

but not until the destruction ends and the people go out to the fields to locate the dead with their faces to the ground. And when they discover their names they may cry 'I love'; and peace is bestowed on the world once again when,

> 'thousands of doves fly out'

and the country will move on,

> 'when you grab a hand
> in the darkness and say goodnight'

life will start over and the émigré will come back to find his family who don't even recognize him,

> 'because he has met death
> because he has met life before life, and

> *beyond death'*

at that moment asking,

> *'and which key will lock up your heart, that with*
> *its two spread open door-leaves*
> *stares at God's star-drenched orchards?'*

Although *Romiosini* is uniquely attractive after it was blended with the music of Mikis Theodorakis, it became a monumental piece of contemporary Grecian life, ultimately because of the success of Ritsos' poetry but also by the power of artful music the soulful composer wove around it.

The book that follows, *Parentheses,* was written between 1946 and 1947 and published for the first time as part of the second volume of *Yannis Ritsos – Poems II*, in 1961. The title itself suggests that this collection of 21 short poems is a sort of intermission between the long poems before it and after it. And like the short poems of *In the Margins of Time,* they unfold the various moods of the poet, and refer to various themes.

In this book we see a playful Ritsos as we read in the opening poem, 'The Meaning of Simplicity': *"it turns like that because I tell you this",* suggests the poet will make a diversion from the seriousness of the long poems where he can develop longer themes and subjects at his leisure. Here he devotes some of his genius to writing short-form poems though the depth and the solemnity aren't diminished with the length – contrarily, we find again, a sensitive and shrewd, an enigmatic Ritsos employing hidden meaning and mystical nuances from what each poem doesn't say, but intends.

The poet reaffirms his humble attitude, and the poems are open to various interpretations, depending on the view and openness of the reader. This further transforms the reader into a poet and conversely the poet to a reader, assimilating the two persons and bridging any chasm between them.

In *Parentheses,* we find a lively and jovial Ritsos, who leaves us to decide what is better: a straightforward approach to things or one that beats around the bush. His quest resembles that of a child trying to locate a hidden treasure in a very familiar, yet well guarded place. A most appropriate poem for such a book is of course, 'The Meaning of Simplicity', where Ritsos opens by saying,

> *'I hide behind simple things so you may find me'*

illustrating his playfulness often referred to by his readers.

Images of windows in this poem appear to relate to openness, to a communication with nature, with the endlessness of light coming into the rooms and thus eliminating the sense of measurement as the immense becomes a room and a room turns into the infinite,

> 'The four windows hang rhyming quatrains
> Made of sky and sea inside the rooms'

Human time appears in the form of a wristwatch showing twelve noon and the person feeling free with his/her 'hair in the hands of the sun, in the light, in the air' Ritsos plays with the reader, as he insists in *Perhaps Someday*,

> 'But I shall insist in seeing and
> showing you – he said
> because if you don't see it is as if I didn't see
> I shall insist at least on not seeing with your eyes'

the poet being the reader and vice versa – both are the creators of the image to be seen or the one they both truly see.

Smoked Earthen Pot was written in 1949, in the prison camp of Limnos and was first published in the collection *Yannis Ritsos – Poems II*, in 1961.

Between 1948 and 1952, the poet was arrested and sent to prison camps in Limnos then to Makronissos and then to Saint Eustratios, also known as Ai Strati. During these years and always under the watchful eye of guards and of other prisoners, he secretly wrote and hid his work in whichever box, bottle, or other means to a safe place for his materials to be preserved. After four years in these places of internment, he was released and he returned to Athens where he devoted time to their publication.

In this book, the poet opens the curtain of a passage leading back to his communist ideas of equality among the citizens, freedom for all and most importantly, food and shelter for all. Greece was still feeling a deep wounding from the civil war, and the conditions of people's lives were deteriorating as well. Devastation and hunger were obvious to every eye. With *Smoked Earthen Pot*, Ritsos displays his wish that he could become a gigantic caldron, a great earthen pot, cooking enough food to feed the hungry people living in his country, hungry people the world over. Bravely, in the opening lines, the poet presents us with his brotherly emotion,

> 'It was a very long road up here very long my brother

The cuffs were heavy on the hands…'

Throughout a discussion between two people or more, the first person voice never refers to himself by saying 'I did this' but always uses 'we' in referring to a brotherhood of people working together or struggling together. Images of the war aftermath are prevalent also,

'The handicapped man next to you takes off his leg
Before he goes to bed he leaves it in the corner
A wooden hollow leg
You have to fill it like you fill a flowerpot with soil
And plant flowers
Like darkness is filled up with stars
Like poverty slowly fills up thought and love'

The universality of his message appears when he says

'Because my brother we don't sing so that
We may stand out in the world
We sing so that we may unite the world'

and he discovers that his fraternal love becomes a river from which just

'two drops are enough to sprinkle the nightmare's face
and it vanishes like smoke behind the trees'

he emphasizes that he only wants to become

'An earthen pot then Nothing else
Earthen, blackened pot
boiling boiling and singing
boiling on top of the sun's fire and singing'

Skirmish is a long poem consisting of eight parts, written in 1952 in Saint Eustratios internment camp and published for the first time as part of the book *Vigilance* in 1954 when the poet lived in Athens and worked for the newspaper *Avgi* (Greek word *Αυγή* means Dawn). With the title *Skirmish*, the poet underscores the animosity and the differences of the political sides of east and west that dominated Greek politics during the civil war and the Cold War that followed. The poem illustrates how affected every person is, one way or another, as though caught up in a skirmish where none is declared a winner and both sides have their casualties; this skirmish sometimes takes place between people, in the minds and hearts of people and of the poet himself.

The poem opens with a desperate cry of anguish, informing the reader about the perils of civil war and imprisonment as well as the influences of foreign interests,

'You know the great loneliness of exile
these infuriated seashores that could be ours
though they are foreign'

the isolation of the prison camp where,

'We saw the dusk spending its loneliness without leaving
anything behind'

and the stillness of time when one is imprisoned,

'Tomorrow seems to be so far the same as yesterday'

The evil of political upheaval and the dichotomy of the Cold War and its effects on Greece; the resulting civil war and the poet's imprisonment along with thousands of other Greeks constitute his strongest cry for justice,

'Then what separates people when you and I are hungry
when we both thirst together or on our own
– we thirst the same way
what separates us that you are a guard and I am the exiled?
when both know the meaning of the word mother'

pain and suffering are over the entire country, none can escape it, shrouding all like a heavy cloud,

'Tell me then what a mother with a smoked up lamp
can understand
with two children killed and the third one missing?'

and yet even in the darkest hour, the poet, the man finds the courage and strength to smile at the world and the stars and that smile transcends every pain and hatred. It is above every evil thought and brings him back to his natural transparent self, who remains unaffected by evil, unaffected by his imprisonment. He is trying to act on a more civilized level than his prison guards and thinking beyond baser instincts while he enlightens the whole prison camp, the country and the cosmos with his forgiveness, his smile.

'One night two nights many nights
we saw the stars behind their bayonets –
do you remember that? Do you remember how
joyous we were seeing them?
It was the first time that we truly smiled my brother'

the smile that transcends even death and turns the dead into immortals,

> '*And George who got killed in the previous war*
> *appeared at the turn of the road In his palm he held*
> *the bullet that found his heart like he was holding*
> *a lead toy soldier trying to gift it to a child He*
> *said goodbye to you He left…*
> *It was because of our smiles my brother*'

and when finally the poet takes control of the skirmish inside him, between his battered ego in the prison camp, leading him into hatred, he finds the strength to rise above it with profound eloquence as,

> '*Two policemen went by*
> *one of them held a small almond branch…*
> *The flowers lighted their faces under their caps…*
> *I tell you the world is beautiful…*
> *There are not any dots on our voices or silence anymore*
> *the world is beautiful*'

In the year 1956, Ritsos makes a serious shift in style when he writes and publishes his famous *Moonlight Sonata*, a long poem, though it will be proven to be his shortest long poem, and one for which he wins the year's Greek State Prize for poetry. In this book he changes to the dramatic monologue and he uses the first person instead of the collective 'we' found in most of his previous works. He uses a short prose as a prologue in order to introduce the characters and the setting, and he also closes the poem with another piece of prose as epilogue.

Moonlight Sonata is very short, just one 16-page pamphlet with the actual text taking just eight pages. Yet in this short poem we find an abundance of important images and memories intertwined and expressing the simple environment of everyday people, on one side an old woman dressed in black, as though mourning for the old age taking hold of her body and on the other side a young man with unbuttoned shirt, counterbalancing the old age of the other character.

When *Moonlight Sonata* appeared for the first time in France, in a translation by Alekos Karatzas, Ritsos was in Athens, still working for the *Avgi* newspaper. Of this small book, surrealist French poet-author Louis Aragon commented, "We must salute him as he rightfully deserves and shout it from the rooftops; he is one of the greatest, one of the most remarkable poets of our time."

The poem opens with the introduction of the luminous character, the moon, having center stage in the title,

> '*Let me come with you What a moon tonight!*'

and leads the reader to a fascinating voyage with deep highs and lows, via the clarity and firmness of verse that unfolds slowly, yet coherently as though fighting through the words via the words, beneath the words, and in the gaps between. The locale is vague, the old woman and young man are unidentifiable, yet such intensity and depth emanate from the plain, terse sentences.

> '...when I pick up the cup from the table
> a hole of silence is left below and at once I place
> my palm over it
> so I don't look inside I put the cup back in its place'

the double meaning of images are not produced via use of '*poetic words*' by resorting to grand ideas or embellishment, but by the disembowelled armchair, the shoes with worn heels and

> '*hanging pots glittering*
> *like large eyes of exquisite fishes*'

Ritsos' shift from other forms of poetry to the dramatic monologue captures the everyday things of simple people and elevates them to the level of the eternal, as when the house imprisons a person and keeps him or her within its virtual old age, a parallel is drawn to the woman dressed in black, the house which is haunted, where

> '*the stucco falls silently like the hat of the dead man*
> *from its peg in the dark hallway*'.

It is in this darkened hallway and old haunted house where the life of an old woman unfolds, amid ghosts and memories filling her loneliness. Then the dreadful phrase comes, like an affirmation of fate, as an unquestionable axiom,

> '*I know that everyone marches to love alone*
> *alone to glory and to death*
> *I know it I tried it It's of no use*',

while all this takes place in an unnamed city that appears airy though made of cement, whitewashed by moonlight.

The poem ends with another piece of prose as epilogue. The old woman dressed in black and left in the isolation of her prison, the haunted house, haunted by her memories while the young man strolls down the road with an ironic and perhaps empathetic smile on his lips, free and away from the darkened house as though some cloud had hid the moon. The only things remaining at the end, are the elongated shadows, as the moon re-enters glowing in the corners of the room.

Helen is another long poem in dramatic monologue format, written in 1970 and published in 1972 while the poet is in Athens, reprieved from his exile in Samos. *Helen* is a lot longer than *Moonlight Sonata*, and follows that pattern by commencing with short prose as prologue, and ending with a piece of prose as epilogue. The setting here is also an old, badly kept and deteriorating house, where just a few things are alive, Helen herself on the pinnacle of old age.

> *'An old – old – one two hundred years old'.*

Her younger servants wait anxiously for her to die so they can absorb her belongings, echoing Nikos Kazantzakis' *Zorba the Greek* when old Madame Ortance dies and villagers enter the house, snatching every-thing away.

In *Helen*, the main character's memories are still alive, taking her to past glorious days when she was irresistibly beautiful, and ships filled with thousands of young soldiers were sailing off to reclaim her. These memories flash through Helen's mind, and by staying suspended there momentarily, they erase the ravages of time, concealing her wrinkles, her aches. The memories constitute masks, gracing the face behind them with a variety of lively expressions to veil her emotions, and save her from her most profound fear and acceptance that her heavenly beauty has vanished.

Now Helen remains in the imprisonment of her house and opposite the *Moonlight Sonata*, where a black-dressed widow appeals,

> *'Let me come with you'*

in a world that she knows she cannot belong, here in this poem, Helen implores her visitor,

> *'Sit down for a while – no one comes around anymore'*

her time spent imagining things, she

> *'examines the black stone of her ring in the endless*
> *hours of the night',*

and as she finds refuge in the glorious bygone days when great war-riors fought for her favors and inevitably, the aimlessness of all that overtakes her when she contemplates all that is temporal, her beauty, and above all, life's events,

> *'so there is no meaning in things or events*
> *the same goes for words although with them we name*
> *more or less those things we miss or those that we never saw*

the airy as we call them the eternal things – innocent words
misleading consoling always ambiguous in their intended
accuracy – what a sad story to give name to a shadow
calling it at night when in bed with the sheet pulled up
to your neck and hearing it we fools think that we hold
its body that it holds us: that we are held together in the world'

The importance of what people project in their lives as valuable and necessary to them is evident in the passage and how people cling to images and myths, and give them life while never questioning why a myth remains so strong and influential in what a person chooses to do or to not do in his/her everyday affairs.

Helen, in the midst of her isolation, as though out of reaction, springs out of her self-pity and into self-indulgence, realizing that all perish, that she'll perish, that when her time comes, she has to face the inevitable heroically, yet alone and thus the book ends with her holding onto her last hope of proof of her tangible beauty,

'And in that scene on the walls of Troy did I truly ascend
letting it fall off my lips? – Sometimes even now
I try
here lying in bed to open my hands to stand on my tiptoes
to stand on air
the third flower'

The poem ends with an epilogue, and we discover that she truly dies and the moon rises exactly as in the *Moonlight Sonata* and the statues in the garden are dimly lit – where would her male visitor go now?

The Caretaker's Desk, a collection of 99 short poems, was written between March and May 1971, and published first in Italy in both Italian and Greek in 1975, and then in French, in France and in Athens, the following year.

Every apartment building used to have a caretaker who usually lived in the basement or main floor, a man or a woman or a whole family and his/her job was to take care of everything needed in the building – from opening the door, to handling and distributing the mail, taking care of the heating and cleaning the building, arranging for the tradesmen for repairs, and for this reason one could say that nothing took place in the building that the caretaker wouldn't know about. For the same reason, the desk where the caretaker worked was a strategic, central point before which everything was transacted or unfolded.

The caretaker observes from behind his desk all the activity taking place, everything the inhabitants of the various units of the apartment do, everything they try to hide from his merciless eyes, giving him the advantage of knowing intimate details of their lives, and sometimes secrets they may have which he keeps to himself. The caretaker's desk transforms into a focal point of importance and becomes like a kingdom within a building, as the person behind it peers at the unsuspecting passers-by and keeps tab of events that would go otherwise unnoticed.

At this stage of the poet's life, Ritsos is a mature, sensitive man who is full of passion and wisdom. He finds himself creating a small world around the focal point of the caretaker's desk, and the person behind that desk is a veritable king in his castle, absorbing, cataloguing, digesting all activity and events; he retains the things that come before his eyes, or passes them on to others; he gives life to life by recording its action, as the poet himself does in his creations, omnipotent within the metaphor of the building, from the microcosm to the universal.

The poems were written during the dictatorship of the colonels in Greece, and this is reflected in this book, in how Ritsos writes as though he constructs a puzzle, trying to keep certain messages concealed, shrouding something he wants to say and leaving it to the reader to decode, to add to, as though the reader has the responsibility of finishing certain images. We read in the opening poem,

> 'You never learned later on
> the purpose and what was the difference'

leaving us to ponder, what difference: between what choices or fates? We feel obligated to piece together images to create a clearer picture. Ritsos is in a very sensitive situation at this stage of his life, and because of his experience of being incarcerated, he writes cryptically in order to hide from the eyes and ears of the ever-present oppressor; he is imperceptible, and vaguely defined though his message is well-framed in his depiction of the everyday sufferings of a family, reflecting into the mirror of universal themes,

> 'The woman went to the bedroom
> opened the drawer and took the receipts
> of the water company the power the phone
> turned her back to the balcony door 'Let them cut them off'
> ...and among all (she heard) was herself as well
> speechless calm standing free joined with
> all vanished killed or alive'

Ritsos' protagonists are common people living in an apartment, a house or in a poor neighbourhood and mostly people starting to form the Greek middle class, they are the trades-people: builders and barbers, electricians and the plumbers with their tools, their dirty hands, sweaty armpits and eyebrows; they are his heroes with their struggles and endless fight for the daily bread, with their everyday events and small pleasures. Some of them are obviously victims of barbarous acts and events of war. Ritsos will write about them from this point on, until the end of his creative life.

The six books which follow were all written between 1978 and 1980, and were released for the first time in 2007 in the collection *Yannis Ritsos – Poems XIV*, except for *The World is One*, which was first published as part of a three-book collection titled *Italian Triptych*, consisting of poems he wrote during his three trips to Italy. The following six books appear in an English translation for the first time.

The poet by now lives in the Agios Nikolaos suburb of Athens; he has put behind him all the painful experiences of the dictatorship years and devotes his time to writing and publishing his works. In 1976, he is awarded the International Poetry Prize of Etna – Taormina in Sicily, Italy and the following year he is awarded the Lenin Prize and elected Member of the Mallarme Academy. Although he was unsuccessfully proposed nine times for the Nobel Prize for Literature, he gratefully accepted the Cross of Lenin (referred to as the Nobel Prize of the East) saying, "this prize is more important to me than the Nobel."

In the final books of this translation, we discover that Ritsos' heroes are still the same laypeople and he writes about them with compassion and hope, celebrating their lives, their dignity and their struggles. At times, his poetry adopts different depths of consciousness, and certain raptures, as though he has been in an altered state and suddenly returns to the wakened realm; the surreal intermingles with the direct and whole, often in an explosion of images and symbols. The images exude lyricism and anguish equally, witnessing the poet agonizing over the human condition, over the displacement of people in time and space. He places special importance on this theme, by naming one of his books of this period, *Displacements*.

Ritsos' experiences and his love for his country touch the reader's heart and mind, as wind that sweeps up dust particles of the landscape, its vegetation's seeds, the flash of its sky, the solemnity of its icons. In the elation of the statue faces, and the wisdom of this land that has endured about every possible disaster imaginable, we witness the sturdy Ritsos, who against all odds remains faithful, looks forward and remains an optimist, a least up to the last decade of his life. He doesn't shy from human suffering, as he personally endured so much, and throughout his works, the stanzas are filled with references to it.

Short Admission is a collection of laconic, short poems; they're short and yet the few words nail expansive thought;

> *'Flags and dead*
> *flags and alive*
> *again flags*
> *comrades/only flags'*

The book opens with the well known images of the Greek landscape, the sea, birds, stones, and the blue sky into which the poet blends all else,

> *'The sea – he said –*
> *I don't have birds in my hair*
> *I hurl a stone*
> *I become light blue*
> *a golden thread/hangs from my ear*
> *I hear clearly/the sleeping turtle*
> *and my awkward silence'*

and ending with the philosophical wisdom of a 69-year-old didactic man he says,

> *'What you offered*
> *what you lost*
> *what they deny you*
> *belongs to you*
> *lift your bed*
> *take off your wings*
> *walk',*

Replacements is also a book of short poems where Ritsos' wit and music reappear as though undiminished, the Greek locale, the statues re-emerge and his Spartan style is enriched with what is missing, with what is not said, but hinted to by its absence. His reference to a third person reappears as though in a conversation taking place between the poet and someone else, and the reader always has to add what is not there, or he needs to decide how many different things may be added to a certain image; the book commences with,

> *'Half a glass of water remains on the table The newspapers*
> *don't adapt to the space at all here I am – he said –*

> *amid the leaves and the stones I can open the door*
> *I can live without any words The stony woman*
> *supported her chin with her fist Suddenly*
> *wind blew the leaves fell covering him',*

and while interjecting some very short poems such as 'Glory'

> *'You don't have to undress anymore to close your eyes for a while*
> *The most bitter substitution for life is glory',*

he ends the book with the eloquent, 'Sharp End',

> *'What you replaced with those and those with others*
> *repeated circle or better a rising helix*
> *swirls motionlessly and turns into marble – a glorious column*
> *sculpted spiral exclusive column of an invisible temple and at*
> *its apex not the thorny Corinthian capital but the Stylite*
> *upright speechless with a bandage around the eyes.'*

The World is One, is a book that reflects on the poet's experiences from three trips he took to Italy with his Greek friend, Nicolas Crocetti in 1978. When back in Athens, Ritsos worked on the poems but left them unfinished for almost two years until 1980 when Crocetti, while visiting Athens prodded Ritsos, who reworked the poems and finalized them before they were released in both languages Italian and Greek in Italy. Ritsos writes,

"For the whole May of 1980, I reworked these poems, I did a lot of
revisions, additions, until, reading them in their final form (if there
is a final form for a poem) I felt the cunning, pleasant emotion that I
was reading the impressions of a different traveler, a different writer, as
though I was reading poems of a conspirator, distant, vague friend".

Of certain delight is the reappearance of his wit, scolding the Italian lifestyle and mocking society's prudence when children are constantly restrained by their mothers, making sure they don't stray or get involved with the wrong people such as in the poem 'Pasolini Street'.

> *'Strange – he said – that in an ancient city with dark*
> >   *red and yellow colors*
> *you find children held by their mother's hand*
> *in these very busy streets under the countless windows*
> *here where Pasolini went for a stroll in the night…*
> *come on all the earth's sinful come on all the earth's sinful'.*

Furnished Rooms is a longer book, consisting of 86 short poems. Ritsos' caduceus opens his world once more to the reader for his witty and funny side to burn and bless readers with momentary delight. The book starts with a bucolic Greek scene of bygone days, perhaps of Ritsos' childhood days when,

> 'At dusk women went down to the spring –
> barrels pitchers next to the river The boys
> were for the horses the mules the eels
> women yelled horses neighed However a deep
> silence steamed up in the air as though you needed
> to separate things in two and choose
> only between a horse and a pitcher',

and the reader has to go between the lively, animate life of the horse and the inanimate silence of the pitcher. It is between these two symbols that everyone must find a balance, as the two are inextricably tied.

One also discovers in this book a lot of short poems of just two stanzas, as in 'After the Dream',

> 'It was smoke it vanished – grey smoke light blue
> the naked body remained all alone on the red blanket'

Ritsos uses the color red again, which he insists unites people with the world, Ritsos' world, and the world of the east.

They Left is a book of 95 short poems, that lead one to ask who are the *They*, Ritsos refers to? *They*, could represent large numbers of Greek immigrants who left Greece between 1970 and 1985: this translator is one of them. For Ritsos *They* are also his comrades being left behind by the emigrated Greeks. *They* also may refer to the years that have gone by, as he is now 70 years old. Perhaps he feels regret for something he has not accomplished by this junction of his life. In any case, his charisma and eloquence keep marching ahead quite undeterred and he appears to be at the top of his craft, producing his relevant and timely books one after another.

They Left opens with the poem, 'The Three' in which the images appear to give a view to all windows. Through open windows on a cold but sunny winter day, one witnesses three women grooming themselves getting ready to meet the soldiers who are to be released from the army camp. His attention to detail captures one of the women breaking her comb in her haste. However the poet's days and years are portrayed as wasted in a mood of cynicism that pans the people remaining in the same spot, with venal interests, just as they were years ago with their pettiness and egos; his disappointment is underlined in the book's final poem, 'The Sin',

'They left they left – he said They stayed – he said
in a while They stayed
They are gullible days lost And there were a few trees…
The absolute – he said is
our profound sin And as the lights were turned on on the ships
in the bars in the patisseries they underscored exactly that' ,

Inhalings, the last book of this translation, consists of 79 short poems written in a different format with very short stanzas, a complete departure from the long poems Ritsos wrote in earlier days. *Inhalings* relates to air to the bloodstream carrying oxygen to the muscles, to movement, to life. With its unusual title, *Inhalings* relates to taking in, taking notice of a breath, as well as the taking notice of events, of life, or differences. *Inhalings* also speaks of keeping, retaining, maintaining of circulation, of events, of faith in wanting to experience a combined life that is at once spiritual and visceral. Once again, we discover this great poet, placing the reader in his orbit and guiding him to breathe, to absorb and adapt while remaining integral.

The book opens with a laconic dedication to poetry,

'Poetry/presentofthefuture/twograinsofwheat/oneapple/thesnake
red/and golden'

show careful and precise expression with an accuracy in its reach and power, bringing the moment to fruit, while he avoids an excess of verbiage,

'Breakfast/under the trees/two cups/a lot of birds/I look at the
statue/it
has a hole/in his right rib – /ah my poor mother'.

A believer in the collective, in comradeship, and at a junction of his life when consumerism and the fast pace of life was obliterating traditional beliefs, ideals and political persuasions,

'For so long/with barely enough bread/with cheap cigarettes/
comrade/
how the world grows bigger/from a glance to a glance/
from a hand to a hand/in one word – comrade'

yet the invincibility of the inevitable strikes him like a thunderbolt as the beliefs he relied on for most his life vanish, and he replies with such bitterness and sorrow,

'This nothing – he said – /is synonym to/everything – he had
a towel

around/his waist/ – was he coming out of the bathroom?
        Was he going
in?/ He had beautiful hair/calligraphic legs/we didn't
        believe him',

and his disappointment is evident,

        'They waited for us there – he said – /the great dead/waited f
                or us there/
        The children who we were/big rocks and salt/women
                with sky blue
        kerchiefs/crumbled balconies/a staircase in the front yard/
                bearded
        rowers/the twelve, very thin fishermen/and they were all
                angry/and we
        at that limit between/memory and forgetfulness/and even the
        sea/vigorous and irreversible/amid its eternity/also angry'.

During the nineteen-eighties, Ritsos is involved in writing novels. Nine books are united under the title *Iconostase of the Anonymous Saints*, and his last years are devoted to the publication of his works. Ritsos laboured in seclusion for the most part. Difficult years in prison camps contributed to his health's deterioration, but the greatest blow to the poet, was the fall of the Soviet Union, and perestroika in the second part of the nineteen-eighties. From this vantage, he watched his world, and the world of ideas he supported all his life caving in, and he succumbed to death in Athens, on November 11, 1990. He was 81 years old.

– Manolis

The Ocean's March
1939-1940

Harbor at night
lights drown in the water
faces without memory or continuance
faces lit by passing spotlights of distant ships
and then sunken in the shadow of voyage
slant masts with hanging dream lamps
like the cracked wings of angels who sinned
the soldiers with helmets
between the night and embers
wounded hands like the forgiveness
that reached late

Prisoners tied on anchors
a ring around the horizon's neck
and other chains there at the feet of children
at dawn's hands holding a daisy

And it is the masts that insist
to count the stars
with the help of calm memory
– a bouquet of seagulls in the morning blue sky

Color deserts the face of day
and light doesn't find any statue
to dwell in to be glorified to becalm

Nevertheless we still shelter
the sun's open wound
that springs flowers out of seeds

in the same march
in the same question
in the fertile veins of spring
that repeats the swallows' rounds
writing erotic zeros
in the invincible firmament?
Which wound
hasn't graced us yet
that we may complement
the godliness of God?

We had the garden by the seashore
The sky slipped through the windows
and mother sitting
on her low stool
embroidered the fields of spring
with the open doorsteps of the white houses
with the dreams of storks in the straw roof
written in the glaucous diaphaneity

You hadn't come yet
I looked at the west and I saw you
– a rosy reflection on your hair
– a shadowy smile deep in the sea

Mother held my hands
But I
behind her tender shoulder
behind her pale hair
smoothed by fragrances of patience and kindness
I looked solemnly at the sea

A seagull was calling me
at the depth of the evening
there in the light blue contour of the mountains

The mirror designing dawn
and garden broke

Day before yesterday we buried the first swallow
with the sorrowful flutes of flowers
Then the children sat alone
before the evening window
staring at the dying sun

Behind the white wall of the yard
the road was waking up
and as the golden light was melting at a distance
the great shadow of mountains was rising
with the silent footstep of death
up to our white hands
to our hearts
up to our bowing foreheads

Mother Who is chiming
the horizon's azure bell?

Silver cloud next to the moon

The old seamen
who don't have caiques anymore
who don't have nets anymore
sit on the rock
and smoke their pipes
voyages shadowed and remorseful

But we don't know anything
about ashes in the taste of a voyage
We know the voyage
and the blue green semicircle of the horizon
which is like the wild eyebrow
of a sea god

We jump on the boats
untie the lines
and sing to the sea
staring at the opened cloud
next to the spring moon

Which diamond city
sleeps behind the mountains?
Which lights shiver in the night
and call us?

There are some small white graves
of innocent seagulls
far away on desolate islands of the unknown
that they alone met
in the illumination of the ocean
We laid down there our first flowers
our first sob our first thought

We heard the song of the sea
and we can't sleep anymore

Mother
don't hold my hand

Sea sea
in our minds in our souls in our veins the sea

We saw ships bringing mythic lands
here in the blond sand
where the evening wayfarers slow down
We dressed our childish loves
with wet seaweeds
We offered to the seashore gods

lustrous shells and pebbles

Morning colors melted in water
dusk fires on the gulls' shoulders
masts showing the immensity
open thresholds in the step of night
and over the stone's sleep
sea songs hover
illuminated unappeased
entering through small windows
designing gardens flashes and dreams
on the steamed windowpanes and in sleeping brows

Rhythm agony and vigil
There on the naked rocks
we the homeless barefoot children
saw Beauty
walking barefoot in the sea
we heard her voice
shivering with the azure echoes
with the phosphorescence of stars
seeding golden stories
in the green sea floor

Venerable heart
unsuspecting childish heart
who never refuses

We were stretching our arms
to gather star flowers
to gather the stars of our pulse
replying to the sea voices
to hold onto Beauty's dress
traveling toward infinity
through the path designed on the pelagos
by the immense summer moon

At noon we wrestled naked on the sand
with the wet bodies of twelve-year-olds
more for embracing than for the win
more for the wresting than the win
only for the victory

Salty hair
sunburned thighs
waves splashing on a kiss
the sea just further than a spasm

The high noon descended buzzing in swirls of fire
to engulf houses of fishermen with white flames
to burn the hearts that don't resist

Outside the windows tranquil guitar playing of sea breeze
the sunlit face of blue sky
in white summer memory
with a purple band of shadow
slant on the velvety cheek

Golden breath of endless water
nets sunbathing on the rocks
boats filled with fruits and flowers
our homes written in the sea
here they are our homes

The red stones
the lilacs
and girls
wave from the seashore

Who is calling us
from the roof of our house?

We built our house by the sea
They are pearls in shells

and they are big coral forests on deserted sea floors

We crafted our flutes
with the bones thrown last night
in front of our yard by the singing storm

Hear our song oh mother
the song of a new voyage

You who lament for death
don't recognize us

The sea doesn't cry
it sings

End of the Sunday mass
whitewashed yard
opposite the sea a silent bell-tower
that chimed souls Saturdays of seamen
and now laughs in the sunshine

We have father's pipe in our lips
under our student hats
the Southern Cross and ancient mermaid
embroidered on the chest

Dark colored navy flannel
up to the neck
and as the girls gaze at us
we assume the wide and open stride
of world-traveled captains

In the girls' glances the echo
of a big morning forest shivers
in musical limpidity
and trust

But as the serene houses wave
to us tenderly

with the stooping acacia on the white wall
the flash of the great sea
will move among us
to win us over once again

Ai captain
eat your dried-up bread quickly
and the black olive
dipped in salt and in the sun
over the vertical rock

Time to set sail

As we breath
the glaucous sail of zephyr unfurls
and its sunlit pleats
wave
up to behind happy breasts
of the distant mountains

There are no borders for our heart
falling in love with the sea

A banner of health
that doesn't hesitate
nailed onto stone salutes the sky
stirring over people
large shadows of dew
from the morning sea
with its white sails and islands
flowering in the midst of May

Behind the rocks crawls the deserted
silver thought of moon

On the child's bed pillow shining shells
in his sleep azure voices of the ocean
the Sirens with lyres made of fish bones

Oh Goddess of the distant island
if the stalactites hymn the sleep of
pale serenity in your pelagic lair
and if your gleaming breast contends
the blue circle of starry sea
and if it is a blond crown of honeybees
around the fountain where light pierces imperceptibly
scenting shadows of all-great trees –
you know the crafty Odysseus will leave

Laertis will wait in vain
with his dog above a rock

As He appeared naked from the sea
golden from the dawn water
with his erected phallus depicted in the sun's cornice
Nausica and the awestricken virgin girls hid
behind the trees
their naked soles vacillating
a crowd of doves made of white light
fluttered over the green reflection of grass

…Out in the sunshine close to the sea
our evening table is austere
Spring-moistened wheat bread in wine
the moon secretly drew scenes
from Troy onto
the Hellenic clay pitchers

Mother you knew that we would leave
and you salted our supper with tears
stooping and sad under the stars
and on the island shelves the girls who
got engaged to Odysseus sighed

We spent blood and sperm
with kites and clouds
over sunlit waters

with small wooden caiques
in the light blue bays
being fragrant with goodbyes
with kisses next to boats of the old dock
behind the tumble-down summer windmill
readying the long voyage to the unknown

And when we returned at dusk
with bloodied hands and broken knees
carrying the loot of tiredness:
watery images denying the shape
rosy bell-chimes of dusk
the spasm of regret
the void of struggle –
there under the shadow of the sea cemetery
our childish eyes smelled the silence
they heard the night's passing
they heard beauty's flute
that consoles the sad forehead
and justifies destiny

Who cuts to pieces God's soul
and our joy
who divides silence
in a thousand names and stars
that stir and light our hands
that incise circles of loneliness
in the same sea
that preserves creative fire
but doesn't take comfort?

Flutter of sea birds
in the voiceless caves of rocks
the angels' drawings
embroidered with stars in the water's crack
close to resistance of pebbles
on green shadows of the dock
under the enlarged eyes

of the pensive boys

The wound of day that left
inscribing the horizons and memory with blood
was drawing God's imperfection
his movement dreams creation

Light blue awareness
in the dilated eyes of children
in the solemn lips of ephebes
who didn't quantify sailor's
awareness that glorifies
the outburst of stars
from the opened wound of God
so it will appease
the wound of man

We closed our eyes
in our white paternal bed

The lamp blown out
in the window frame
secret reflection of the sea
Behind fences and trees
we heard
her great voice calling us
filling our sleep with azure landscapes
all flowered with snow white sails
with gardens of gulls in silent reverie
sitting on the stony edge of the unknown
above the magnetic dark abyss

God's cry named us from there

Tomorrow we'll swim again
tomorrow we'll travel more
tomorrow the dawn will ask for our endurance
and we'll respond to the sea

We wrote our first verse in the sand
while the insisting masts looked at us solemnly
and the wave whispered the eternal homecoming

We stood on the rock like busts of escape
staring at the moon designing circles
asking our secret
about ships carrying white shadows
about the endless voyage
about the anchor that didn't nail the water
We touched our wound and time
and we escaped

The voyage always remains with us
and the endless clamor of the sea

The ships had come with the dawn
loaded with wheat coal and wine
for the dreams of captains
for the food of fire

You threw the bread the wine and coal
and remained naked in the sea
without cloth covering your ribs
without love hiding your eyes

The hour had the color of secret pearl
sunk in the thought of dawn
with distant voices filled with danger and promise

You looked at your body in the water
and you loved the water forgetting your body

Oh voyage without any burden
with fire without coal
with hunger without bread
with thirst and elation without wine

It is too late to go back now

If the wave is warmer than love
and the ship warmer than the harbor
you know it
as escape sings in your hair
opposite the horizon with the sea horn
of eternal migration

The ships left and left us
without bread wine and coal in the midst of the sea

All night long we cried
stooping over the white coffin of a seagull

From the corner mother's
lamp lighted us
a thin limb of light
in the middle of the Virgin's diaphanous palm

Heavy sleep around daybreak
in the conches' history
melted candles
in the sea's church

And it was the ship waiting
with its bow incised in the light of dawn
sword of the wind
tonight go to sleep with a bitter heart
like the bread of fishermen in the storm

Tomorrow we'll uproot the crosses
of the sea cemetery
to engrave children's boats
and to incise in headstones
small statues of beauty and of the sea
to fill the deserted house
to beguile life and ourselves
in spite of the negative god
under the blessing of God

The masts vanished
the smoke had sunk
behind the voiceless contour of water
that resembles the knee of a mother asleep
and the voyage vigilant in our breasts
vigilant like the wind and the sea
in winter's dusk

Soft hills travel
in the mist
and the sick sun is sleepy
on the moist stones of evening

The storks high up
in a triangle of repentance

A small lonely prayer book
under the evening rain
the Saint Nickolas cenotaph by the shore
where Autumn stops
to throw a coin of bitterness in and a yellow leaf
while the roar of rough sea distances the misted sandy beach
to the teary starlight of silent September

Gather the azure marbles
from childish days with games and cries
to carve the ocean's statue
bloodying hands in the cloudy afternoon
where the pale reflection of pelagos
writes a circle of sunlit guilt
high up in the vacant air

Winter caught up with us all alone
in the small green seaside house

The deserted balconies
and on the pale seashore
the fog walks noiselessly

Decay of yellow leaves
silent death of chrysalis –
the seaweed blocking doors and roads
verdant memory of cypresses

At the turn of the road the shadow of silence

We saw through the window the last
summer visitors leaving
and the small caique with the empty baskets
Ships sleep in the harbor
and the ash-colored flags of wind
are fluttering on naked masts

In a little while the sorrowful rain
will come
to cleanse the lyric names
the childish plans
and the sea reflections
from the summer boats

With the light of lightning
we'll read fate
in our open palm
and we won't have
not even a word to feed loneliness
not even two crumbs
to feed the few sparrows
dying by the deserted road
The dock trees
slant and alone
in the looted twilight
– wooden busts of summer

Where did the young girls' orchestra go?
to the seashore garden where
at night the sailors drank
amid the trees

and pounded their feet in the air
for a gold coin of moon
in her hair behind the basil plants?

In the nights
only an enormous green reflection of the sea
roams on deserted steep rocks

We pass silently by
the dark rooms
opposite foggy mirrors
that don't recognize us anymore
and we listen to the footsteps of silence
of the wind and of the sea
on our sleepy touch

It is something of the void's safety –
a locked door at night
the sketch of a procession of cypresses
in the silver obscurity
of autumn starlight

And when the solitary full moon
rains resignation and forgetfulness
we open the window
and pray

God we thank you
that we are thus alone and sorrowful
so we may look at the sky without any awe
serene and endless like the firmament
forgotten and unrecognizable like the unknown

Night The invisible mountain range at a distance
I stand in the black frame of the door
and call the name of God
in the snowstorm of stars
amid the diaphanous shadow of people
who sleep and die

in the wilderness which recasts my voice
into thousands of voices

Where did they all go leaving me here
to stare at my empty palms
to keep company to silence and rain?

Deeply grieved up to the point of death
I see the desolate sky
and I salute a big cloud
and I am like a sad little lamb
that they left alone
in the dark valley

Oh God why have they all left from my side?

In my ripped clothes
I have a tender heart
made of birds and flowers
(How many nights I cried secretly
for the wound of the butterfly)

Let all leave Let all leave
I will again stay
opposite the wide sky
opposite the great sea
without bitterness and grumble
and I shall sing
Let all leave
The more I stay alone
the closer to people I get
the closer I am to God

I listen to my voice
set free in the wind
and I warm up my days

A childish dance
returns from the night
it undresses silence
it resurrects the spring

But I am still cold oh mother

Evening has already come
The last autumn crickets
carve shadows on fences
with their unsuspecting short voices

Search in your heart
to find the sun that left

And as twilight fades away
the rose's fragrance will
drip in our soul
a drop of dew on the eyelids
the last light of dusk
on two naked crucified hands
on a frozen face
opposite the silver bow of the open sea

They took our sea song
they tied our sea legs

Silent and awestruck little children
with our salty eyelids
with our big light blue eyes
scared we passed the large plazas
under hospitals smelling of sleep and sweat
under houses with red lamps
under smoke-blackened high-rises
that smell of blood darkness and snatching

Mother mother
whose tender tears' wisdom
we denied
where is your forbearing hand
with the expression of patience
where is your hand
to hear the dawn and the sea
to re-warm loneliness?

Mother
the sky crumbled
in the innocents' tears

We who walked during the nights
in the white forests of pearls
we who carved the azure face
of a dream in the stone
we don't know to walk
on roads that get painted with
the blood of blond Jesus every day

Behind the walls they lurk
A lot of terrified wild doves fly
away from the corners

Doors gape in the night
Swords shine
A moon: decapitated

People using human bones
build ladders
so they can ascend

Kyrie Kyrie
and us here
in the middle of the long roads
sorrowful and clumsy
with the empty haversack in hand
with a nightingale cage on our back
with the wide memory of the sea on our forehead

with innocent surprised hands that don't beg

Mother we have nothing left
Where shall we find shelter?
Where shall we sleep?

There where the hands and houses empty
the sea takes her first place
in the black rooms of night

The dark armor the gypsum
masks the honey-colored
smile of love the greenery
portraits don't hang from
walls anymore

Only the free proud cool
inexhaustible reflection
of the ocean waves there

Dark-complexioned boy with light blue eyes
with thick hair combed by the sea
boy with the irresponsible straddle that never asked the earth
proud boy who denied the Sunday mass
who crafted kites and ships with math notebook sheets
do you remember the old captain
who forgot the harbor staring at the stars
to regain his youth by singing of the sea?

At the time that
the last smile of night left us
and we didn't have any ship to embark
and the docks without lampposts and passengers
we met our shadow oh boy of the sea
we met you with a spring moon in your hands
walking alone amid the rocks of the seashore

where serene crabs and seals reverie

Eyes content with water pictures
that still hunger for water
parades of stars in the memory of gulls asleep
sudden assault of dolphins panic of aqua world
on cracked water mirrors
the circular escape of galaxy

Let startled silence leave again
to the distant asleep shore
 – white daughter of sunken captains
living in the ruins of the ancient dock
and every night as the moon fills
she is chased by the drunk sailors

Master of the sky of earth and of the sea
until when shall we vigil
until when shall we thirst
until when shall we die?

To reach where the light
stops shattering
on wounds and roses
to silence the footsteps
of tired swallows
you would have to get tired
to the last step of twilight
with your breath shattered until death

Among the cracked evenings
when the oil-lamps of houses dripped tears
where the children prayed
in front of the sick Virgin Mary bed
in the snow where a
large lonely moon died

amid winds that crucified
the erotic wings of birds
we harvested warmth and light
to bloom a spring eulogy

And yet victory didn't come it didn't end

So thus alone alone
so much that death enamors us
and our shadow walks on the blond shore
like a peaceful oceanic bird
content with reflections and silence
abandoned by night and love

And yet the predawn didn't arrive

Now who will bring to us
the emigrated ships
loaded with dawns and doves
with children's smiles and tears?
Who will bring back to us
the long convoy of stars
that sunk in our lighted eyes?

Kyrie Kyrie
bring back to me
the sky dress of prayer
bring me the heart
that ignores rain
and blooms swallows
bring me the departures and returns
to find the strength to cry
for the wound of a firefly
to find the strength to sin
and repent
when our island bell
chimes over the sea
the snow-white Sunday innocence

our lost ignorance
our lost health

In the sweet eyes of birds
the vision of fields will stay still
with the scarlet poppies
and the golden abundance of wheat ears

Love and geraniums will bloom again
in small windows by the shore
and a young Jesus will come take us by the hand
where we'll play under the lilacs until twilight
with storks sea breezes and sun

And when evening comes we shall jump in the white caiques
and with the nets of sad biblical fishermen
we shall catch a watery moon
to lie down peacefully with it
so that it lights our sleep with silent angels
who haven't yet learned to laugh or cry
but to only smile in the dream
of the unborn Creation

Islands with trees silent during evening vespers
where peaceful doves fall silent
there we fall silent gathering the day's roses
while the evening shadow falls on white paper
where we incise life next to the seashore

We won't read what we wrote
We shall raise our eyes
yearning for the galaxy's waterfall
behind the almond tree of a white cloud
lingering above the sea

The time without hours and
repentance has arrived again
Azure echo of the light water
foggy walk of fishermen on sand

children sleep in the boats
and Angels bathe in their sleep

Fragrance of grass and star fragrance
At a distance mountaintops vanish in the opulent sky

Our tired hands are sprinkled
with the new dew
and our hair scented with
the shadow of yesterday's grief

Mother the world has no borders

The big harp of twilight
is abandoned in the thick shadow of forest
A rosy cloud burns
in the conflagration of dusk

My god retain this color a bit longer
so that we know our thought
that is defeated but not subdued

We still need this
distant fondness
that cares for what perishes
that upholds the dream
of immortality

The evening goes by
the deserted shore
with the lecythus containing ashes
on her naked shoulder

A smile just shines on her thoughtful figure
that feeds the question our vigil
and hastens the glimmering oracle
of our destiny

Tonight the whole firmament is fragrant
with the sleepless god's sperm

We water roots
in the eternal spring
rising from the bowels of night
and filling the skulls
of dead people with roses

Light fires on the distant docks
embroider stars on the sea's sleep
raise your ravished arms

Here silence regains a voice
Here the departed live forever
Here there is no flight and ravaging

Evening song over the open seas
accompanied by the absence of things
blooming in eternal circles
of silence and love

The sea stares at her face
in the sea

Take the subdued idols
Take knowledge that wrinkled up our youthful touch
Take the fruitless tired serenity
that sat on the rock
to build her temple and her grave
with the wood of our ancient ships

Leave us only
the night's ecstasy
when mothers wait in
front of the bloomed door for
their strange and insubordinate children
who missed their evening meal

who swim naked all day
who search for the gull's nests
and night-long whisper in their sleep
undecipherable words about ships and Angels
for some crazy Angels who live
in purple coral plantations
about some blond Angels who
got engaged to the sea
and forgot God
Angels playing wild trumpets
made
with the bones of castaway poets

Leave us only
the night's ecstasy
when the children fish for stars
in the snow white caiques
when naked and handsome ephebes
stare straight at beauty's eyes
without suspicion or fear
Return to us
the paper ships
to moor in a well known harbor
of our first homeland

For a moment
we shall kneel on the sand
and we shall pray
in front of our indomitable shadow
while the sea's sad Virgin Mary
will quietly open the front door of the church
and will lean to kiss our hair
drenched by the slender dew of stars
of silence and of the night
Although we
shall again deny
the kiss of love
that soothes and ties

We are unknown in the unknown

we the handsome and insubordinate
shall travel forever
in the silver forests of the moon
in the deserted islands of stars
without knowing God
without finding God
like the pulse of that same deity
who creates wearing herself out

Nightly harbor lights
sunken in water
faces without memory and continuance
successively lit
by spotlights of passing
distant ships
and then sunk
in the shadow of eternal voyages
slant masts
with hanging lamps of dreams
like the cracked wings
of Angels who sinned
soldiers with helmets
between the night and coal
wounded hands like the
forgiveness that reached late

At the peak a great fire
burning the hearts of shadows

Prisoners tied on anchors
in a red flash
a ring
tight around the neck of the horizon
and on the dawn's hands
holding a daisy

Color deserts the face of day
and light doesn't find any statue
to dwell in to be glorified to becalm

Brothers
how can I stay away from you?

Sea sea
books don't impede the question
a question doesn't heal the wound
Pelagos starts from our wounds

The voyage dreams
at the last contour of tears

Who banishes the sun
from our children's hair
and our great hearts?

Unfurl the sails
raise the anchor
March and the old harbors vanish
March and the dawn gleams
with all our ancestors' tears

Cuffs cannot stand in the ankles of sea
cuffs cannot stand in our sea heart

Goodbye loves and homelands

Pelagic birds in light and salinity
dreams of voyages large sails
our ears unsealed to the Siren's songs
our eyes vigilant
There is neither smoke nor Ithaca
Horizons don't have any other horizon
The eternal song of open sea answers to the void
and fills the nothing with heart and sun

Oh nights of storms
whipping illuminated winds
wave-froths on the windowpanes
the smoky lamps of fishermen's houses
terror of sorrowful girls
mending socks of émigrés
sleepless lighthouses with eyes of mothers
and the immense sea is merciless
like the thought of god
wild tender and untamed
like the hearts of poets

Specters of castaway captains
with pipes still between their lips
on the lighted horse of lightning
sunken ships returning
to night's harbors
the lost crews
standing outside closed doors
waiting
searching their lives silently
holding tropical pictures
azure fields with enormous lilies
and ebony naked women

Those cry and don't see

But we
who spoke to the sea for hours
we who always retain
on our lips damp deep and young
the voyage's sweetness
we accept the eternal gifts of death

And when mothers
curse the sea
and when the old captains
walk step by step worrying
in closed rooms
we

open the doors

run to the big rocks
and raise our cry
in the night
overpowering the tempest
forgetting bread and house
freshening up the fevered forehead
with the wide anger
of the sea

Sea sea
as you are
we are
we shall not succumb to the night
and to sleep

We shall not condescend to cry:
we have won forever

Joy of rough seas
of calm sea
of departing
joy of the eternal voyage
let the dock lights turn off
let us enter the ocean's heart
in the endless song of nightly waves
while God
from the height of his great loneliness
stones our courage
with illuminated dreams

Oh endless pain Oh universal joy
fire of the firmament
that burns down the black hair of night
and lights the dawn over white sails

over the high masts
where the poets climb
to salute the new face of God
reflected smiling in the waters
amid the frame of two drunken seagulls

Sun sun
that paints the sea with blood
I offer myself naked to your fire
to light the eyes of men

My brothers
listen to your voices to my voice
listen to the song of the sun and seaplace

Notes on the
Margins of Time
1938-1941

Doxology

He stood at the far end of the road
like a leafless dusty tree
like a tree burned by the sun
praising the sun that cannot be burned

Hour of Song

Next to the wine jugs
next to the fruit baskets
we forgot to sing

On the evening of our separation
with the consent of
the evening star alone
we sang

Healing

Years of sky The street and the sundown
The white houses are serene
like the memory that doesn't feel sorry for you anymore

Two poplars vanished at dusk
two poplars
two poplars

And the sun like a wound that heals

Fear of Life

Stony day
stony sun
stony silence

The horses died on the mountain
the trees died in whitewash
you didn't die

Sound of their distant hooves
sound of the old panting
in petrified noon

And the fear that perhaps you wouldn't die
and the fear of water trickling
fear water breath – life

One Dead

He said: The light with the enlarged eyes
with the enlarged arm hairs
with the magnified voices of builders on the opposite
construction site with the blinding sea
between their naked ribs is terrible

You have to get saddled with a mountain – he said –
so that you may pass standing through the sun's responsibility

However down in the basement – he said –
are the large empty barrels like coffins of your ancestors
there is the conciliatory shadow
and the oil stains on the floor
and the roots of the tree that pushes through the wall
its contorted fingers

The security of death – he said

There you hear the distant words of vineyards and seeds
you taste the silence and the moisture
you get used to being dead

And he was truly dead without being accustomed to it
When the long days came with flags
when light knocked on his door
no one opened

He was dead without being accustomed to it

Punishment

Moments – moments
uncounted
tamed by the sun
countless

Then we counted them
With the palm of a dry grapevine leaf
we secured the summer

On the Eve of Autumn

The last vacationers sit in front of windows with
    crossed arms
the few in love and dry leaves sit on benches
    of gardens

When the coach was heard from the road
no one went down to open
only a dog came out of the door
and looked straight in the eyes of the afternoon

Perhaps she was in there the sick lady
who is always cold and holds a bouquet of violets
on her knees

It was she – the hotel manager said and spat out the window
Then he wiped his lips and closed the shutters

Floating in Air

With the first cold spells the trees leave stooping in the wind
In the evening the sky becomes a large closed glass door
In there many have gathered talking in low tones and smoking
because we see behind the steamed up glass
some insignificant flashes flickering
From time to time someone throws his cigarette from above
and we kept our fingers in check before we got burned
None of us had some soil of his own anymore
a small field or a grave

Winter is Approaching

With each tick of the clock a yellow leaf falls
You had a straw hat with lilac flowers
Now in there chickens lay eggs
and a snail climbs on the chair leg

The snow will be cold cold cold
like the father's high collar
that is hidden in the chest for years

The trees already smell of mothballs

Myth

At night we lighted the oil lamps
and took the roads asking the passers-by

She wore a dress we said
in the color of dreams Didn't you see her?
She wore two light blue earrings

No one had seen her Only in the cabin at the end of the village
the old woman the lumberjack's mother pointed her finger
and showed us the river behind the trees

Down to where two light blue stars flickered

Memory

Father came home late He didn't say good evening
Mother was concerned with her children   She didn't pay
attention to him
The children enjoyed her care They didn't pay attention that he
didn't
        say good evening He
had his hands clasped behind him
had talked to the rain in the harvested fields
behind the woodsman's cabin He had a double barrel shotgun
        across his shoulder

He stood near the window alone
and when a strong lightning strike lit the glass
I saw the cross of the window incised in his forehead

Perhaps we learned of that separation tonight
perhaps the same cross is incised since then
in the lit wall of our silence

An Invitation

Come to the luminous beaches – he murmured to himself –
here where the colors celebrate – look –
here where the royal family never passed
with their closed carriages and official emissaries

Come – it is not good if they see you – he would say –
I am the deserter of the night
I am the burglar of darkness
I have filled my shirt and my pockets with sun

Come – it burns my hands and my chest
Come let me give it to you

And I have something to tell you
that even I cannot hear

Portrait

His eyes are angry his hair sticks up
like the shattered glass on the fence wall of a tree garden
Your hand cannot clamber up there – it will be scratched
His hands are two petrified rivers

In his silence a young girl had drown some years ago
and his mouth remains tightened – not tightened
just that he licks like a child does a red sugary cockerel

Don't show that you saw him – he will go away
with his hair sticking up like the glass on the fence wall

Proportions

The stars are muddy in the cistern
the cistern in the middle of the old yard
like a mirror of the closed room

The doves sit around the cistern
whitewashed flowerpots sit end-to-end in the moon
around and around our wound our songs

Succession

The sun doesn't think about your hesitations –
it wants you naked and it takes you naked
until the night comes to dress you

After the sun there is repentance
after repentance the sun again

Etesian Winds

Ship after ship after ship –
The pushcart man looks down the slope
The pines throw themselves into the sea
The sea climbs up the mountain
And the pushcart man splattered
with white foam mounts the sun

Delay

The summer ended quickly We ran out of time
Big clouds hung on top of the mountains
like masks of an ancient tragedy What should we do?

Our shoes no matter how old   are always a bit tight
The light is narrow and the cloud is cinched down
We stop before the bloomed tree
before the nourishment and water
in front of tomorrow's window
somewhat embarrassed panting
in the emotion of an eternal delay

With pinched feet how did we come this far?

Summer in the City

In this place the light is beyond hope This heartless month
doesn't allow us not to be two You are not enough
The monotonous clank of the streetcars turning the corner
the marble masons cutting stones in high noon

Above the fence wall you could see the conventional funerary
stele
with marble flowers marble ribbons
the bust of a banker
the face of a child shadowed by an angel's wing

On these professional sculptures the Attic sun incises
        its seal
the shadow adds unbelievable extensions –
so it wasn't strange at all that yesterday afternoon
returning home from your office
holding the net with bread and tomatoes
not at all strange that yesterday as the sun went down
you met the marble ephebe in the small park
sauntering slowly and smiling

You sat on a bench by the lake throwing bread to the goldfish
        and all night long
though you didn't have any food   you were not hungry at all

Nude

Here in the untidiness of the room
between the dusty books
and the old people's portraits
between the yes and the no of so many shadows
one band of motionless light
here in this position
where you undressed one night

Copper Engraving

Lone bells chime of silence
bunches and bunches of memories under the trees
the cows sad at sundown

Behind the young shepherds
in the west a cloud bleated

April

Spring Your eyes are two drops of sea
A canary up and down a wooden cross

Admission

Defeated by the light blue
with his head leaning on the knees of silence
dead tired of life
dead tired of youth
sunken inside his fire
and the seaweed stirring in his armpit –

The wave of day didn't find resistance
not even on a pebble of his thought

So he was ready for love
and for death

Old Waltz

The sundown shed on the face of a young woman so gracefully
like a red lily sheds on the piano during the final
    chord

An orange angel was left in the street
before his long shadow

In a while the entrance lights were turned on
the noise of cars was heard
and the sound of silk on the stairs

Frailty

A shredded light is wind-tossed on a tumbled fence wall
Behind the fence wall the workers urinate
    at the end of their shift

One window is opened Someone sang
And the night fell asleep again amid the stars
like a naked woman amid the osiers

Her body must be full of moisture

Moon

Moon moon The moon
yellow round glass in the middle of spring night Behind it
faces of the night shadows gather
and see you – you don't see them They own you

Here are all the unknowns: unknown pacified
in the silent admission that they shall not be known
calm silent and pale as if known and left behind

Childish

In the little harbor the sea copies
the leaves and the clouds and birds
beautifully carefully and like calligraphy –
from time to time the wind hastily underlines her
mistakes with some thick light blue lines

But the one who writes all day long staring at the sea
Makes no mistakes – my embittered serenity –
and speechless he always yearns for love
to underline his heart – the only mistake

Three Lines

The sky entrusts you with all his light blue
How will your shoulders endure it all day?
How will the ribs of your song endure it?

Exchange

Midnight stooped over us
like a commercial vessel stoker
sweaty stoker full of coal dust

For a moment he laughed His teeth shined like
        stolen diamonds
And we wanted to see his face under the smudge

We drew our finger on his forehead
Since then a white line makes the night darker
Since then a black line stays on our finger

After the Flood

Those days it rained unceasingly Torrential rain
The river flooded You couldn't see the bridge
People stood by the banks They waited The rain wasn't stopping
Some did away with their underpants and shoes so they
        could cross the river
Then they stayed like that They didn't cross They stayed in the
rain
naked until night came and we didn't know anymore: did they
stay there? Did they
        cross? Did they drown?

The next day it was sunny The river receded
Love went back and forth on the bridge playing with the leaves
and no one remembered anymore the deeds of ones who fought
        the water
neither the cries of those who the river separated
nor those who drowned in the night

One shoe sailed calmly on the river
like a boat or a bird amid games of water and sun

For You

He had no time – how could he listen? Fighting for his bread
he didn't see that the wheat ear grew tickling the sun's ear
he didn't see the blond mustache of summer
he didn't see that he also grew

I sang for you – the other told him
Come song talk to me still even if he doesn't listen – he said to
him
Come moon   kiss him for me even if he didn't kiss me

This moon like a blond shepherd – alone
lies down beside the little lamb of his soul

Duty

One star gleams in the twilight like a lit
        keyhole
you glue your eye on it – you look inside – you see everything
The world is fully illuminated behind the locked door

You need to open it

Assistance

The wind converses in front of the windows
like those who are going to separate
The furniture becomes like the poor girls gathering
fallen olives The evening walks under the olive trees
all alone and the field with harvested wheat
is a denial The shed husk of the cicada
resembles a small bell-tower fallen on dry grass

The drizzle comes later – it hunts the sparrows
slowly the moon lies down under the cypresses
like the abandoned plow The plowman
sleeps beneath the soil –
his wife alone with the dog and the thin ox

The hands of silence are frozen
as she ties her black headscarf under her chin
But the trace of his hand stays on the wood of the plow
        more strong than his hand
and the chair's back keeps the warmth of his broad shoulder
        blades

About these insignificant things – I don't know –
I want to write a small song that will show I don't know
anything about all these only that they are as they are
alone completely alone and they don't ask for any mediation
between themselves and someone else

Silent Separation

She took down her jacket and left without any tears –
like she took down the moon from the summer sky

He didn't believe He waited the same night
the next day and the one after that He waited

After two weeks went by with the moon-change
he knew that she wouldn't return Only the mirror was left
to remember like an open window
in a moonless sky
that she took her jacket with her

Obstacle

Drizzle on the roofs of the countryside
One closed up house Inside it a man undresses
The creak of the bed was heard the fall of shoes
a plate they broke in the kitchen

Then the shadow of the train passed over the dusty
    laurels
and it was as if they closed the door discreetly so that we
    couldn't see
    who went through the hallway

In the other room was loneliness with her big book
and all light was concentrated in half a glass of water

Someone tried to pierce the mirror with his finger
    The drizzle stopped
They positioned the cameras on the seashore
Snapshots memories disturbances
and this insistence that you want to pierce the mirror to look
at the other side so that the view wouldn't obstruct your idol

In the Barracks

The moon entered the barracks
It rummaged in the soldiers' blankets
Touched an undressed arm Sleep
Someone talks in his sleep Someone snores
A shadow gestures on the long wall
The last trolley bus went by Quietness

Can all these be dead tomorrow?
Can they be dead from right now?

A soldier wakes up
He looks around with glassy eyes
A thread of blood hangs from the moon's lips

The Victor

He unlocked his dark room hesitantly
to try once more to hear the sound of his footsteps
on the snow white stone pavement of day

All expected him to come out through the sun's door

He wore a golden denture of light
and tried to learn off by heart a few green leaves
but he felt that this way his empty mouth was more visible
and for this reason he neither spoke nor smiled

The others listened to their cheering
They never sensed that he stayed silent
Then he stooped down he took a stone and went after
the last loyal dog who followed him

The people raised him on their shoulders in the sunshine
And like that raised above their heads
no one saw him crying

The Defeated

He didn't fear the light anymore at all   He went out to the street
No one paid attention to him   A contented sun
smoked his cigarette over the city

He wrapped his laughter in a piece of the night
and vanished at the turn of the street defeated by his victory

The Hill

Someone had a lot of dead people
He dug the ground he buried them himself
Stone by stone earth on earth
he built a hill
On top of the hill
he built his cabin facing the sun

After that he opened pathways
he planted trees
carefully geometrically thoughtfully
His eye was always smiling
His hand wasn't trembling
The hill

There on Sunday afternoons mothers climb
pushing their baby carriages
the workers of the neighborhood in clean shirts
go there to sunbathe and breath some fresh air
There at twilight pairs in love saunter
and learn to read the stars
Under the trees a child plays harmonica
The pop vendor yells about his lemonade

On the hill they all know
that they are closer to the sky

But no one knows how the hill was built
no one knows how many sleep in the hills' bowels

Romiosini

1945-1947

I

These trees don't take comfort in less sky
these rocks don't take comfort under foreigners'
    footsteps
these faces don't take comfort but only
    in the sun
these hearts don't take comfort except in justice

This landscape is merciless like silence
it hugs its fiery rocks tightly in its bosom
it hugs tightly in the sun its orphan olive trees
    and grapevines
it clenches its teeth There is no water Only light
The road vanishes in light and the shadow of the fence wall
    is made of steel

Trees rivers and voices turn to marble
    in the sun's whitewash
The root stumbles on the marble The dusty
    bulrush
The mule and the rock They all pant There is
    no water
They've all been thirsty for years and years They all
    chew one bite of sky over their bitterness

Their eyes are red for lack of sleep
a deep wrinkle is wedged between their eyebrows

like a cypress between two mountains
       at sundown
their hands are glued to their rifles
their rifles are extensions of their hands
their hands extensions of their souls –
they have anger on their lips
and grief deep within their eyes
like a star in a pothole of salt

When they clasp a hand the sun is certain
       of the world
when they smile a small swallow flies away from
       their rough beards
when they sleep twelve stars fall from their
       empty pockets
when they are killed life follows the uphill with
       flags and drums

For so many years they've all starved they've all thirsted
       they've all been killed
besieged by land and sea
sweltering has devoured their fields and salinity has
       drenched their homes
wind pushed down their doors and the few lilac shrubs
       of the plaza
death goes in and out the holes of their overcoats
their tongues are astringent like cypress cones
their dogs died wrapped in their own shadows
the rain pounds on their bones

Petrified on their battlements they smoke
       the cow dung and during the night
they keep watch on the furious pelagos where
the broken mast of the moon sank

The bread running out the ammunition spent
now they load their cannons with only their
       hearts

So many years besieged by land
    and sea
they are all hungry they are all killed and yet
    nobody died –
on their battlements their eyes shine
a large flag a great conflagration
    totally red
and every dawn thousands of doves fly out
    from their hands
to the four gates of the horizon

II

Every evening with the thyme scorched on
    the rock's bosom
there's a water-drop that for a long time has been digging
    silence to its marrow
there is a bell hanging from the ancient plane-tree
    calling out the years

Sparks sleep lightly in the embers of solitude
and roofs contemplate on the golden fine down
    on the upper lip of Alonaris [1]
– yellow fine down like the corn tassel smoked up
    by the grief of the west

Virgin Mary leans down on the myrtle her wide
    skirt stained by grapes
On the road a child cries and the ewe who lost her
    lambs answers from the meadow

Shadow by the spring The barrel frozen
The blacksmith's daughter with soaked feet
On the table the bread and the olive
in the grapevine the night lamp of evening star

---

[1] *Month of Wheat Harvest – June*

and high up there turning on its spit
      the galaxy is fragrant
by the burnt-up lard garlic and pepper

Ah what silky stars the pine needles
    will need still to embroider
over the scorched fence wall of summer
      "this will also pass"

how a mother will still squeeze her heart over
      her seven butchered brave lads
until light finds its path to the uphill
      of her soul

This bone sticking out of the earth
measures the earth yard by yard and
      the lute's strings
and the lute from dusk to dawn with
    the violin
grief by grief they sing it to rosemary
    and the pines
and the ropes ring like lyres in the boats
and the seaman drinks bitter sea in
      Odysseus' wine cup

Ah who then will fence the entrance and which
      sword will sever the courage
and which key will lock up your heart that with
      its two door-leaves wide open
stares at God's star-drenched orchards?

Long hour like the Saturday evenings of May
      in the seamen's tavern
long night like a roasting pan on the tinsmith's wall
long song like bread on the sponge diver's
      dinner
And here is the Cretan moon rolling down
      the pebble mount
goup goup with twenty lines of nails on the soles
      of his leather boots

and here are those who go up and down
     the Palamidi[2] stairs
filling their pipes with roughly cut leaves
     of darkness
their mustaches star-sprinkled with thyme
     of Roumeli[3]
and their teeth pine roots in the Aegean's
     rock and salinity

They were thrown in iron and fire they conversed
     with rocks
they offered raki[4] to death in their
     grandfathers' skulls
on the same threshing floors they met and shared their dinner
     with Digeni[5]
slicing their grief in two like they sliced their barley bread loaves
     on their knees

Come you oh woman with the salty eyelashes with
     your hand gold-plated
by your concern for the poor and by the many
     years –
love is waiting for you in the bulrushes
the seagull hangs your black icon in his cave
     and the bitter urchin kisses your toenail

In the black grape of the vineyard the red
     bright must bubbles
shoots of the burned bulrush bubbles
under the earth the root of the dead man begs for water
     so it will grow a fir tree
and under her wrinkles a mother holds the knife
     tightly

---

[2] *Venetian castle of Palamidi in Nafplion with one thousand steps*
[3] *Part of Mainland Greece between Peloponnesos and Thessaly*
[4] *Moonshine*
[5] *Literary meaning, one of two races; however also a mythical*
figure, invented during the Medieval years of Turkish
occupation, who was   destined to free Greeks from slavery

Come you oh woman who broods on the golden
        eggs of thunderbolts –
when an azure day comes you'll take off the headscarf
        and again take up arms
that May's hailstorm will beat your forehead
that the sun will break a pomegranate in your cotton apron
that alone you will divide seed by seed
        among your twelve orphans
that the shore will shine around you like the edge of a sword
        and April's snow
so that the crab will come out from the rocks to sunbathe
        and cross its claws

III

Here the sky doesn't lessen the oil of our eye
        not even for a moment –
here the sun lifts on his shoulders half the weight of rocks
        we carry on our backs
the roof tiles break without any ah under the knee
        of noon hour
people walk in front of their shadows like dolphins
        in front of the boats of Skiathos
when their shadow becomes an eagle painting
        his wings at dusk
 and later he roosts on their heads and
        thinks of stars
when they lie down on the sun-drenched roof
        next to the black raisins

Here every door has incised a name in it for some
        three thousand years
every stone has been painted with a saint with wild
        eyes and hair made of straw
every man has a red mermaid etched on his left arm
        stitch by stitch
every Kore has a handful of salty light under

her skirt
and the young men have five-six little crosses
    of bitterness over their hearts
like the footsteps of seagulls on the seashore
    in the afternoon

You don't have to remember We know it
All paths lead to the High Threshing Floors The wind
    is pungent up there

When the Minoan fresco of the west flakes
    in its solitude
and the conflagration of the barn by the
    seashore is put out
old women climb up here stepping on the carving
    in the rock steps
they sit on the Great Rock knitting the sea
    with their eyes
they sit and count the stars like they count their
    ancestral silver spoons and forks
and slowly go down the path to feed their grandchildren
    with gunpowder from Mesolongi[6]

Yes truly Elkomenos[7] has two hands so sorrowful
    in their shackles
though his eyebrow stirs like a boulder ready
    to break away
from over his bitter eye

---

[6] *Famous city besieged by the Turks during the Independence War of
1821*

[7] *The Pulled One. There is a church in Monemvasia, Greece, dedicated to
Jesus the Elkomenos, Redeemer, who is dragged, chained and carrying
the cross, along the streets of Jerusalem before the crowds on his way to
Golgotha. He bears the cross and metaphorically the spectators' sins. A
parallel can be drawn between this and the ancient ritual of dragging
the scapegoat; a goat that was decorated with flowers and beads and
pulled along the streets of Athens; Athenians symbolically threw their
sins at it before pushing it out of the gates of the city to the unknown of
the elements, (scapegoat), thus redeeming the populace from their sins
until the following year when the event was repeated.*

From the sea bottom rises a wave that doesn't
    know of begging
from high above flows this wind with veins
    of raisin and sagebrush lung

Ah may it blow once and obliterate the orange
    trees of memory
Ah may it blow twice to spark the iron rock
    like a percussion cup
Ah may it blow three times and drive mad the
    fir forests of Liakoura [8]
may it punch once with its fist and blow
    tyranny up in the air
and pull the bear night's nose ring that it may dance
    a tsamikos [9] for us in the middle of the bastion
and the moon would play the tambourine that it may fill the
    island balconies
with bleary-eyed youth and mothers from Souli [10]
A messenger arrives from the Big Glen
    every morning
the sweating sun shines on his face
he holds romiosini tightly under his
    armpit
like the worker holds his cap inside
    the church
"The hour has come" he says "Be ready
Every hour is our hour"

IV

They went straight to dawn with the haughty
    air of the hungry
a star had curdled in their motionless eyes
on their shoulders they carried the injured summer

---

[8] *Forested area in Peloponnesos*
[9] *Northern Greece folk dance*
[10] *Northern Greece village well known from the Independence
War of 1821*

This way the army went with banners glued onto
     their flesh
with stubbornness bitten by their teeth like
     an unripe wild pear
with the moon-sand under their heavy boots
and with the coal dust of night glued in their
     nostrils and their ears

Tree by tree stone by stone they passed the world
with thorns as pillows they spent their sleep
They carried life like a river in their parched hands

With every step they won a yard of sky – to
     give it away

On watch they turned to stone like the
     conflagrated trees
and when they danced in the plaza ceilings
     shook inside the houses
and the glassware clinked on the shelves

 Ah what songs shook the mountain peaks –
as they held between their legs the earthen dish of the moon
     and had their dinner
and broke the sigh amid their heart pleats
like they would break a louse with their
     thick nails

Who will now bring you the warm loaf of bread so that
     you may feed dreams in the night?
Who will stand in the olive tree's shade
     company to cicada so that it won't go silent
now that the noon whitewash paints all around the horizon
     a stone wall
erasing their great manly names?

This soil that was so fragrant at dawn
the soil that was theirs and ours –
     their blood – how fragrant the soil was –
and now how our vineyards have locked their doors

how the light has thinned on roofs and trees –
who would have said that half of them are under
        the earth
and the other half in jail?

With so many leaves the sun greets you good morning
and the sky shines with so many banners
and these are in jail and those lie under
        the earth

Silence any time now the bells will chime
This soil is theirs and ours
Under the earth in their crossed hands
they hold the bell rope – waiting for the hour
        they don't sleep they don't die
they wait to ring the resurrection This
        soil
is theirs and ours – no one can
        take it from us

V

They sat under the olive trees in early afternoon
sieving the gray light with their big
        fingers
they took off their cartridge belts and measured the
        anguish fitting the path of night
how much bitterness fits in the wild mallow's knot
how much courage in the eyes of a shoeless child
        holding up the flag

Past its time the last swallow remained in
        the plains
weighed himself in midair like a black band
        on the sleeve of autumn
Nothing else remained Only the burnt up
        houses smoldering

The others who left us for sometime

lay under the rocks
with their ripped shirts and their oaths written
        on the fallen door
No one cried – we had no time Only silence
        became deeper
and the light gathered down the shore like the
        orderly house of the dead woman

What will become of them when the rain comes amid
        the rotten plane leaves in the soil?
What will happen to them when the sun dries up in
        a blanket of cloud
like a crushed bug in a villager's bed?
when the snow stork stands embalmed on the chimney
        of last night?

 Old mothers scatter salt in the fire they scatter soil
        over their hair
they have uprooted the grapevines of Monemvasia[11] so that
        not a black grape
        will ever sweeten the enemy's mouth

they placed in a sack the grandfather's bones along
        with their knives and forks
and they go around outside the walls of their country looking
        where to grow roots in the night

It'll be hard to find a tongue less powerful
        less stony
than the cherry tree's –
those hands that were left in the fields or
up on the mountains or down under the sea
do not forget they never forget –
it'll be difficult for us to forget their hands
it'll be hard for the hands that grew calluses
        on the trigger to ask a daisy
to say thank you on their knees or on
        the book

---

[11] *Southern part of Peloponnesos*

or in the bosom of the starlight

It will take time And we need to speak up
until they find their bread and their rights

Two oars rooted down in the sand at dawn
       in rough seas Where is the boat?
A plow embedded in the soil and the wind
       blowing
burnt up earth Where is the plowman?

Ashes the olive tree the grapevine and the house
Night stitched on with her stars inside
       the sock
Dried laurel leaves and oregano in the middle-self
       on the wall Fire couldn't reach it
Smoked up cooking pot in the fire – and the water
boils by itself in the locked up house They had no
       time to eat

The forest's veins on their burnt door leaf –
       blood flows in the veins
And here is the familiar footstep Who is he?
Familiar footstep on the uphill nails in the soles
Crawl of root in the rock Someone is
       coming
The password the response A brother Good
       evening

So then light will find its trees the tree
       will find its fruit
the flask of the killed still has water and light
Good evening my brother Good evening

The old Lady West sells herbs and embroidery
       in her wooden shack
no one buys them They went up high
It's difficult for them to come descend anymore

It's difficult for them to fit in their own height

On the threshing floor where the braves ate
        one night
the olive pits and the dry blood of the moon
        remain
and their fifteen-syllabic armory
the cypresses and laurels remain all around

Next day sparrows ate the crumbs
        of their army bread
children made toys out of the matches
that lit their cigarettes and the stars' thorns

And the rock where they sat under olive trees
        in the afternoon opposite the sea
it will become whitewash in the kiln tomorrow
day after we'll paint our houses and the bench
        of Saint Savior
the day after that we'll plant the seed
        where they fell asleep
and a pomegranate bud
will flash its first baby smile on the breast
        of sunshine

After that we'll sit on the soil to read all their hearts
as if we read from the world history for the first time

VI

Thus with the sun in the heart of pelagos whitewashing
        the opposite pleat of day
the latching and the anguish of thirst are counted twice
        or three times
the old wound is counted over again
and the heart is slow roasting in the heat like an onion
from Kythera [12] left by the doors

---

[12] *Island where famous strong onions are produced*

More and more their hands resemble the soil
more and more their eyes resemble sky

The oil storage jar is empty Just a bit of bottom
        dregs And the dead mouse
The mother's courage emptied along with the
        earthen jar and the cistern
The gums of solitude harden from the gunpowder

There is no oil for the candle of Saint Barbara
there is no mint for incensing the golden
        icon of twilight
there is no bite of bread for the beggar evening to play
        her star-song on the lyre

In the upper castle of the island the cactus pears and the
        asphodels become ghosts
The soil dug up by the cannonballs and
        the graves
The demolished government building gapes patched
        with sky There is no place anymore
for more dead There is no place for sorrow to
        stay and braid her hair

Burnt up houses with empty sockets gaze on the
        petrified pelagos
and bullets wedged in the walls
like knives in the ribs of the saint tied to
        the cypress

All day long the dead sunbathe on their backs
and only when evening comes the soldiers crawl
        on their bellies over the smoky rocks
sniffing with their nostrils the air beyond
        death
they search the moon's shoes chewing slowly
        a piece of sole
they strike the rock with their fists perhaps
        some water may spring out
but the wall is hollow on the other side

and they hear again the sound of the bombshell
        swirling and falling in the sea

and once more they hear the scream of wounded
        in front of the gate

Where can you go? Your brother is calling you
The night is built around the shadows of
        foreign ships
The roads are closed by walls
There is only one road to the mountain peaks
And they make an insulting gesture to the ships
        biting their tongues
to hear their pain that hadn't as yet turned into bone

On top of the terraces the dead captains stand and guard
        the castle
their flesh melts under their garments
        Ai brother didn't you get tired?
The bullet sprouted up a bud in your heart
five hyacinths poked through the armpit of
        dry rock
breath by breath the fragrance talks of the fairytale –
        don't you remember? –
bite after bite the wound talks to you of life
the chamomile germinating in the dirt of your
        big toe's nail
talks to you of the earth's beauty

You grab the hand It is yours Dampened by
        salinity
The sea is yours Once you uproot a hair from
        the head of silence
the fig tree's milk drips bitter No matter where you are
        the sky looks at you

The evening star rolls your soul in his fingers
        like a cigarette
so that you may smoke your soul like that
        lying on your back

wetting your left arm in the starry sky
and your right glued to your rifle –
        fiancé
to remember that sky never forgets you
when you take from your inside pocket the
        old letter
and unfolding the moon with burnt up fingers
        you'll read of manliness and glory

Then you'll climb up the highest guard post
        of your island
and lighting a star as a percussion cup you'll
        fire one round in the air
over the walls and masts
over the mountains that stoop like wounded
        soldiers
so that you scare the sprites and they run
        to hide in sleep's blanket –

you'll fire one round straight to the sky's bosom
        to find the azure mark
as if trying to find over the blouse the nipple
of the woman who tomorrow will suckle
        your child
as if trying to find after many years the knob on the gate
        of your paternal home

VII

The house the road the cactus pear tree the sun
        peels in the yard pecked by the chickens
We know them They know us Here on the ground
        amid blackberry bushes
the tree snake has abandoned its yellow skin

On this ground is the shack of ants and the tower
        of wasps with its many embrasures
on the same olive tree the shell of last year's cicada
        and the voice of this year's cicada

in the bulrushes your shadow follows you like a
        tormented silent dog
a loyal dog – at noon he sits next to your earthen
        sleep sniffing the laurels
in the evening he coils himself by your legs
        staring at one star

This is a silence of pears multiplying between
        the legs of summer
a sleepiness of water that always gapes amid the roots
        of the carob tree
spring has seven orphans sleeping in her apron
a half-alive eagle in her eyes
and there up high behind the pine forest
the lonely chapel of St. John the Abstinent like a sparrow's
white dropping drying out in the sweltering heat
        on a flat mulberry leaf

This shepherd wrapped up in his sheepskin
has a dry river in each hair of his body
has a forest of oak trees in every hole of his flute
and his cane has the same knobs
with the oar that first dove in the blue of
        Hellespont

You don't need to remember The plane tree's vein
has your blood as have the island asphodel
        and the caper

The silent water well raises up from depths to high noon
a round voice made of black glass and white wind
a round voice like the old storage jars – the same
        ancient voice
and the sky washing away the rocks and our eyes
        with indigo

Every night in the fields the moon turns the great dead
        on their backs
searching their faces with rough frozen fingers
to locate a son from the chin's shape and from

the stony eyebrows
she searches their pockets She will always find something
        We always find something
A locket with a piece of the holy cross One tattered cigarette
One key one letter   a watch stopped
        at seven o'clock
We wind up the watch again The hours walk

Day after tomorrow after their clothes rot away
and they remain naked amid their army
        buttons
like pieces of sky remaining among summer
        stars
like the river stays among the fragrant laurels
like the path goes among the lemon trees
        early in the spring
then we shall perhaps find their names and
        we shall perhaps cry out: I love
Then But again these things are a bit too
        remote
and a bit too close like when you grab a hand in the
        darkness and say good evening
with the bitter attitude of the exiled returning
        to his paternal home
where not even his family recognize him
because he has met death
because he has met life before life and
        beyond death
and he knows them He's not bitter Tomorrow he says
        And he is certain
that the longest road is the road closer to the
        heart of God

And now is the time when the moon kisses him sorrowfully
        close to his ear
the seaweed the flowerpot the stool and the stone ladder
        say good evening to him
and the mountains the seas and cities and the sky
        say good evening to him
And then finally shaking the ash off his cigarette

over the iron railing
he may cry because of his assurance
he may cry because of the assurance of the trees and
the stars and his brothers

Athens, 1945-1947

Parentheses

1946-1947

The Meaning of Simplicity

I hide behind simple things so you may find me
if you don't find me you will find these things
you will touch what my hand touched
the traces of our hands will join

The August moon shines in the kitchen
like a tin-plated saucepan (it turns like that because I tell you
this)
it lights the empty house and the kneeling silence of the house –
silence stays always kneeling

Every word is an exit
for an encounter often postponed
and then the word is true since it insists on the encounter

Hunger

The night passed its mouth stuffed by speechless water At daybreak
the sun shone wet on the coiled cables
Faces – shadows masts – shadows voyages –
perhaps saw them perhaps not – our hunger was never satisfied

Someone yelled behind the mountain someone else
behind the trees and yet another one
all along the length of sundown – where should we run?
Would we have enough time? Perhaps it is us yelling? And
    the mountains
became bigger and sharper like the teeth of the hungry man

A Face

It is a bright face silent all alone
like the entire loneliness like complete victory
over loneliness This face
looks at you between two columns of still water

You don't know which of the two convinces you the most

Summer

The four windows hang rhyming quatrains
made of sky and sea inside the rooms
A lonely daisy is a small wristwatch
on the arm of summer showing
twelve at noon Thus you feel
your hair entangled in the hands of the sun
keeping you free in the light and in the air

Perhaps Someday

I want to show you these rosy clouds in the night
But you can't see It is night – what can you see?

So I can see through your eyes he said
that I won't be alone that you won't be alone And truly
there is nothing to the direction I pointed

Only stars crowded together in the night tired
like people on a picnic who come back on a truck
regretful sleepy nobody singing
with wilted wildflowers in their sweaty palms

But I shall insist in seeing and showing you he said
because if you don't see it is as if I didn't see –
I shall insist at least not seeing with your eyes –
and perhaps someday from different directions we shall meet

Self-sufficiency

This morning has taken the sun on its back
climbing up the rolling Attic hills
like a young man carrying his accordion

And last night with its joy is gone
and her fear of her joy Gone is also
the sorrow that didn't hope for her end

The cypresses the sun the windows – and we see them
Under the trees two chairs Why two?
Ah yes one is for you to sit the other to stretch your legs

Final Agreement

When the rain struck the window with one of its fingers
the window opened toward the inside Deep inside
an unknown person a sound – your voice?
Your voice distrusted your ear The other day
the sun went down the fields like a descent of farmers
with scythes and pitchforks You went out to the road
yelling not knowing about what you were yelling
stopping for a moment with a smile under your voice
as if under the rosy fully illuminated umbrella of a woman
sauntering along the railing of the park
There suddenly you recognized that this was your true voice
agreeing with all the unsuspecting voices floating in the air

Transformation

This which you call serenity or discipline kindness or apathy
this that you call a closed mouth with clenched teeth
showing the sweet silence of a mouth hiding the clenched
      teeth
is just the metals' fortitude under the useful
      hammer
under the formidable hammer – it is because you know
that from the amorphous you pass to the formed

Suddenly

Silent night Silent And you had stopped
waiting It was almost quiet
And suddenly on your face so intensely you felt
the touch of the absent He will come Then
you heard the window shutters hitting each other
Wings came up And a bit farther down the sea
was drowning in its own voice

Racecourse

Racecourse during the night the lights the music
the glittering cars along the whole length of the avenue
When the neighborhood lights go out
when the last music note falls like a dry leaf
the racecourse facade becomes
like a huge taken-out denture Then
the bronze instruments sleep in their cases
animals wailing are heard over the city
the tiger in her cage concentrates on her shadow
the animal tamer takes off his uniform and smokes his cigarette

And the neighborhood moment by moment is lit
as the eyes of the lions glitter behind the iron bars

Afternoon

The afternoon is full of fallen plaster black stones dry
    thorns
The afternoon has a difficult color of old footsteps stopped
    halfway
of old storage jars buried in the yard and over them tiredness
    and grass

Two people killed five killed twelve – so many so many
Each hour has its own killed Behind the windows
stand the ones who are missing and the pitcher with water they
    didn't drink

And this star that fell at the edge of the evening
is like the severed ear that cannot hear the crickets
that cannot hear our excuses – it disdains
in hearing our songs – alone alone
alone detached from others indifferent to condemnation or
    justification

Understanding

Sunday Buttons shine on coats
like small laughter The bus is gone
Some cheerful voices – strange
that you can hear and you answer Under the pine trees
a worker is trying to learn harmonica A woman
said good morning to someone – so simple and natural
    good morning
that you would like to learn how to play harmonica under
    the pine trees

Neither division nor subtraction To be able to look outside
yourself – warmth and serenity Not to be
'just yourself' but 'you too' A small addition
a small act of practical arithmetic easily understood
that even a child can do successfully playing with his
    fingers in the light
or playing this harmonica so the woman can hear it

Miniature

The woman stood up before the table Her sorrowful
    hands
slice thin pieces of lemon for the tea
like yellow wheels for a very small carriage
of a child's fairytale The young army officer opposite her
sunken deep in the old armchair He doesn't look at her
He lights his cigarette His hand having the match trembles
lighting up his tender chin and the little hand of the teacup
    The clock
stops its heartbeat momentarily Something has been postponed
The moment passed It is late Let us have our tea
So then is it possible for death to come on such a small carriage?
To pass by and go away? So that this small carriage with
the yellow small wheels is left behind alone stopped
for years in a side street with shut-off lampposts and
then a short song some mist and then nothing?

Women

Women are very distant Their bed sheets smell of goodnight
They place the bread on the table so that we won't miss them
Then we understand that we did something wrong We get up
        from the chair saying:
"You are very tired today" or "don't worry let me light the lamp"

When we light the match she turns slowly going to
the kitchen with an inexplicable concentration Her back
is a sad little mountain loaded with many dead –
the family dead her dead and your death

You hear her footsteps creaking on the old floor planks
you hear the plates crying in the plate rack and then the train
is heard carrying soldiers to the front lines

Triptych

1. Until Evening Came

He was holding her hand in his hand He wasn't talking
He was listening far away and perhaps inside him
to the ample pulse of the sea
The sea the pine trees the hills were her hand
If he didn't say this to her how could he hold her hand?

They kept quiet until evening came Under the trees
there was only a statue with his two hands severed

2. A Woman

This night is unapproachable doesn't kiss anybody –
Alone in her fear as though no one may come to kiss her

With five stars – fingers she hides a strand of white hair
and thus she's like a negation of her most beautiful self

3. What is our fault?

Under your tongue hide the thin little dill stems
the grape seeds and the peach strings
In the shadow created by your eyelashes
rests a warm earth I can lie down
and rest without any questions – he said

Then what is the meaning of this 'farther away'?
And what is your fault unsuspecting that you stay with the leaves?
Beautiful and plain in the gold beauty of your warmth?
And what is my fault that I walk in the night
captive of my freedom he said me the punished punishing?

Rainy

Poor music is heard coming from the neighborhood dancing
school
      on Saturday night
poor music frozen with its clogs –
every time the unpainted door opens music springs out to the
street
shivers under the corner lamppost
glances to the high window or the night
then it lowers its eyes to the mud
searches for something anticipating something
as though someone is sick and the doctor is delayed

Poor music It is very cold No one opens the window
to befriend you with some light of a lamp a few black raisins
to tell you I remember – some twenty-thirty years ago
some sounds from old carriages in the rain
a hazy landscape drawn on Tellos Argas' glasses

But the muddy shoes have holes
the couples pass by the street in a hurry they don't listen
Someone stopped very close to the wall He doesn't listen to you
no
He glues something on the wall Only the knife
on the table is a thought and a flash

Poor music if you can fit in it
enter through the hole of the neighborhood elbow

The Same Star

The drenched roofs glitter in the moonlight Women
wrap their shawls around them They rush to hide in their houses
If they stay a bit longer by the front door the moon will see them
crying

He suspects that in every mirror there is
another diaphanous woman bound by her own nakedness
– no matter how much you want to wake her up she won't
She fell asleep smelling a star

And he smells that same star staying awake

Conclusion

This window is alone
This star is alone
like a forgotten cigarette on the table –
it smokes it smokes lonely in the light blue

I am also alone he said
I light my cigarette I smoke
I smoke and think I am not alone

Waiting

Night falls late in the neighborhood We can't sleep
We wait for daybreak We wait
for the sun to strike like a hammer the tin roofs of the sheds
to strike our foreheads our hearts
to turn into sound that can be heard – a different sound
because silence is filled by gunshots from unknown points

Can You?

We saw him kneeling in the most upright position blowing
        his breath
under the big caldron to keep up with the fire
consuming his own fire Impatient – he was getting out of breath
pressed by his skin not fitting into his own skin

The light trembles on the horizon as its ribs butterfly
its pulse plumps up the grapes
and makes the new leaves swirl motionlessly

This way stooping he spent himself that we stayed upright
you and I without ever thinking
that someday we should be obligated to him somehow

Then how can you not at least stay upright?

Thank you

You won't say thank you to me
as you don't say thank you to your heartbeats
which carve the face of your life

But I shall say thank you to you
because I know what I owe you

This thank you is my song

Smoked Earthen Pot
1949

It was a very long road up to here Very long my brother
The cuffs were heavy on our hands In the evening
when the small lamplight moved his head saying "time has
        passed"
we read the world history written with small names
in some years incised with a nail on the prison walls
in some childish drawings of those about to die
 – a heart a bow a ship slicing time with certainty
in some verses left half finished that we would finish
        them
in some verses that were finished so that we wouldn't finish
It was a very long road up to here – difficult road
Now this road is yours You hold it
like you hold your friend's hand and you count his pulse
on this mark that the cuffs have left on him
Regular pulse Confident hand Confident road

This handicapped man next to you takes his leg off before
he goes to bed he leaves it in a corner – a wooden hollow leg –
you have to fill it like you fill a flowerpot with soil and
        plant flowers
like darkness is filled up with stars
like poverty slowly fills up thought and love

We have decided that one day all people will have two legs
a joyful bridge connecting eyes with eyes
connecting a heart with a heart Thus wherever you may sit
among sacks of the deck on your way to
        exile

behind the iron bars of the transportation department
near death which doesn't say "tomorrow"
among thousands of crutches of bitter crippled years
you say "tomorrow" and you sit quiet and certain
like a just man sits opposite other men

These red marks on the walls may be made
        of blood
– all the red of our days is blood –
 maybe from the sundown hitting the opposite wall

Each dusk things become red before they vanish
and death is ever closer Outside the iron bars
voices of children and the train's whistle
Then cells become even narrower
so you have to think of the light in a field of wheat
and bread on poor people's tables
and mothers smiling by the windows
so you may find some room to stretch your legs

Those hours you clench your comrade's hand like
turning into a silence full of trees
a cigarette cut in half goes from mouth to mouth
like a flashlight searching in the forest – we find the vein
that reaches spring's heart We smile

We smile to our inside This smile we hide now
Illicit smile – like the sun that has become illicit
and the truth illicit We hide our smile
just as we hide the picture of our beloved in our pocket
just as we hide the idea of freedom between two leaves
        of our heart
Here we all have one sky and the same smile
Tomorrow they may kill us This smile and
this sky they can't take away from us

We know that our shadow will remain over the fields

over the earthen fence of the poor house
over walls of big houses that will be built tomorrow
on top of our mother's apron who dresses fresh green beans
in the fresh air by the front door We know it
Let our bitterness be blessed
Let our brotherhood be blessed
Let the newly-born world be blessed

My brother sometime ago we were very proud
because we weren't confident at all
We said big words
we placed many gold stripes on the arm of our verse
a tall crown waved on the forehead of our song
we were noisy – we were afraid and for this we were noisy
covering our fear with our voices
we pounded our heels on the sidewalk
long strides reverberating
like those in parades with empty cannons
that people look at from doors and windows
without any of them clapping
Then they gave speeches on wooden platforms on balconies
the radios blared they repeated speeches
fear was hiding behind flags
the dead kept vigil in the drums
no one understood what was happening
though the trumpets kept the rhythm of the parade
they were out of time with our hearts We searched the rhythm
The reflection of the rifles and windows for a moment
        shone something into our eyes – nothing else
then no one could remember a word   remember a face or
        a sound
At night when the lights went out and the wind blew small
        paper flags in the street
and the heavy shadow of a street roller stayed on the door
we kept vigil
we gathered the scattered buzz of streets
we gathered scattered footsteps
we could find the rhythm the heart the flag

And yes my brother we learned to talk quietly and simply
Now we understand each other – nothing else is needed
And tomorrow I say we shall become even simpler
we shall find those words that assume the same weight
        in all hearts and all lips
thus we call the figs: figs and the trough: trough
that others will smile and say: "these kind of poems
we can craft for you a hundred per hour" And this we want also
Because my brother we don't sing so that we may
        stand out in the world
we sing so that we may unite the world

So there is no need for me to yell that they may believe me
so they may say: "whoever yells is right"
The right is on our side and we know it
and no matter how quietly I talk to you I know you will
        believe me –
we got used to quiet-talk in holding rooms and in the meetings
        in the conspiratorial work of occupation years
we got used to it in the short straight words over the fear and
        above the pain
day hour password in terrible deaf corners of night
in intersections of time that for a moment were lit by the
        floodlight of future –
hasty words a short version of life just the important
        parts
written on the cigarette package or on a such a small piece of
        paper
hidden in the shoe or in the hem of our jacket
a small piece of paper like a big bridge over death

Ah of course they shall say all these are nothing
But you my brother know that from these simple words
from these simple acts from these simple songs
the body of life grows the world grows we grow

And don't say I achieved something important
only that I passed by and leaned on the same wall that you

my young comrades did
that I only read in the transportation papers the names
     of our heroes and our martyrs
that I was only put in the same cuffs you were put
that I hurt only with you and dreamed with you
that I only found you and you found me comrade

Uncle Christos was building the oven of an army camp
He had stood and looked at his old confident hands
these simple wise hands of a comrade –
hour by hour the oven grew higher
the world grew higher
love grew higher
and when I tasted the first piece of our warm loaf of bread
with this taste I took into me
something from the old builder's wise hands
something from his calm smile that doesn't want retribution
something from the hands of all our comrades who knead
     the world's bread
that serene confidence of a man
who creates useful and necessary things

Later on we learned a lot more but if I sat and recalled
     all these
my song would never end
like our love of life the sun never ends

And I come only to embrace you and to cry my brother
like a person in love who comes back to his sweetheart after years
and with one kiss he describes all the years she waited
and all the years waiting for them beyond their kiss
We have stared at the same mark for a long time
for many lives we have searched for this mark
as though to entrust it with our hearts and our hands
And this mark stared at by thousands of hurt people
takes something from our eyes and from the contact of our eyes
and grows bigger it rises it rises
like the dough in the trough the tree under the sun
     hope in our hearts

And again other things the great ones the unreachable and
        unseen
since we have looked at them so intensely and we have loved
        them so deeply
they have become ours one with us we have had them next to us
like the salt cellar like the fork the plate
and now the same way wholeheartedly and serenely we look
        at a leaf or a star
the stone where we sit or high up at the smokestacks of futures

Today my heart neither resembles any golden cloud bursting
        into flames at dusk
nor an angel who sets a table among the trees
        of Heaven
shaking off with his white feathers the crumbs of stars from the
        beards of ancient saints
Nothing like that Now my heart is a wide earthen pot
that was placed over fire many times
that cooked a thousand times for the poor
for the farm workers for the passers-by
for the laborers and for their bitter mothers
for the hungry sun for the world – yes for the whole
        world
– a poor smoked up blackened earthen pot that does
        a good job
that boils wild mountain dandelion and once in a blue moon
        a piece of meat
and under it my hungry brothers poke the fire
        – each one putting in his wood
each one waiting for his share

They sit around along with the sheep and cows
like you sit here around me
they talk about the weather about seeding the crop
they talk of rain sun peace
for that sign more and more eyes stare at
for that star no wind can blow out
and the dead people gather around our table
and they wait for their share as well

And this earthen pot boils and boils singing

These days the wind haunts us
Around each glance the barbwire
around our hearts the barbwire
around hope the barbwire It's so cold this year

Closer Come closer Drenched kilometers gather
        around them
In the pockets of their old overcoats
they have small fireplaces to warm up children
They sit at the bench and they steam off from the rain
        and the distance
Their breath is the smoke of a train going away far away
        They converse
and then the discolored door of the room turns into a mother
        who crosses her arms and listens

I listen too and I become more and more –
and I throw a word here and there
like we throw wood in the fire –
the fire is blazing up becoming more light than fire – wood
        after wood –
the walls turn red the wind subsides the window shutter
        creaks
a young donkey on the grass is heard outside
and the dog sits quietly before the feet of the dead
We all wait for dawn

The wind has subsided Silence In the corner of the room
a plow deep in thought – waits for the plowing
The water is heard more clearly bubbling in the pot

Those who wait on the wooden bench
are the poor they are ours they are the strong
the farm workers and the proletariat
 – every word of theirs is a glass of wine
a corner piece of black bread
a tree next to the rock

a window open in the sunshine

They are our own Christs our own Saints

Their heavy shoes are like train cars full of coal
their hands are the confidence –
worked up hands tough hands calloused
with worn-out nails with wild hairs
with their big finger as wide as man's history
with their wide palm like a bridge over a cliff

Their fingerprints are not only in the logs of the
        prisons
they are kept in the annals of history
their fingerprints are the dense rail lines
crossing the future And my heart nothing more
my comrades but an earthen smoked up pot
that does its job right – nothing else

So my children now I think like a grandfather
        telling fairytales
(and don't get angry that I call you my children
I may be older just in years
not in anything else
and tomorrow you may call me "our child" and I won't get angry
because as long as there is youth in the world I'll be young
and you may call me "our child" my children) –
so my children now I think
to search for one word to suit the height of freedom
neither a taller nor shorter
 – the excess is false
the barely-enough is shy
and I don't intend to feel proud
any more or less than a man

We shall find our song We follow the right way What do you
have to say comrade?
It is good It is good
The dandelions are boiled The olive oil is scarce It doesn't matter
The appetite and the heart are enough It is time

Here is a brotherly light – the hands and eyes are simple
Here I am not above you or you above me
Here each of us is above himself
Here is a brotherly light flooding like a river next
        to the big wall
We hear this river even in our sleep
And when we sleep with one arm hanging outside the
        blanket
it gets wet in this river

Two drops of this water are enough to sprinkle
the nightmare's face and it vanishes like smoke behind the trees
And death is nothing but a leaf that fell to sustain
        an ascending leaf

Now the tree looks straight in your eyes amid its leaves
its root shows you its path
you look straight in the world's eyes – you have nothing to hide

Your hands are clean washed by a thick bar of the
        sun's soap
you leave them uncovered on top of the comrades' table
you entrust them in the hands of your comrades

Their movement is simple full of accuracy
And when you pull a hair from your comrade's jacket
it's as though you peel a page off the calendar
revving up the rhythm of the world
Though you know that you'll still cry a lot
until you teach the world how to smile

An earthen pot then Nothing else
Blackened earthen pot
boiling boiling and singing
boiling on top of the sun's fire and singing

Kontopouli – Limnos, Febuary 1949

Skirmish
1952

I

You know the great loneliness of exile
these infuriated seashores that could be ours though
     they are foreign
this air that harasses the window shutters
these window shutters that we have never opened
     or closed
though they still trust us with all afternoons

The moon rises very early stumbling on clouds
The house of the teacher is all alone by the shore
and the light of the lamp behind the windows is more lonely
     than his daughter's heart
when she saunters in the plaza of the island at twilight
among the pulled up boats
among the fishermen who listen to the cafe gramophone
     while mending their nets

We saw the sea dusk spending its loneliness without leaving
     anything behind
We saw the tents flying away with the wind   without reaching
     there where they wait for us
But we had arrived at home
we had lighted the lamp
we had spread a wide smile on the table
and had waited They didn't come
Then it makes no sense to remain in tomorrow – even if you

had arrived
Tomorrow seems to be so far the same as yesterday
Fold this big light like a tablecloth The supper
        later on
The flag mast leaning on the ground
The railings of the courtyard drenched by the drops of rough seas
the same as the wooden steps and the green balcony

The paint doesn't hold together – salinity eats away at it
the wind and sun   rain The paint doesn't hold together on these
        worn-out planks
Every so often we need new repairs
Nothing goes right Poor patch-up jobs

The policeman goes by with the evening meal in his mess tin
his greatcoat flaps in the wind like sheet metal in the refugee
        settlement
Then what separates people in this afternoon when the lights
        are turned on so early
when a brazier is put on in the front door of the poor dwelling
when a long tail of red sparkles blows up in the wind
and it could be a horse galloping in fairytales
a horse that you and I can ride on
and it can take us wherever we want – to a poppy field
where girls laugh – whatever we want – one horse –

Then what separates people when you and I are hungry
when we thirst together or on our own – we thirst the same way
what separates us? That you are the guard and I am the exiled
when we both know the meaning of the word mother
when both our ears freeze by the wind
and when we hold a few colors of dusk in our pockets
like money of another era that can't buy you
        anything these days?

II

They say that the sea is great
it ties the separate cities with strong arms of water
They say that the sea is beautiful
when sundown spreads on the horizon
and the whole horizon is a ship
freshly painted with rosy oil paint –
a ship traveling all over the world with everyone – so they say
We don't know how immense is the sea
when the bread on the table is scarce – we don't know
it is harder to count dividing a bite into five
than count the size of the sea And the windows
don't look at the horizon We notice that windowpanes are
       missing
You glue cartons on them the wind comes through
That rosy ship never passed through our windows

George went missing in the war The youngest
is serving his duty now Mother dyed
all her dresses black even the one
she wore as a bride She has saved the black lining
of father's old overcoat – it's always useful
Every so often she cuts a piece and she hems our sleeve
       or lapel
There are also the other mournings that aren't visible
and for these we never wore the black band on our lapel
speechless mourning even heavier than
a plate of dandelion for supper without any olive oil
a patch on Maritsa's elbow
a hand that delays in caressing and when it does the hour has
       already passed
a thank you that you didn't say a thank you that they didn't
       tell you
a mark on Petros' arm on his wrist – it is from
       the cuffs he says –
we change our subject of conversation – we don't insist

Every evening there are thousands of crutches pounding the
       sidewalk

What is it my son? What is it? Mother cannot sleep
And farther down to the field there are large graves dug
There they threw them piles on piles The crutches cannot
    be heard there
A great silence crucified on a tree An angry silence
    What is it my son?
Keep quiet mother – it's the wind – nothing
Mother mends the socks of the jailed
those ones from the killed man If you try to talk to her of
    the sundown
of the rosy ship – mother doesn't understand
The room smells of tar and diesel oil The lamp is dimmed
Tell me then what a mother with a smoked up lamp
    can understand
with two children killed and the third one missing
with the scarce bread and the socks you cannot patch It is
    the wind mother
It becomes stronger as it goes What can you say of the ship?

Ah we should buy a bit of horizon for mother
just enough that can fit through a broken window
She would then have a sweet shy smile over her
    wrinkles
like this light of St. Stratis over the tied fishing
    boats

III

My brother the path we have followed has no return
Behind us there is only death
In front of us it may again be death
A different death in the sun my brother that is
    like life
There is no need for more words We keep silent

It was so cold those days And it was hard
to dream of the sun in such cold Most of the times you
could make one out of old newspaper cuttings
with statistics about the industrial development of foreign

countries
with shredded flags that couldn't dress anyone
　　anymore
You could understand this And you insisted To get warm
There is a sun you were saying dismounting from the
　　mountains
and the long hours pounding their shields on the walls –
this coppery sound that even if it wasn't the final answer
at least it could block the ears Some short very short whispers
couldn't be heard although they had so much strength and
if you heard them from very close
they were like a finger very close to your eyes
hiding the sky the trees the city your friends
For this reason they play only drums and trumpets in the parades
　　You understood
but you didn't want to ask – to reach to the end What would be
　　the use of it?

It was very cold those days The discolored curtain
swayed in the room with the chipped stucco
so discolored like the vegetable vendor's voice in the winter
　　sundown
As far as the notebooks with verses were concerned they couldn't
　　patch up the cracks of the door
and a lot less the holes of the soul It was then that Lefteris
　　took his own life
And no one asked why – it was as though we knew the reasons
　　well

All the rest were familiar pretenses We were very
　　proud
so that we could disregard them And tired enough
so that we didn't touch them Petros says he lost
one of his legs in the struggle Petros –
Nick says he saw him – sauntering in the wheat field
spring was holding his arm says – he had a bright light
on his forehead – so bright like a large double loaf of bread
　　in the neighborhood house
and a big smile in his eyes – like the square of the sun
　　in the factory We knew it

Petros was in the front we didn't ask anymore
No matter how cold it was We persisted

For this I tell you my brother the path we have followed has no
    return

IV

It is always tedious to converse with the wind alone
to create shadows with your fingers on the naked wall
a stool a little donkey a rabbit – they don't have anymore
their first innocence – the heart is being dug and furrowed so
    much these years
many wounds so much blood – the shadows of your hands don't
    create a reason for a fairytale in the darkened village
where the large whitewashed room smelled of wool cloth
    warmed by the fire
and the two wet thick shoes steaming by the fireplace
when we were saying that with these shoes
you could walk with silence and with the river
even with death – and if you hesitated a bit
it would be so that you could smile
                    And no matter what you say it is always tedious
and memories from so much suffering and the ancient sacrifice
are not enough to fill your hands It's not enough

All the voices in tears All the books sleepy
The statues in the dark hallway are dusty

The two who play backgammon at the cafe on Saturday
    night and yawn
The one who searches for the rent money and forgets his debt
The one who searches for a bar of soap and leaves his fingernails
    greasy He and him
who has many dead in his house and two people always
    in his heart
two people who don't agree on anything who all the time
    stab each other
in a smutty way like the cutthroats in the tavern

and none of them ever gets killed And then they embrace
     each other like drunkards
they clink their glasses and cry cry cry We are sick and tired
     of these crying voices

these quarrels that defile the sun A sun like
a scabby cat crawling on the roof tiles
and the windows still painted gray by the night
and the blood painted gray One sun ray then a sword
to cut from top to bottom this gray cloth in
     front of the door
We cannot endure these voices anymore we don't endure them
A different voice like a hammer may it be rough may it be
     discordant
hammering away at the fiery darkness like copper
making door handles for large doors
making wide beds for two for three for more
     – not just for one
not just for one – making morning roads for the children's
     outings
for outings of couples in love for our outings
and a thick sun with large mustaches wheat ears and
     keen ears
a voice like the steel saw in the big carpentry shop outside
     the city
making furniture for the new high rises of the poor

I cannot endure it I tell you I cannot endure it
But since we want this voice this voice is ours
the sun is ours and the dream is ours
the future and the death ours

Give me your hand Come let me kiss you
Not the cheek On your lips Shout with me then
Shout shout shout

We shouted
The opposite window opened
The door opened

Old Helen went out to feed her chicken

V

It may be very quiet my brother or very noisy
you may have your eyes closed in the night
or sunken in your wound like two pebbles in
    a deep well
however the sun is not a foreign story
even if you don't stare at it even if you don't remember it The
    sun is
Even if you forget it sometimes you know it The sun is
For this reason you have appetite for supper for work for a book
A rose is always a rose and then after many nights
    in vigil
sometimes it may be a large drop of blood
sometimes a rosy flashlight on the old door of
    a poem
sometimes an innocent fist of a child in his mother's shadow
sometimes a deep wound on the ribs of spring or a kiss
    you didn't give
but a rose is always a rose And the sun is

And many things can happen Many No matter what they did
they didn't fail to learn this For this reason we smile
    my brother
for this we have no malice inside us
for this we don't have any hatred They don't understand

They don't understand at all Their knives cannot find their target
because we don't have a target my brother
Their knives can't pierce the sun
Their knives are blind All knives are blind

One night two nights many nights
we saw the stars behind their bayonets –
do you remember that? Do you remember how joyous we were
    seeing them?
It was the first time that we truly smiled my brother

But they didn't see our smile among their
    bayonets
This was our revenge Not revenge
And I say this word and perhaps they'll understand
This is not our job my brother Not revenge

Only that we'll bring this smile
like we bring a warm loaf of bread to the house
like we open a door in the sunshine
like we say the sky is light blue
and we give a handshake without talking
and we saunter under the peppers being certain about everything
    agreeing
about time about place about the kiss
about tomorrow's words which are same as our smile
when we raise our head a bit following
a dove's flight in the forest Petros passed by like that
with his crutches underarm
as though he was swinging from two bloomed pear trees

And George who got killed in the previous war
appeared at the turn of the road In his palm he held
the bullet that found his heart like he was holding
a lead toy soldier trying to gift it to a child He
    said goodbye to you He left

It was because of our smile my brother

VI

In the evenings when the shadow falls over trees and rocks
like the clothes of a tired man fall on the chair and the man
    remains naked
in the evenings then we feel that this stone fence still remains
    between us
I hear your voice behind the stone fence "you haven't
    fallen asleep yet?"

I don't answer I know that you wouldn't hear me I know

you spoke so that only you could hear your voice Only you
    discern
your words in my voice I don't say it – it is the same with me
    It's this stone fence

We look at it carefully so that we forget it
we read the store posters with the big letters
Cashmere The Latest Trendy Ties Radios Combs
and then the graffiti of the struggle
often wrongly written and most times misspelled
On these we linger as they're not like the others with the thin
    water paint
they are incised in the fence wall – they have overtaken the wall
in these letters we see through to the other side
    of the wall – and that way among them
I see you in pieces – sometimes one of your hands taking
something –
    a tool perhaps or a flower
sometimes your feet with your tattered shoes worn-out
    on illicit streets
sometimes your unshaven chin
enduring like a clumped up field now ready for the plow
or your hairy nostrils smelling the future through
    a key hole

and more than anything else your eyes turned my way
meeting my eyes gazing your way
and they are in total agreement to destroy this stone
    fence
so I can see you whole – so you can see me whole
without the radio and the theatre commercials
– whole We agree It is our oath
The other differences are unimportant

From here on I hear your voice
I answer you We dream together comrade

Our evenings are beautiful Our day proved to be good
the bread is good the light is good the sleep good –
we shall craft a small wooden ship for George's young sister

who was killed
we shall weave a blanket for Uncle Lampi who is cold
we shall plant trees around the old people's home
we shall open a big window on the night's facade
so as to see from the backside of night so that there'll always be
     day time
many wide windows without the crossed iron bars comrade

Have you noticed how relaxed people walk in the sunshine?

VII

These nights we spent have made fear useless
when you jumped to one side   bullets flying next to
     your ears and ribs
when you stayed in vigil among the dead
wounded to your bone marrow by the scream of the torturer
     and the silence of the tortured

That we still speak that we still walk up the hill with the thorny
burnets is something you cannot weigh
like you cannot weigh life and death
like you cannot weigh the light coming in every morning and
     taking the whole spot of the departed
But now you speak more calmly more certainly
as though you talk to the sun that sits in the opposite chair
and your words are so simple
as if they carry the voice of the ones who can't talk anymore
of the ones who will talk tomorrow

For another night we run with the night lamps Where is he?
Where
     is the drown man?
A piece of the sea is lighted The acetylene The world
Packed heads with flat caps stand out here
over this lighted piece of sea
The water is green – we noticed – the seaweed was stirring
We stoop over the drown man They have pulled the spear off
     his neck We look

at the deep wound Because of love he says Yes because of love
His pullover pushed up to his chest Why you undressed him?
His belly is bloated His penis is bloated
as if having intercourse Why you undressed him?
 – No no he is not cold anymore
                              Girls from the seafood market gather
Next to the wooden textile factory the electrical generator
dap doup dap doup it insists – life carries on
life is good – dap doup dap doup goes the motorboat
        starting on –

He is not cold He is not cold Dap doup – the girls go
        around the corner
laughing Naked like that He is not cold Perhaps the motorboat
carries oranges Dap doup dap doup
The oranges we were saying like large drops of winter
        sundown We were cold

We don't want our children to be cold We don't want that
        And the
        drown man – He is not cold He is not cold Dap doup
dap doup We must hurry comrades the world is cold the
world is on fire – we must hurry

One day people have to be joyous We have to be joyous
Maybe by dying – no by drowning not by drowning – maybe
        we shall be joyous by dying

VIII

The cloud and the sun – half of the landscape in light half in the
shade
The afternoon is as soft as a forgiveness that came on time
The windows look at the seashore – the short curtains pulled

Someone must have knelt here – two small depressions remain
        in the sand
like two open palms holding two warm fresh eggs
        almost transparent

A man wants to laugh He tries he tightens his mouth not
        finding his laugh yet
We all want to laugh At the shore the exiled people saunter
they talk – they prepare the laughter of the world The sea
        is calm Two policemen went by
One of them held a small almond branch They must have been
        talking about
their girlfriends – since one of them was holding an almond
        branch
The flowers lighted their faces under their caps

I tell you the world is beautiful No matter what you say no
        matter
        what you do it is beautiful
The future is secure my brother No matter what happens it is
        secure

There are not any dots on our voice or our silence anymore
        The world is beautiful

Can you turn back the wheels of the sun?
No matter how they use their rifles as levers
no matter how they use their shoulders – it cannot happen

And not only that but your teeth that shine when you laugh
        and wash your face in the morning
and your hair that drips water for your decision
and your hands whether holding the spade or the book
whether still clenched in your empty pockets
whether caressing the wind's hand in the evenings when the
        light dims
        and you want to caress

the evenings when the light dims like when the bucket rope
breaks and you hear the sound of water swallowing a bite of
        silence
like the hungry man swallows his saliva
and you don't know what to do anymore with your hands that
        want to caress
you don't know which dream which hand to caress first

how to caress the head of day that fell asleep
    on your lap

Time is never enough for you Time cannot contain you And time
    doesn't exist
Sleep never forgives This peaceful scream this
    responsibility
not only to caress the hand of the wind quietly
not only to place your hand on the shoulder of night – my god
    these stars
that demand of you their existence that demand
to take blood from your voice and circulate
in the people's veins My god these stars
thousands of stars – and you pull up the wick of the lamp
with just your two fingers – our lamp inside the tent
lighting happily the faces of sleeping comrades
illuminating in the huge glass of silence in the
    middle of the firmament –
our lamp comrade illuminating the happy face of
    the world
the face of the world that will become happy Because you
    want it and we want it

This is our job comrade

Saint Stratis, 1952

Moonlight Sonata

1956

*Spring evening Large room of an old house A middle-aged
woman dressed in black talks to a young man They haven't
put the lights on A merciless moonlight enters through two
windows I have neglected to say that the Woman in Black has
published two-three poetry collections with religious subject
So the Woman in Black talks to the Young Man*

Let me come with you What a moon tonight!
The moon is good – it doesn't show my
gray hair The moon will turn my hair golden again
You won't see the difference
Let me come with you

When the moon is up the shadows in the house grow longer
invisible arms pull the curtains
an invisible finger writes forgotten words in the dust
on the piano – I don't want to hear them Keep silent

Let me come with you
down the road to the brick factory's wall fence
to the point where the road turns and the city
appears airy though made of cement whitewashed by moonlight
so indifferent and fleshless
so positive like beyond flesh

that after all you can believe you exist and don't exist
that you have never existed that time and its ravaging
        never existed
Let me come with you

We shall sit on the ledge of the knoll for a while
and as the spring breeze blows on us
we may imagine we shall fly because
many times even now I hear my dress rustling
like the sound of two powerful wings flapping
and when you enclose yourself in this sound of flying
you feel firmness in your neck your ribs your flesh
and thus firmly put within the muscles of the blue wind
within the vigorous nerves of the height
it doesn't matter whether you leave or return
and it doesn't matter that your hair has turned gray
(this is not my sorrow – my sorrow
is that my heart hasn't turned white)
Let me come with you

I know that everyone marches to love alone
alone to glory and to death
I know it I tried it It's of no use
Let me come with you

This house is haunted it pushes me away –
I mean it has aged so much the nails fall off
the pictures fall as if diving to the void
the stucco bits drop silently
like the hat of the dead man off its hanger
        in the dark hallway
like the worn-out wool glove of silence falls off her
        knees
or a band of moonlight falls on the old worn-out armchair

Once even that was new – not the picture you
        stare at with such disbelief –
I mean the armchair so comfortable you could
        sit for hours
and with closed eyes dream of anything

– a smooth sandy beach wet and polished by the moon
more polished than my old leather shoes that every
        month I polish at the corner shoe store
or a fishing boat's sail that vanishes in the horizon rocked
        by its own breath
triangular sail like a handkerchief folded on an angle only twice
as though it didn't have anything to cover or to keep
or to wave unfurled like saying goodbye I always had a
        fixation with handkerchiefs
not for keeping anything tied in them
like some flower seed or chamomile gathered in the fields
        at sundown
or to tie it in four knots like the cap workers wear
        in the opposite construction site
or to wipe my eyes – I maintained my vision properly
I never wore glasses Just a fixation with handkerchiefs

Now I fold them in four in eight in sixteen
to keep my fingers busy And now I remember
that's how I kept the beat in music long ago at
Music School with a blue uniform and white collar with
two blond braids – eight sixteen thirty-two sixty-four
held by the hand of a small peach tree a friend of mine
        full of light and rosy flowers
(forgive me for these words – bad habit) – 32 – 64 – and
        my family had
so many hopes for my music talent So I was saying to you
        about the armchair –
disemboweled – the rusted springs are visible the straw –
I thought of taking it to the furniture shop next door
but who has the time the money and desire – what can you
fix first? – I thought of throwing a sheet on it – but I was afraid
of the white sheet in this moonlight Here sat
people who dreamed great dreams like you and like me
and now they rest under the earth without being disturbed by
        rain or moon
Let me come with you

We shall stop for a while at the top of the marble stairs
        of Saint Nicolas

then you will go down the road and I'll return
having on my left side the warmth from touching your coat
        by chance
and even some square lights from the small neighborhood
windows
and this snow white vapor from the moon that resembles a big
        procession of silver swans –
and I don't fear this expression because during
many spring nights I talked to God who appeared to me
dressed in the haze and glory of moonlight such as this
and I sacrificed to Him many young men even more handsome
than   you
thus white and unreachable I became vapor in my white flame
        in the whiteness of moonlight
conflagrated by the insatiable eyes of men and by the hesitant
        ecstasy of ephebes
besieged by graceful sunburned bodies
vigorous limbs trained in swimming in oaring in gymnastics
        and football (though I pretended I didn't notice)
foreheads lips and necks knees fingers and eyes
chests and arms and thighs (and truly I didn't notice them)
– you know sometimes in admiring you forget what you
admire
        your admiration is enough –
my god what eyes filled with stars and I rose in an apotheosis
        of denied stars
because besieged as I was from outside and from within
I had no other path but only upward or downward
        – no it's not enough
Let me come with you

I know it's late Let me come
because for so many years day and night and purple noon
I remained lonely unyielding adamant and immaculate
still in my marriage bed immaculate and lonely
writing glorious verses on the knees of God
verses that I assure you will remain as incised in
        impeccable marble
beyond my life and your life farther beyond It's not enough
Let me come with you

This house cannot contain me anymore
I can't endure carrying it on my back
you have to always be careful very careful
to support the wall with the large buffet
to support the buffet with the very old engraved table
to support the table with the chairs
to support the chairs with your arms
to place your shoulder under the dangling beam
And the piano is like a closed black casket You don't dare open it
You have to always be careful very careful so that they won't fall
so that you
      won't fall I cannot stand it
Let me come with you

This house despite all its dead it doesn't intend to die
It insists on living with its dead
to keep on living off its dead
to live in the certainty of its death
and to take care of its dead in decrepit beds
     and shelves
Let me come with you

Here no matter how lightly I walk in the haze of evening
whether with slippers or barefoot
something will creak – a window cracks or a mirror
some footsteps are heard – they are not mine
Perhaps these footsteps are not heard outside in the street
the repentance they say wears wooden shoes
and if you look in this or the other mirror
behind the dust and the cracks
you'll discern your face even hazier and more fragmented
your face that above all you wanted to maintain clear
     and indivisible

The rim of the water glass shines in the moonlight
like a circular razor – how can I bring it to my lips?
When I thirst so much – how can I bring it? – You see?
I am still in the mood for similes – this has stayed with me
this still assures me that I am not absent
Let me come with you

Sometimes as evening comes I have the emotion
that outside the windows the bear handler goes by with
        his old heavy she-bear
her hair full of thorns and thistles
creating dust on the neighborhood road
a lonely cloud of dust that rises like incense in the sundown
and the children return to their homes for supper and
        are not allowed out anymore
although behind the walls they guess the old
        bear's footsteps –
and the tired bear marches in the wisdom of her loneliness
        not knowing where or why –
she has grown heavy and she can't dance on her hind legs
anymore
she can't put on her lacy bonnet to entertain the children
        the loafers or the ones who are hard to please
and the only thing she wants is to lie down on the ground
letting them step on her belly thus playing her
        last game
showing her formidable power for resignation
her disobedience to others' interests the rings in her lips
        the needs of her teeth
her disobedience to pain and life
with her certain alliance with death – even a slow death –
her final disobedience to death with the continuance
        and knowledge of life
that ascends with wisdom and action above her slavery

But who can play such a game up to the end?
And the bear gets up again and marches
obeying her leash her rings her teeth
smiling with her ripped lips at the small change that the beautiful
        unsuspecting children throw at her
(beautiful exactly because they're unsuspecting)
and saying thank you Because bears who have aged have
learned to say only one thing: thank you thank you
Let me come with you

This house suffocates me Especially the kitchen which is
like a sea bottom The hanging coffeepots glitter

like round large eyes of exquisite fishes
the plates move slowly like jellyfish
seaweed and shells clutch at my hair – I can't unstuck
    them any longer
I can't rise up to the surface again –
the platter falls off my hands soundless – I slump
and see bubbles from my breath rising
    and rising
and I try to have fun watching them
and I wonder what one standing above could say seeing
    these bubbles
perhaps that someone has drown or that a diver explores the
    sea floor?

And truly it is not just a few the times I have discovered it
    the depths of drowning
corals and pearls and treasures of sunken ships
unexpected encounters and events of yesterday today and
    tomorrow
a verification almost of eternity
a certain breather a certain smile of immortality as they say
certain happiness a euphoria even some enthusiasm
corals pearls and sapphires
only that I don't know how to give them – no – I do give them
only that I don't know whether they can receive them – anyway I
    give them
Let me come with you

Just a moment let me get my jacket
These capricious days however we have to take care of ourselves
There is dampness in the night and the moon
don't you think that really makes it colder?

Let me button your shirt – how strong your breast is –
how strong the moon – the armchair I say – and when I lift the cup
    from the table
a hole of silence is left below and at once I place my palm over it
so I don't look inside – I leave the cup back in its place
and the moon is a hole in the world's skull – don't look inside
it has a magnetic power pulling you – don't look

don't any of you look
let me tell you – you will fall in it This vertigo is
beautiful is airy – you will fall –
the moon is a marble water well
shadows and silent wings stir mysterious voices – don't you
      hear them?

Deep-deep the fall
deep-deep the ascend
the airy statue firm in its unfurled wings
deep-deep the merciless generosity of silence –
quivering illuminations of the other bank as you pendulate
      in your own wave
breath of the ocean This vertigo
is beautiful and airy – be careful you will fall Don't look at me
my role is wavering – the exquisite vertigo This way
      every evening
I have a little headache some dizziness

Often I run to the pharmacy across the street for aspirin
other times I feel lazy and I stay with my headache
and I hear inside the walls the hollow sound of water running
      through the pipes
or I boil a coffee and always absentminded
I forget and I prepare two – who is to drink the other? –
It is funny really and I leave it to cool on the ledge
or other times I drink the second cup looking outside the window
      at the green pharmacy light
like the green light of a silent train coming to take me
with my handkerchiefs my worn-out shoes my black purse
      my poems
without any suitcase – what can you do with them?
Let me come with you

Ah are you leaving? Goodnight No I won't go with you
Goodnight
I'll go out in a while Thank you Because after all I have to
get out of this dilapidated house
I would like to go and see a bit of the city – no not the moon –
the city with its calloused hands the city of a day's work

the city that takes an oath on its bread and its fist
the city that endures all of us on its back
with our littleness our malice our animosity
with our aspirations our ignorance and our old age –
to hear the heavy footsteps of the city
that I don't hear your footsteps anymore
not the footsteps of God not even my own footsteps Goodnight

*The room darkens It seems that some cloud has hidden the moon
Suddenly as though a hand increased the volume of the radio in the
neighborhood bar a well know music phrase was heard And then
I understood that all this scene was accompanied by a low toned
"Moonlight Sonata" just the first part though The young man
probably goes down the road with an ironic and perhaps empathetic
smile on his calligraphic lips and with a feeling of being freed When
he arrives exactly at Saint Nicolas before he descends the marble
stairs, he will laugh – a loud uncontrollable laugh His laughter
won't be heard as inappropriate under the moon Perhaps the only
inappropriate thing is that it is not inappropriate at all In a while
the young man will become silent he will become serious and will
say "The decline of an age" Thus completely calm once more he
will unbutton his shirt again and he will march on his way As far
as the Woman in Black is concerned I don't know whether she went
out of the house or not The moonlight shines again And in the
corners of the room the shadows become tense out of an unbearable
regret almost anger not as much for life as for the useless confession
You hear? The radio carries on*

Helen

1970

Even from a distance the wear and tear was obvious – walls
with plaster half fallen discolored window shutters the balcony
railings rusted A curtain stirred a little outside the upper floor
window yellowed and in shreds at the bottom When he approached
– hesitating – the same sense of abandonment in the garden:
overgrown plants fleshy leaves unpruned trees the few remaining
flowers choked in the nettles the fountain dry and moldy lichen on
the beautiful statues A lizard stayed motionless between the breasts
of a young Aphrodite warmed up by the last sun rays of dusk How
many years had passed? He was young back then – twenty-two?
twenty-three? And her? You could never tell – her radiance was
so strong – it blinded you it pierced you – you never knew who
she was if she was if you were He rang the doorbell He heard the
sound of the doorbell ringing he felt so lonely in this familiar place
now differently arranged with unknown entanglements painted in
dark colors They were slow to open the door Someone leaned over
from the upper window It wasn't her A servant – very young She
seemed as though she was laughing She left the window They were
still taking their time Then footsteps were heard on the stairway
inside They unlocked the door He went up Certain smell of dust
rotten fruit dried-up soap urine This way Bedroom closet Metal
mirror Two tattered engraved armchairs A small table made of
tin with coffee cups and cigarette butts And her? No no – it isn't
possible An old – old – one two hundred years old But just five
years ago – No no The bed sheet full of holes There motionless
sitting on the bed bent over Only her eyes – larger than ever
autocratic piercing empty

Yes yes – it's me Sit down for a while No one comes
          around anymore
          I almost
forget the words Not that they are needed I think summer
          is almost here
the curtains stir in a different way – as if to say something –
          stupidities
          One of them
has already gone out the window pulling as though to break
          the rings
to fly over the trees – perhaps to take the whole house
someplace else – but the house resists with all its corners
and me along with it although I have felt these last few
          months liberated
from my dead people and from myself and this resistance
          of mine
incomprehensible unintentional not mine the only thing I have –
          my bond
with this bed with this curtain – and it's my fear as if
          my whole body
is anchored by this ring with the black stone I wear on my
          pointer finger

Now I examine this stone closely in the endless hours
          of the night –
black without any reflections – it grows it grows it fills up
black waters – the waters overflow rise I sink
not to the bottom but on an upper bottom and from there
I discern my room down below myself the closet the servant girls
arguing speechless I see one of them standing
on a stool and with a rough spiteful expression cleaning the glass
of Leda's picture I see the dusting cloth leaving behind
a trail of dust made of delicate bubbles rising and bursting
with a silent murmur around my ankles or knees

I also see you being awkward with your thunderstruck distorted
          face
by the slow undulations of the black water – sometime widening
          sometime elongating your face
with yellow streaks Your hair writhes upward

like an upside-down Medusa But then I say: 'it's only a stone
a small and precious stone' Then all blackness contracts and
        dries up
and localizes in the smallest knot – I feel it
here just below my throat And here I am again
in my room on my bed next to my familiar little
        bottles
that look at me one by one agreeing – they are my only helpers
for insomnia fear memories forgetfulness asthma

How are you doing? Are you still in the army? Be careful Don't
        stress yourself too much
for heroism for honors and glories What'll you do with them? Do
        you still have
that shield with my face engraved on it? You were so
        funny
with your tall helmet and its long tail – you were
        so young
so shy as if you had your beautiful face hidden on the hind
legs of a horse and its tail hung down your bare
back Don't get angry again Stay a little longer

The time of antagonism is gone the desires have dried up
perhaps now we can look together at the same point
        of futility
where I think the true encounters get realized – however
        indifferent
but always soothing – our new community deserted quiet empty
without any displacement or oppositions – we just stir the ashes
        in the fireplace
sometimes making out of ash long thin burial urns
or sitting on the ground we hit the soil with soundless palms

Bit by bit things lost their meaning became empty on the
        other hand
did they ever have any meaning? – loosened up hollow
we filled them with straw or chaff so they take shape
they thicken they stand – the tables the chairs
the beds where we lie on the words – always
        hollow

like the cloth sacks like the vendor's burlap bags –
from the outside you already know what's inside
potatoes or onions wheat corn almonds or flour

Sometimes a sack catches a nail on the stair
or on the prong of an anchor down in the harbor a hole is
opened
the flour spills out – a foolish river The sack empties itself
The poor gather the flour in handfuls to bake
some pies or batter The sack collapses Someone
picks it up lifting from two corners He shakes it out in the air
a cloud of white dust engulfs him his hair becomes white
more so his eyebrows The others look at him
they don't understand anything They wait for him to open
        his mouth to talk
He doesn't He folds the sack in four he leaves
as he is white inexplicable speechless as if disguised
like a lustful naked man covered with a sheet
or like a cunning dead man resurrected in his shroud

So there is no meaning in things or events – the same
        goes for words although
with them we name more or less those things we miss or those
that we never saw – the airy as we call them the eternal things –
innocent words misleading consoling always ambiguous
in their intended accuracy – what a sad story
to give name to a shadow calling it at night when in bed
with the sheet pulled up to your neck and hearing it
        we fools think
that we hold its body that it holds us that we are held together
        in the world

Now I forget my most familiar names or I mix them up –
Paris Menelaus Achilles Proteus Theoclymenos Tefkros
Castor and Polydeuces – my moralizing brothers who
        I think
have turned into stars – so they say – beacons for ships –
        Theseus Pereitheus
Andromache Cassandra Agamemnon – sounds just formless
sounds their images never written on a windowpane

on a metal mirror or on the shallows of a shore like that time
on a quiet sunny day with many masts after the battle
was over and the creak of wet ropes in the pulleys
raised the world up high like the knot of a sob stopped
in a crystalline throat – and you could see the knot
        sparkling trembling
without becoming a scream and suddenly the whole landscape
with ships sailors and carriages sunk into light and
        anonymity

Now another deeper darker sinking – from which sometimes
some sounds surface – when hammers were pounding wood
nailing together a new trireme in the small shipyard when
        a huge
four-horse carriage passed by the stony road carrying on
        the ticking
of the cathedral clock in a different duration as if there
were a lot more than twelve hours and as if the horses
were running around inside the clock until they tired or one
        night
when two handsome young men sang under my windows
a song for me without words – one of them had one eye
        the other
wore a large buckle on his belt – shining in the moonlight

Words don't come so easily to me now – I search for them
        as if I'm translating
from a language I don't speak – nevertheless I translate
        Between the words
or among them deep holes remain I peer through
        these holes
as though I peer through knots that have fallen from the boards
        of the door
completely closed nailed here for eons I don't see a thing

No more words and names I can only discern some sounds – a
        silver candleholder
or a crystal vase echoing by itself and suddenly stops
pretending that it knows nothing that it didn't echo
        that nobody

struck it or touched it that nobody passed by it A dress
falls softly from the chair to the floor turning the attention
from the previous sound to the simplicity of nothing
        However
the idea of a silent conspiracy although diffused in the air
floats denser in a higher level almost leveled out
so much so that you feel the incising of wrinkles around
        your lips grow deeper
exactly because of an intruder's presence who takes
        your place
turning you into an intruder here in your own bed in your
        own room

Oh this alienation in our own clothes that get old
in our own skin that gets wrinkled while our fingers
cannot grip anymore cannot even wrap around our bodies
the blanket that rises by itself disappears disperses
        leaving us
naked in the void And then the guitar hanging on
        the wall
forgotten for years with rusted strings begins to quiver
like the jaw of an old woman quivers from cold or fear
        and you have to
place your hand flat on the strings to stop their
contagious chill But you cannot find your hand
        you don't have a hand
and you hear in your stomach your own jaw
        quivering

In this house the air has become heavy and inexplicable perhaps
from the natural presence of the dead A chest
opens on its own and old dresses come out of it rustle
        stand upright
and saunter quietly two golden fringes remain on the carpet
        a curtain
opens – nobody is revealed – though he is there a cigarette
burns on its own in the ashtray with short interruptions –
        the man
who left it there is in the next room somehow
        awkward

with his back turned looking at the wall perhaps at
        a spider
or a water stain – he is turned toward the wall so that the
dark hollow under his protruding cheekbones
        isn't visible
The dead don't feel any empathy for us – that's strange eh? –
not so much for them but for us – this neutral familiarity
        of theirs
with a place that has denied them and where they don't
contribute anything to its upkeep aren't concerned with its wear
        and tear
they're finished and unchangeable though just a bit older

This is what sometimes surprises us – the overgrowing of
        the unchangeable
and their silent self-sufficiency – not at all dignified they
        don't try
to force you to remember them to please you The
        women
leave their bellies slacken their stockings loose
        they take
pins from the silver box they pin them one by one
in two straight rows on the couch's velvet then they
        pick them up
and start again with the same graceful attention A
        very tall person
comes in through the hallway – his forehead hits against
        the door frame
he doesn't make any grimace – and no sound is heard
        at all

Yes they are as foolish as we are more quiet Someone
        else
lifts his arm solemnly as if to bless someone
he pulls off a crystal piece of the chandelier brings it to his mouth
simply like a glass fruit – you think he will chew on it or he will
        start
a human function again – no he keeps it between his teeth
so the crystal shines with futile flashes A woman
takes her face cream from the small round jar

with the expert movement of her two fingers and writes
two thick capital letters on the windowpane – something like H
        and D –
the sun warms up the glass the cream melts drips down the wall –
and this doesn't mean anything – two greasy short furrows

I don't know why the dead stay in here without anybody's
        sympathy I don't know what they want
going around the rooms in their good clothes their good
        shoes
polished smooth and noiseless as if they don't touch
        the floor
They take up space they lie down wherever they like in the
        two rocking chairs
down on the floor or in the bathroom they forget the water
dripping and they forget the scented soap melting in the water
The servant girls going among them sweeping with the
        big brooms
don't notice them Only sometimes the laugh of a servant
seems somehow confined – it doesn't fly up high out of
        the window
it looks like a bird tied by its leg with a string that someone
        pulls downward

And then the servants get inexplicably very angry with me they
        throw the broom
here in the middle of my room they go to the kitchen –
        I hear them
boiling coffee in big pots spilling sugar on the floor –
the sugar crunches under their shoes the smell of coffee
spreads through the hallway floods the house looks at itself
        in the mirror
like a silly dark impudent face with uncombed locks
        of hair
with two light blue false earrings that blows its breath on
        the mirror
the glass clouds I feel my tongue rolling around
        my mouth
I feel that I still have some saliva "a coffee for me too" I
        yell at the servants

"a coffee" (I ask only for a coffee nothing else) they
pretend that they don't hear me I yell again and again
without bitterness or anger They don't answer I hear them
        sipping their coffee
from my porcelain cups with gold rims
and delicate purple flowers I keep silent and gaze at
that broom thrown on the floor like a stiff corpse
of that tall and slim young vegetable seller who some years ago
showed me his big penis between the railings of the garden

Ah yes sometimes I laugh and I hear my hoarse laughter
        rising
not from my chest anymore but much lower from my feet
even lower from the earth And I laugh that everything was
so pointless purposeless ephemeral and meaningless – wealth
        glories wars and
jealousies jewels and my own beauty
                                    What silly legends
swans Troys loves and gallantries
                                I met again
in mournful night feasts   my old lovers with white
        beards
with white hair with bulging bellies as if they were
already pregnant with their death to devour with strange
        greediness
the roasted goats without looking into the shoulder blade – what
        would they look for? –
a leveled shadow had filled all of it with just a few white stains

And I as you know I still had my former beauty
as if by a miracle (but also with tints herbs and salves
lemon juice and cucumber water) Though I was just terrified
        to see in their faces
the passing of my own years At times like that I tightened
        my belly muscles
I tightened my cheeks with a false smile as if
steadying up two crumbling walls with a thin beam

Thus shut in confined stretched I was – Oh god how tiring –

every moment confined (even in my sleep) as if I was inside
a freezing armor or a wooden full-bodied corset or inside
my own Trojan Horse narrow deceptive already knowing
the futility of deceit and self-deception the aimlessness
of fame the aimlessness and transience of every victory
                              Just a few months ago
after my husband's death (months or years ago?) I left my
        Trojan Horse
down in the stable forever with his old horses so that
the scorpions and spiders would roam around inside them
        I don't dye my hair anymore

Big warts have grown on my face Thick hairs have
grown around my mouth – I touch them I don't look at
        myself in the mirror –
long wild hairs – as if someone has found his throne
        inside me
an impudent malevolent man and his beard
grows through my skin I let him be – what can I do? –
I'm afraid that if I chase him away he would drag me along
        behind him

Don't go Stay a little longer I haven't talked for so long
No one comes to see me anymore They all left in a hurry
I saw it in their eyes – they were in a hurry for me to die Time
        doesn't pass
The servants hate me At night I hear them opening
        my drawers
taking the lacy things the jewels the gold talons –
        who knows
whether they would leave me a good dress for the necessary
        occasion
or a single pair of shoes They even took my keys from
under my pillow – I didn't move at all I pretended I was
        asleep –
one way or another they would have taken them – I just don't
        want them to know that I know

What would I do if I didn't have them? "Patience patience" I say

"patience" – and even that's a small victory when
they read my old letters from admirers or the poems
that famous poets dedicated to me – they read them
with stupid emphasis and mispronunciation
        the accents the meter
and the syllabification – I don't try to correct them I pretend I don't
        hear Other times
they draw big mustaches with my eyebrow black crayon on
        my statues
or they place an ancient helmet or the night chamber pot
on their heads I look at them calmly They get angry

One day when I felt a bit better I asked them again
to make up my face They did I asked for a mirror
They had painted my face green with a black mouth I said to
        them "Thank you"
as if I didn't see anything strange They were laughing One
        of them
stripped right in front of me put on my gold veils and just
        like that
in her bare feet with her fat legs started dancing
she jumped on top of the table – frenzied she danced danced
bowed as if mimicking my old movements High up on her thigh
she had a love bite from a man's strong even teeth

I looked at them as if I were in a theater – never humiliated
        or grieved
not even indignation – what for? I only repeated deep
        inside me
"one day we shall die" or better "one day you will all die" and
        this
was a certain victory in revenge fear and consolation I looked at
everything straight in the eye with an indescribable apathetic
        clarity as if
my eyes were independent of me I looked at my own eyes
being just a meter away from my face like the glass
of a distant window behind which someone else sits and
observes whatever happens on an unknown street
with closed up cafes photo studios perfume shops
and I had the feeling that the beautiful small crystal bottle

broke and the myrrh spilled out in the dusty showcase
            Passers by
stood vaguely smelling the air they remembered something good
and then vanished behind the pepper trees or the end of the street

Sometimes I smell the scent even now – I mean I remember it
strange isn't it? the things we consider great vanish
            disappear –
Agamemnon's murder   the slaughter of Clytemnestra (they had
            sent me
from Mycenae one of her beautiful necklaces made of
small gold masks linked together with rings from
the upper tips of their ears I never wore it) You
            forget them
some other things remain unimportant   meaningless things – I
remember
            that one day I saw
a bird sitting on the back of a horse and this inexplicable thing
seemed to explain (to me at least) a certain beautiful mystery

I still remember as a young girl on the banks of Eurotas
            next to the sun-warmed oleanders
the sound of a tree peeling its bark by itself The peelings
fell softly in the water floating away like triremes
and I waited one way or another for a black butterfly with
            orange stripes
to sit on a piece of bark amazed that although motionless
            it moved
and it entertained me that butterflies though experts in the air
have no idea about traveling in water or of rowing And so it came

There are certain strange lonely moments almost funny A
            man
walks at midday having a huge basket on his head
            the basket
hides his whole face as if he is headless or disguised
with an enormous eyeless plural-eyed head A different man
as he saunters romantically in the dusk stumbles on something
            curses
turns back searches – a very small stone he picks it up

he kisses it then
he remembers to look around him he leaves as if guilty
        A woman
slips her hand in her pocket she doesn't find anything
        takes her hand out
raises it observes it carefully as if it was steamed up by
        the powder of emptiness

A waiter has caught a fly in his palm – he doesn't
        squeeze it
a customer calls him he forgets opens his palm
        the fly
flies away and sits on the glass A piece of paper rolls
down the street hesitantly with many interruptions without
attracting attention from anybody – and it likes this But then
every so often it makes a certain crackle opposing itself as if
        looking
for an unbiased witness for its humble secret route And
        all these things
have a desolate and inexplicable beauty and a deep pain
because of our own known and unknown gestures – don't they?

The other things are lost as if they never existed Argos Athens
        Sparta
Corinth Thebes Sykion – shadows of names I pronounce and they
        echo as if they are sunken
in the incomplete A stray well-bred little dog stands
before the window of a poor dairy A young woman passing by
        looks at it
it doesn't respond its shadow is spread on the sidewalk
        enlarged
I never learned the reason I doubt it truly exists There remains
only that humiliating compulsive (from whom?) approval
like when we nod yes as if we greet someone
with incredible servitude although nobody goes by
        nobody is there

I believe that another person told me one night with a totally
        colorless voice
all my life's events and I was so sleepy I wished inside me

that he'd finally stop so that I could close my eyes
and sleep And as long as he spoke just to do something
    to resist sleeping
I counted one by one the tassels of my shawl in a certain
    rhythm
with a silly childish game of the blind fly until its
meaning was lost in the repetition But the sound remains –
noises thuds crawling – the buzz of silence a discordant
    cry
someone scratches the wall with his nails a pair of scissors fall
    on the floor planks
someone coughs – his palm on his mouth so that he may not
    wake up the other
who sleeps with him – perhaps his death – he stops then
    again
that spiral buzz from an empty shut-off water well

At night I hear the servants moving my big furniture
they take it downstairs – a mirror carried like on a
    stretcher
reveals the worn-out plaster designs on the ceiling
a windowpane hits the railings – it didn't break
    the old overcoat on the hanger
raises its empty hands for a moment then it places them back
    in the pockets
small wheels of the couch legs creak on the floor
    I feel
here in my elbow a scratching on the wall made by the
    closet's corner
or the corner of the large engraved table What will they do with
    them? "Goodbye" I say
mechanically as though bidding farewell to a visitor always
    a stranger
    only
that vague buzz lingers in the hallway as if from the horn
of down-and-out old lords hunting after rainfall in a burned
    forest

Really so many useless things collected with such greed –
blocking the space – we couldn't move because our knees

hit against wooden stony metal knees Oh of course we
       have to
grow old very old until we shall become just to reach
       that
serene impartiality the sweet lack of interest in comparisons
       in judgments
when our share exists in nothing else except this
       serenity

Oh yes so many silly battles heroic deeds ambitions arrogance
sacrifices and defeats defeats and other battles for this that
       already
had been decided by others when we were absent And the
       innocent people
poking hairpins in their eyes hitting their heads on
the towering wall knowing so well that the wall won't fall
or even crack so they can see through a little fissure
a bit of shadowless light blue sky free from time and their own
       shadows
       in the meantime – who knows –
perhaps there where one resists without hope perhaps there
       human history
commences as we say and the beauty of man
among rusty pieces of steel and bones of bulls and horses
among ancient tripods where some laurel still burns
and the smoke rises swirling in the sundown like a golden
       fleece

Stay a little longer Evening is coming The golden fleece we
       spoke of
       – Oh what a thought
it comes slowly to us women – but it relaxes us somehow On the
other hand
       men
don't stop to think – perhaps they are afraid perhaps
       they don't want
to look their fear straight in the eye to see their tiredness
       to rest –

spineless vain busy they walk in darkness Their
        clothes
always smell of smoke from a conflagration they survived
or passed by without even knowing They undress quickly
        toss their
clothes on the floor go to bed But even their bodies
smell of smoke – it intoxicates them When they finally fell
asleep I used to find among their chest hairs some thin burnt-up
leaves or some black-gray fluff from killed birds Then
I would gather these and keep them in a small box – the only signs
of a secret communication – I never showed to them – they
        wouldn't have recognized them

Sometimes they were oh yes beautiful – naked as that in
        deep sleep
totally unresisting loosened up with their big strong
        bodies
moistened and softened like the roaring rivers running down
from high mountains to serene plains or like abandoned
        children At such times
I truly loved them as if I gave birth to them I observed their
        long eyelashes
and I wanted to pull them back to me to protect them or
this way to couple with their whole bodies They slept And
        sleep expects
your respect because it is so rare These too are gone Forgotten

Not that I don't remember anymore – I still remember but
        memories
are not so emotional anymore – they don't touch us – faceless
        serene
clear right to their bloody corners Only one of them
still retains some air that breathes around it
                                        That evening when
I was surrounded by the endless cries of the wounded
and whispered curses of old men and their wonder
        amid
the smell of overpowering death that from time to time
        glittered
on a shield or the point of a spear or the metope

of a neglected temple or the wheel of a chariot – I climbed up
alone onto the high walls and sauntered
                                          alone totally alone between
the Trojans and the Acheans feeling the wind pressing my fine
veils onto my body caressing my nipples holding my whole
        body
both dressed and totally naked with only a wide silver belt
pushing my breasts up high –
                                thus beautiful untouched
emancipated
at the time that my two lover-rivals dueled and the fate
        of the long
war was decided –
                                I didn't even see the strap of Paris'
helmet being cut – instead I only saw a flash of its
        brass
a circular flash as the other swung it around his head
in anger – an illuminated zero
                                It wasn't really worthy of looking –
the outcome of the war was already arranged by the gods
        and Paris
who without his dusty sandals very soon would be in bed
cleansed by the hands of a goddess waiting for me smiling
pretending to hide a false wound on his ribs with a
        rosy bandage

I didn't watch anymore I hardly even heard their
        war-thirsty cries –
high up on the walls I was above the heads of mortals airy
        made of flesh
belonging to no one without need of anyone
as if I was independent absolute love – free
from fear of death and time with a white flower
        in my hair
with a flower between my breasts and another in my lips
        hiding for me
the smile of freedom
                        They could
have shot at me from both sides with their arrows
                                        I presented

an easy target walking slowly on the walls completely intact
in the golden purple evening sky
                              I kept my eyes closed
to make every hostile gesture from them easy – knowing
        deep inside
that none of them would dare Their hands trembled with awe
at my beauty and immortality –
                          (maybe I can add now that
I didn't fear death because I felt him so far away)
                              Then
I threw down the flowers from my hair and my breasts
        – the third one
I kept in my mouth – I tossed them down on both sides
        of the walls
with a completely intolerant gesture
                                Then the men inside the walls
and outside
threw themselves against each other friend and opponent to grab
those flowers   to offer them to me – my own flowers
                        I didn't see
anything else after that – other than stooping backs as if all
        of them
were kneeling on the earth as the blood dried up from the sun –
        perhaps they
had already stepped on those flowers
                        I didn't see
                        I had my arms raised
and rising on my tiptoes I ascended
letting the third flower fall from my lips

This still remains with me – like a consolation like a remote
        justification and perhaps
this will remain I say somewhere in the world – a momentary
        freedom
even illusory of course – a game of our luck and our ignorance
        in that exact
position the sculptors (as far as I recall) tried to create
my last statues – and they are still in the garden
you must have seen them coming in Sometimes I also see them
        (when the servants

are in good moods and they hold me by my arms and take me to
that chair by the window) They gleam in the sunlight
        White warmth
rises from the marble right up to here I don't think anymore In a
        while
even this tires me I prefer to gaze at part of the street
where two-three kids play with a ball made of rags or
        some girl
lowers a basket tied with a rope from the balcony across
        the street

Sometimes the servants forget me there They don't come to
        help me back to bed
and I stay all night looking at an old bicycle left
in front of the lit window of the new patisserie
until the lights go out or until I fall asleep at the windowsill
        Every so often
I feel that a star wakes me sliding through space
like saliva from the open mouth of a toothless old man
                                                    Now
they haven't taken me to the window for a long time I stay
in bed sitting or lying down – this I can do To kill time
I touch my face – a strange face – I touch it I examine it
        I count
the hairs the wrinkles the warts – who is inside this
        face?
                Something acrid rises in my throat – nausea and fear
the stupid fear my god that perhaps we may lose the nausea
        Stay for a little while –
some light comes through the window – they must have lit
        the streetlamps

Wouldn't you like me to ring the bell so they may bring you
something? –
        some sweet black cherries
or a bit of candied bitter orange peel – perhaps I still have some left
in the big jars turned into congealed sugar by now – if of course the
greedy servants have left some The last years I've been making
sweets – what else could one do?
                After Troy – our life in Sparta was

so boring – really isolated All day long closed in
        the houses
amid the crowded loot of so many wars and memories
faded and annoying crawling behind you in the
        mirror
while you combed your hair or in the kitchen emanating
from greasy steam of the pot and you hear with the water
        boiling
some dactylic hexameters from that Third Rhapsody
while a rooster crows discordant nearby from the neighbor's
        coop

You surely know how monotonous our life is Even the
newspaper
headlines have the same shape and size – I don't read them
anymore
        Every so often
flags on balconies national celebrations army parades of
wound-up soldiers – only the cavalry maintained something
        improvised
something personal – perhaps because of the horses Dust was
rising
        like a cloud
we closed the windows – what's the use after one had to dust
one by one all the vases little boxes porcelain statuettes mirrors
        buffets

I stopped going to these celebrations My husband would come back
        sweaty
he threw himself on the food making noise eating and
        chewing over
old boring glories and worn-out animosities I observed
        carefully
the buttons of his vest that were about to pop out – he was
        very fat
Under his chin a large black mark flickered

Then I touched my own chin carrying on with my food

                 absentminded
feeling in my hand the movements of my lower jaw
as if it was severed from my head and I held it naked
        in my palm

Perhaps for this reason I gained some weight myself I don't know
        Everyone looked scared –
I saw them sometimes behind the windows – they walked
        sideways –
somehow limping as if hiding something under their arms
        In the afternoon
the bells rang solemnly The beggars knocked on doors
        At the far end
the whitewashed facade of the Maternity Hospital that in the
        evening
        seemed whiter
more distant and unexplainable We lighted the lamps quickly
        I would alter one
of my old dresses Then the sewing machine broke so they
        took it down
to the basement along with those old romantic oil
        paintings
with well-known mythical images – Nymphs rising from the
        sea Eagles
        and Ganymedes

One by one our old friends left Even the mail slackened
only around festivities or birthdays a brief postcard –
a stereotypical scene of Taygetos with its ridged peaks
        light blue
a piece of Eurotas with white pebbles and oleanders
or the ruins of Mystras with the wild fig trees But more often
        than anything else
telegrams of condolences And no answers Perhaps in the
meantime the recipient had died – we never learned further
My husband didn't travel anymore He never opened a book In his
        last years
he had became very nervous He smoked a lot During the night
        he would pace around
the big living room with those tattered brown slippers

and his long nightgown Noon at the table he would
    recall
Clytemnestras' unfaithfulness or Orestes' justified act
as if he wanted to threaten someone   But who cared?
    I didn't even listen to him
however after he died I missed him a lot – I certainly missed
    those silly threats
as if those would arrange for me an unchangeable position
    in time
as if they would stop me from aging
                                        At that time I would dream
of Odysseus that same one with his agelessness with his smart
    triangular cap
delaying his return that crafty man – with excuses of imaginary
    dangers
while he let himself (as though a shipwreck)
sometimes in the arms of Circe
    sometimes
in the arms of Nausica so they would take the barnacles off
    his chest
    and would bathe him
with tiny rose soaps they would kiss his knee scar and anoint him
    with oil

I believe he also reached Ithaca – she must have covered him
    in her woven things
the charmless fat Penelope Since then I never received his
    messages –
perhaps my servants tear them up – of what use are they anymore?
    Symplegades
have moved someplace else in a secret more internal space – you
    feel them
motionless softened – even more fearful than before – they
    don't crash
they suffocate you in a thick black fluid – none escapes them

You may go now Night has come I feel sleepy – Oh to close
    my eyes
to sleep so that I don't see either outside or in to forget

the fear of sleep and awakening I cannot I jump up –
I am afraid I won't wake up again I stay up listening
to the snoring of the servants from the living room the spiders
        on the walls
the cockroaches in the kitchen or the dead people snoring
with deep breaths pretending they're asleep they have calmed
        down
I even lose my dead people now I have lost them – they are gone

Sometimes past midnight the rhythmic hooves of horses
are heard from down the road from a delayed carriage as if
        returning
from a morning matinee of some rundown neighborhood
        theater
with its plaster fallen off the ceiling with the peeling walls
with a huge discolored red curtain drawn
that has shrunk from so many washings and in the gap
        it leaves under it
you could see the bare feet of the stage manager or the
        electrician
perhaps rolling up a paper forest so that the lights go out

That crack is still lit while in the auditorium
the clapping has vanished and the chandeliers have turned off
        The air
Stays heavy with the breath of silence and the buzz of silence
under the empty seats together with shells from sunflower seeds
        and the rolled-up tickets
with some buttons a lace handkerchief a piece of red string

...And that scene on the walls of Troy – did I truly
        ascend
letting it fall off my lips? – Sometimes even now
        I try
here lying in bed to open my hands to stand on
my tiptoes – to stand on air – the third
        flower –

She stopped talking Leaned her head back Perhaps fell asleep The
other got up He didn't say goodnight It was already dark As he
walked through the hallway he felt the servants glued to the wall to
eavesdrop they didn't stir at all He went down the inside stairwell
as if descending a deep well having the sense that he wouldn't find
the exit door – any door His fingers contracted already searched for
the doorknob Indeed he imagined his hands were two birds gasping
for air yet knowing that this scene was nothing but an expression of
self-pity that we usually juxtapose opposite a vague fear Suddenly
voices were heard from upstairs The electric lights came on in the
rooms the hallway the stairs He went up again This time he was
certain The woman was sitting on the bed with her elbow steadying
on the tin table and her cheek in her palm The servants came and
went noisily someone was making a phone call in the hallway
Women from the neighborhood rushed in "ah ah" they went and
they hid something under their dresses And again the phone call
The policemen came up they sent away the servants and the women
who on their way out grabbed the canary cages some flowerpots
with exotic flowers a radio transistor and an electric heater One of
them held a big gold picture frame They placed the dead woman on
the gurney The head man sealed up the house – "until they locate
the rightful owners" he said – although he knew that there were
none The house stayed sealed for forty days and then her belongings
– whatever was saved – would go to the auction for the public good
"For the Old Folks Home" he said to the driver The covered vehicle
went off Suddenly everything vanished Total silence He was left
alone he turned and looked around The moon had risen The statues
of the garden were dimly lit – her statues alone next to the trees
outside the sealed house And a serene deceitful moon Where would
he go now?)

Karlovasi, Samos May-August 1970

The Caretaker's Desk
1971

If

Had you left at the appropriate moment
you wouldn't need so many pretexts later on
so much humiliation and indignity By the entrance
two pails tipped over The wet shoes
hidden under the bed Ashes
glasses mourning announcements You never learned
the purpose and what the difference was Searching
you postponed you always postponed Perhaps
even that was one way like the cigarettes
like the glance behind the curtain at the hour
when three naked women multiplied in the sky
with their white arms behind their hair –
and you to carry on your stay here
between two completely unlike statues
that both resemble you – one
painted completely red and the other black

Athens, 15-3-71

Subsistence

What last display did he prepare like that? –
having his empty pockets inside out
like the dirty bags of dead beggars
not having where to hide his hands not
having where to hide the inevitable and useless while
under his tongue he kept a broken match
a key for the big wardrobe and his sperm

Athens, 16-3-71

The Unknown

He knew what his successive disguises stood for
(even with them often out of time and always vague)
a fencer a herald a priest a ropewalker
a hero a victim a dead Iphigenia He didn't know
the one he disguised himself as His colorful costumes
pile on the floor covering the hole of the floor
and on top of the pile the carved golden mask
and in the cavity of the mask the unfired pistol

Athens, 16-3-71

Dead End

In the fall we heard horns of the ancient hunters
blare from under the arches The dowser
    sat by the door
In front of Government House they burned kites Farther on
the statue was alone naked completely shivering on its pedestal
(the one that had endured so much to become a statue)
now totally forgotten secretly contemplated in the rock
a new amazing straddle that would draw
the hunters' attention the butcher's baker's widow's
disproving what he'd dreamed of the most: his unblemished
his glorified his made-of-marble comfortably crucified
    motionlessness

Athens, 17-3-71

Transformation

He opened his palms There were no stigmata
Wounds heal The nails remain inside
Even deeper Nothing shows
               He smokes
He blows the smoke His teeth are of copper Are those not
the nails? Does he chew with them? Or perhaps
they are those under boots of the soldiers?

Athens, 17-3-71

Known Outcomes

For years and years he yearned he undressed
in front of small or large mirrors
in front of every window he carefully tried
one or another pose trying to choose to invent
his own most natural so that he'd become
the perfect statue of himself – although he knew
that usually statues are prepared
for the dead and even more often
for some unknown non-existent gods

Athens, 17-3-71

The Undecided

With time performances become less and less Same as the
        furniture
The subfloor hollow gives way It cannot hold up the
weight of a stone or a footstep A man
slowly-slowly removes the excess so
he can at least hover in midair He walks
next to the telegraph wires Sometimes in the evenings
he touches street lights up high trying
to see the reaction to his touch Between his teeth
he keeps the scissors of total blackout without
ever using them Perhaps he is afraid of
the twisting together of the wires or even more so
the one sitting down there on the last chair
on the sidewalk of the well-lit patissiere
drinking with thoughtful calm slow gulps
a yellow drink from the large shining glass

Athens, 18-3-71

Spring of 1971

The man had long gone to his work The woman
went to the bedroom opened the drawer took
the receipts of water service the power the phone
turned her back to the balcony door "Let them cut them off
all all – she said – let them cut off" as though she didn't know
they'd already been cut them off
                                        An inflated sun
flooded the big bed The shadow evaporated
on the opposite wall A fly sat on the washstand
with the ashtray the alarm clock the blue ribbon
of the dead child The two well-lit sheets
resembled two blind statues lying down
for a half-hearted morning coupling
                                   "All all" she repeated
and among them "all" (she heard it) was herself as well
speechless calm standing free joined with
all the vanished killed or alive

                                        Athens, 19-3-71

And Another Night

That silver candleholder placed
between two empty spaces He tried
to put the candle out and go to bed Then he
compared the strength of his breath
by the resistance of the flame
he discerned the flame's contour – its faint
bow (to him) a consent
and then the trembling upright pose
                              He didn't lie down
He stayed observing within the flame
in an immeasurable forgotten depth
that same body naked invincible
in a new ascension not at all illuminated
while on the right foot of the ascending the same
rope was tied and kept following him

Athens, 20-3-71

Afternoon in the Old Neighborhood

They place the cafe tables on the sidewalk
The old men come and sit every afternoon Sunshine
leans onto newspapers erases news
They can't read anymore – perhaps they'll even get
angry perhaps they'll even forget why death always
occupies the back page of newspapers
the same as backyards with the sealed-off water wells
And everything is quiet this afternoon in the old
neighborhood as though all pregnant women have left

Athens, 20-3-71

Passage

They pass them next to the barbwire They had no faces
On their backs there were large numbers written The sergeant
was fishing on the calm seashore The poem persisted
like the hooked fish shining up in the air
among the yelling of those who kept silent Nothing was
warded off by the seer and her sacrificed cock
Empty urchin shells and sunshine remained on the flagstones

Athens, 23-3-71

Refutation

So it seems they were not all lost The window
still looked out on a part of the city an available
part of the sky The carpenter the builder
dangling off the scaffold they come closer again
Then the nails the planks have another use
and the dream again the wall and the faint resurrection
and the sorrowful glory useful again reminding
those toothpicks in the small vest pocket
that so many years ago we had secretly taken
from the cheap restaurant one winter night

Athens, 24-3-71

A Road

Even glory is a road – he says –
it is the breaking of the road and also the bridge
there where you lay the basket with the bread
the knife and napkin on the ledge
in an obvious spot and you hide
behind the wall late at dusk
waiting for the first passerby to eat his dinner
to look at his teeth to see his appetite to hear
the sound of crumbs falling off the cliff
as he wipes his lips (or your lips?)
with the reverse side of his palm with
no effort to unfold the white napkin

Athens, 25-3-71

Resurrection

He looks again observes discerns
through a distance that has no meaning at all
through endurance that doesn't humiliate anymore
the moth balls in the paper bag
the dry grape leaves in the leaky pail
the bicycle on the opposite sidewalk
                                Suddenly
he hears the knock behind the wall
that same one coded totally alone
the deeper knock He feels like an innocent
who forgot the dead
                    At night he doesn't
use earplugs anymore – he's left them
in the drawer along with his medals
and with his last most unsuccessful mask
Only he doesn't know this is the last one

Athens, 27-3-71

Dispatch
(A poet speaks to a future poet)

If I didn't know that you would listen to me one day
I wouldn't have anything to say I couldn't talk
and the spider who taught us the vertical ascend
on the bare wall would have stopped on my mouth
pushing straight inside my larynx
the three black buttons of my coat
and the other the white ones from the nightshirts of the dead

Athens, 28-3-71

Nightly Event

He hammered the nail on the wall He didn't
have anything to hang He stared at it sitting
on the old chair opposite He couldn't
think or remember anything He got up
covered the nail with his kerchief and suddenly
he noticed his bruised arm painted by
the moon standing by the window The killer
had gone to sleep His legs
naked and strong with perfect toenails with a callus
on the small toe visible under the blanket
and his hairs were curling erotically The statues
always sleep like that with open eyes and
you don't have to fear any dream or word –
the true witness you needed you have him
the precise and trustworthy because you know
statues never betray they only reveal

Athens, 30-3-71

Water Wells and People

We had our water wells inside our houses
We drank the rainwater bathed in it
kept some order and cleanness One night
someone got up emptied his cup
of bitterness in the well The others pretended
they were deep asleep Later one by one
they got up in turns emptied
their cup of bitterness At dawn
no one drank the water Until finally
the ladder sunk in the well The tenants
climbed on the roof opened their mouths
motionless there for hours just hoping
that raindrops would fall The wandering photographer
passed by down the street He didn't see them He read
the funereal announcements glued on the poles
and on big doors of the shut-up stores

Athens, 31-3-71

Review

The one who slept with his shoes and clothes
wet to the bone and that other who
put his head in the black bag
feeling the roughness of the cloth on his chin the one
who stole the shoes of the dead man in the bedroom
and found they were small – he never wore them and
couldn't sell them from fear of revealing himself the last one
who constantly stomped his foot on the rotten planks
in a rhythm that all knew and none
wanted to reveal and from above
the smoked lamp and the drunks' voices
the card players the big copper ashtray
with the Prince of Lilacs engraved on it – when
the bossy waiter entered in a rush he
swept up with a movement of his bony left arm
the whole table of guests throwing down the trapdoor
glasses playing cards packs of cigarettes the players
astonished hastily transformed their anger
into a sleepy pleasure lighted straight on the forehead
by a gigantic crystal chandelier that was suddenly turned on
there at the end of the room behind an unknown glass door
inside the huge empty hall of the dignitaries

Athens, 1-4-71

Exactly Now

Now that you have nothing to say nothing
to show to emphasize to defend now
that everything is lost (and not just for you) exactly now
you may speak roaming among the
tools of torture turning around with your
small finger the meaningless wheels of
broken clocks or that huge hovering
non-resistant wheel still a bit wet
as they raised it from the sunken ship –

exactly now pulling ropes from the ceiling
listening to the sound of pulleys above you
in vague places like the stars during that night
when we came back from the countryside and in
the marble courtyard they had set in exact order
two rows of black wooden highchairs
and in the middle the king's golden closed casket
without any flags without the crown and the sword

Athens, 1-4-71

Unconvinced

And again the perplexed yearning (knowing its return)
to define where from where and why to find justification
as though it was its fault – although it knows that there
is neither excuse nor mistake in an almost spring afternoon
when the dilapidated Music School of the neighborhood is shut
down and the poorest girl in the world got permission to stay
there a bit longer playing the big black piano very loud
in the third floor room with the narrow windows
some immense impromptu scales that
make the faded red velvet curtain
flap above the bus ticket collectors with
the used tickets on the sidewalk of the bus stop
and with the cloud in the chimney though rosy

Athens, 2-4-71

On the Lower Level of the Basement

The springs of old sofas the twisted wires
dressed by the austerity of rust thrown away
in the lower level of the basement – useless for years Sunday
noon and you said "Good morning sir my regards to your wife"
because you had to say something even though no one listened
        to you
looking through the low window the slow legs of the dead
with their freshly polished shoes and down on the floor
that still smelled of very old spilled grape must a severed hand
tied with a yellow string and a hand in the hole of the wall that
pulls the string making the other arm jump
uncontrollably unexpectedly sorrowfully and somehow funny –
a jump higher than possible – a jump as if out of this world

Athens, 2-4-71

Inapplicable

He passes through continuous noise like among
rafters of caved-in houses broken chairs
broken picture frames glass letters – he searches
for some silent sound straight in the shape
of a thin absent pole from where he could
climb up high using arms and legs
while at the same time he feels completely incapable
of such a climb and even more he would look hilarious
climbing while trembling while the others below
would look at the holes of his shoe soles And if he ever
managed to reach the top – what vertigo what fear
how could he look at the higher cloud how he'd look at
the streets below the lampposts his familiar cafe
still having passed around his elbow
that old worn-out shopping net

Athens, 3-4-71

The Wound

To simplify things he would prefer
clean counters the white smooth
finished lines of statues
to carry on with his correspondence (he
acquired enough paper and envelopes last night)
forgetting that small turtle tied
by one of its legs with a string hung from the tree
that he never dared set free though there was
no one around to see him

Athens, 3-4-71

Spineless

The woman before the mirror Naked
She has nothing to discover – she knows it
The replication unsuccessful very tired memory
Scratched record albums glasses
penises sketched on cigarette packs
empty cognac bottles the chairs
apples scattered on the big bed
sounds of heels of the other woman on
the upper floor above her head –
when the lights went out and the walls became narrower
and the servants yelled in the staircase
Mister Mister embalmed stork
we who cut the rope with our teeth
we who cut the wire with our nails –

Athens, 3-4-71

Supervision

He saw the backs of houses lit in the afternoon
high from the terrace with the spread bed-sheets
he hoped again before night for the color
of a distant leniency his own like an erotic
shadow almost covering to their nails
the two dead people lying down naked alone
on top of the marble kitchen table One of them
had a slant appendix incision on his belly the other
had on his right hand third finger a faint
white circle from the ring that they took from him
Perhaps these were the marks of his immortality?

Athens, 4-4-71

The Secret Guard

They waited in the plaza They had erected
a makeshift platform in the middle Paper lanterns
little paper flags hanging from the poles
In the afternoon a strong rain started The plaza
got filled with black umbrellas and wet shoes
The faces weren't visible at all It became dark
The one who was to give a speech didn't come Then
slowly in order one by one they went away
folding their umbrellas leaving them by the platform
and they left in the rain under the lampposts
Only the last one with the big mask
stayed guarding the platform also holding
his folded umbrella like a bayonet
amid the sopping paper flags

Athens, 5-4-71

Expanse

There was nothing else in the night but
the immense dark expanse and the straight road
imperceptibly lit from within There
a big crashed bus
with one of its headlights on flooding
the five awakened startled chickens
and a dry branch of the inviolable

Athens, 6-4-71

Displacement

I don't know anything – he says – nothing anymore I move
in almost roomy spaces without echoes
with no question or answer Distant lighting –
perhaps a hidden spotlight projecting in the air
or on a white non-existent wall slow gestures
by hovering strings grimaces of nothing pulleys
two leaves one Monday one ring
                              I move
between events of the unexplainable I feel
almost explained I hold my breath I strike
the knocker of the ancient garden The servant comes out
He secretly gives me the chain I place it on my neck
under a yellow shirt I don't salute I leave

Athens, 6-4-71

Falsification

The empty open drawers after the search
Darkness of the room with deep inhaling of the mirror
Opposite the fully lit display of the butcher shop
and the old handbarrow with a wax semblance
of Alexander the Great without a spear and helmet
lying on his back over the rotten oranges

Athens, 6-4-71

Midnight

The lawyer's briefcase left on the floor
The boxing gloves on the hanger The guard
had turned against the moon to light his cigarette
Then three thieves with their sack entered
They didn't turn on the light I had just enough time
to throw the keys in the water well

Athens, 6-4-71

Alien Death

When he walked to the upper room of the hospital
he saw the sick man totally covered
with a white starched sheet – perhaps he had
been dead for a while Right above the bed
on the bare wall his pants were hanging
with two legs opened and nailed
like a triangular arch of cloth From there
you could pass straight into the garden of the museum
with replicas of ancient statues
with couples on benches and roasted chickpea sellers

Athens, 7-4-71

So Much White

Behind the glass display window the empty store snow white –
snow white walls benches on the benches
snow white egg cases with snow white eggs Only
a large black fly alone bouncing on the window glass
And you were almost convinced that the store owner
had recently died in the washroom
having in his pocket coins from the sales
of the last eggs – so much white unsold
so much white unwanted lonely and dazzling

Athens, 7-4-71

Sincerity

At dusk we saw him coming behind the windows
with lights from an unknown approaching the display window
with calm people holding in their hands
unwrapped fabrics dragging on the ground
and a woman holding a piece of the invisible
supported like a violin under her chin
and perhaps that was somewhat hard on her because
that way she couldn't raise her head at all
and it was she who dyed her dress black
in the copper caldron in the basement where
they had piled the hoops of big barrels
our wooden childish horses the old lamps
and that first owl on the yard's tree
stuffed disguised into three nightingales

Athens, 8-4-71

Deeper

A lot deeper – he said – a lot deeper still
(though in descending rhythm in continuance) – there
the only point of steadiness Bit by bit
the eye gets used to darkness You discern
the absence of walls the absence of roof
and the missing stairs Neither glass nor mirror
not even the old wardrobe The curtains are held
in the air by pins And the vibrations
of your previous footsteps so faint
on the copper milk jug left
early in the morning in the freshness of spring
before the white dilapidated garden gate
or on top of the other clay vessel held up high
on the forehead of the silent woman

Athens, 8-4-71

Toward Dawn

Late at night when the traffic slows down
and the traffic wardens leave their posts he
doesn't know what to do anymore from his window
he looks down at the big glass of the cafe front steamed up
by the breathing of sleeplessness he looks at the
spectral refracted waiters changing clothes behind the cash
he looks at the sky with its wide white holes
discerning in them the wheels of the last bus And then
that: "nothing else nothing else" He enters
the totally empty room He leans his forehead
on the shoulder of a statue resembling him (unnaturally taller)
feeling the freshness of morning on the marble while
down in the courtyard with the broken flagstones the guards
gather and cut strings off packages of the exiled people

Athens, 8-4-71

Grudge

To speak to admit to that specific
to admit to what you don't have to say – to say it
what you don't know what doesn't exist
spreading the legs of the hanged slowly
like you open the blinds at dawn
and you put out your head looking down
at the empty road where lights are still on
while the hunched man glues on the pole
a large yellow poster upside down

Athens, 10-4-71

Poem

The garbage dump below the Observatory
and the crazy man all alone striking
an old rusted tin bucket
in exquisite homophonic rhythm with the stars
and with the old key-keeper in vigil next to
the derelict train where poisonous nettles grow
hiding the boots of the soldier who undressed
before he climbed and stood at the temple pediment

Athens, 11-4-71

Terminus

He goes of course looks elsewhere tries to avoid
what follows him like a coat on his back
and he can't even undress – it's cold
especially in intersections where shopkeepers
behind display windows or even outside on sidewalks
look with a demanding glance at every passerby And he
feels their glances inside his pockets
even deeper until finally he reaches
the far plaza deserted swept
by the strong wind of purposelessness There
remain only the pedestals of busts of unknown heroes
that one stormy night angry women took
in their embraces and left by train

Athens, 13-4-71

Fake Passport

The woman shakes a blanket from the window
The blanket slips off her hands spreads in the air
slowly orderly horizontally The woman looks on smiling
she jumps on the blanket off the window The blanket becomes
heavy closes like a sack hovers and stops This sack is
lifted by a calm man going upward to the sky
in wide strides He also knows that he lied
For that reason he has turned his back toward
the big door of the printing company from where
three newspaper sellers come crying without newspapers

Athens, 14-4-71

Among the Lost

He always searches He doesn't find He searches Not
that he lost something – among all that's lost – something
        he needs
or something that someone else needs and he should go
on a set deadline to a specified spot
and place it under the flowerpot or by the lip
of the stone frog in the garden pond with the air pump at dusk
when three children of the owner force
the little daughter of the garden keeper to stay lying
behind the tall chrysanthemums pretending
to be dead until the moon rises behind the hill

Athens, 14-4-71

Observation Post

That peaceful speechlessness of faraway compassion
along with the key of the demolished house and the inside staircase
and the stool and the gold cigarette case – you don't know who to
    give them to
You sit by the window behind the blinds You look at the street
The car goes by the knife sharpener the street sweeper the
    customs officer
The girl has black hair The limping person – trying not to limp
limps even more You want to tell him that He stops
for a moment raises his head He surely saw your
face marked with golden stripes behind the blinds
and perhaps for that reason he smiled He goes ahead again
    Doesn't pretend
Now he limps so freely that he doesn't limp anymore And you
imagine your face in his eyes looking pale saintly
with two closed up grooves between the eyebrows However
you hesitate to get up and look in the mirror perhaps the
golden grooves will disappear and black grooves will
remain from where a spider hangs climbing down inside

Athens, 14-4-71

Absence

The wooden horse wooden queen wooden tower the trees
on the white and black tiles incised accurately
the discipline of wooden soldiers Reduced initiatives
The chess set left on the terrace Moisture There is a moon
of affected spring and the ancient owl The hands
opposing and of equal strength hovering invisible united
in a coerced handshake of a shared non-existent victory
over the void the measured void supposedly The two players
perhaps went to the bathroom Sound of water is heard The
    servant
comes out with a big candleholder places it on the table
he sits in the posh armchair takes off one of his shoes
closes his eyes listens carefully to the moths around
    the flame
the slimy worms under the soil amid roots
opens his eyes looks at the candle and takes off his other shoe

Athens, 14-4-71

Morning Fog

Vaguely without any purpose blindly
without any pressure of blindness or feeling
of disengagement The immense view –
roofs and roofs TV antennas spectrums
of time and of the clouds on shut windows
the rusted drainpipes the kiosk owner
selling aspirins paper and envelopes matches
cigarettes clothespins he's completely framed by
the hanging newspapers like a picture of
a bankrupt king when he is busy
with house chores when he hangs
a worn-out shirt he washed himself
while in the kitchen next to the small stove
he has left his big gold ring
with its beautiful stone with which he used to seal
so many foreign decrees without reading them

Athens, 15-4-71

Partial Resignation

It was that the day suddenly clouded over The juggler
lost his tall hat with the birds The man walking the tightrope
ties his rope on the table leg In the hallway
playing cards lie scattered from the night before
In the upstairs room the dead man alone is lying on his back
in his shoes and clothes on the made up bed
his arms crossed his eyes open
staring at the ceiling with that obvious nausea
for so many pretenses turns and disguises
for so many buttons on his pants especially on the vest
when death is one invincible alone
and the elevator with the broken mirror is out of service

Athens, 15-4-71

Empty Bottles

These empty beer bottles and the others
of wine lemon juice or oil down in the basement
in wooden crates dusty mildewed –

if you took them out on a sunny day –
you need not wash them – if they were to be warmed up a bit
if a shadow of a bird flew over their sides –

No this is not a new excuse I am saying
about those bottles for years in the basement One of them
had I believe two strange glass hands
and held her temples as though she had a headache

Athens, 15-4-71

Strange Times

Three messengers came They climbed upstairs
The heralds left from the back door One dog
passed by along the wall Fragrance of the lilac
entered the room of the dead man The soldiers outside
took off their helmets and swords   placing them
on rocks warmed by the sun
                                      I wonder if the killer
had crossed the river? Would he have gone out? Was it
him? Because lately there have been a lot of look-a-likes
You'd think the customs the same orders the epidemic –
when one looked at the others got the impression
of looking in multiple mirrors That almost cooled
things off – a general guilt or forgiveness
and sometimes a general indifference
                                      But now
no one wanted to shoulder such responsibility
and they started one by one   no two looking alike
                                      In the afternoon
we all followed the funeral procession When on the opposite side
before the gate between two tall columns
the killer was standing   holding reverently
the biggest wreath made of white and red lilies

Athens, 16-4-71

Silence

When people turned deaf you understood
that they had finally learned the truth or at least
they had touched that secret pride
not to repeat the well-memorized lie

In the evening they sit in the dark inside the house
having both their feet in a earthen basin
with warm water and listening to the old train
going by on time loaded with barrels
sacks of cement rebar fridges soldiers
and a gigantic whale cut in even pieces

Athens, 17-4-71

Then?

"You of course would have been more believable should you
have died should you…" he didn't continue Staring at him
        taking off
his clothes one by one orderly as always When he
was totally naked he crossed the room wound up
the table clock went to the kitchen and returned
with a glass of water – thus naked he placed it
on the side table He smiled "Then?" He said only
"Then?" And he wet one of his fingers in the water

Athens, 17-4-71

Good Old Man

He stared at the opposite riverbank I don't discern – he said –
the colors the sounds the flags Perhaps they celebrate
perhaps they mourn I cannot see The fog relaxes me
Kosmas is saying little I like him I remember
an old rosy house in the forest The windows
were sealed How many words we said uselessly –
perhaps we're afraid that someday we'd turn silent
And the crow was always distinguished nailed in the cloud
above the wooden crates left there for a long time
before the entrance of the collapsed storage room
The homeless cats gather there every night and give birth
There in one crate I also sit I half close my eyes
waiting for someone to pass by and see me

Thebes, 19-4-71

Big Hypocrite

On so many calm or tormented faces (we knew it
he couldn't fool us) he dissolved his own face and perhaps
undisclosed bitterness and passions
                              What beautiful deeds
attributed to others Such modesty was
regarded suspiciously
                    And now with a hook in his teeth
he lifted in a humorous parody of a weight-lifter
just one matchbox from which
three matches were missing that minutes earlier
the three solemn spectators used to light their cigarettes

Athens, 20-4-71

His Last Profession

This is it – he says – my last profession – one villager's
handkerchief large with blue and white squares
I unfold it I fold it I wipe off my sweat
or even my eyes sometimes Here I gather my belongings
some books one armchair my cigarettes the lighter
the magnifying glass for shaving and the other one
a size reducer as if to look at unpleasant things
or those others that they call unachievable
                            In this handkerchief
exactly in the middle there is a hole Through there
during darker nights the secret bird comes in
my bird hops on my shoulder or my knee
and feeds me with an ear of grain with a star or with a worm

Athens, 20-4-71

At the Edge of the Bridge

Suddenly the lights came on The train went by A chimney
was left alone in the night The man returned home early
he didn't find anybody at home The immoral woman
stood by the bridge's edge under the lights
She had her two dentures in her purse She looked at
the traffic on the road The cyclist approached
stood next to her They didn't exchange any words She
took her dentures from her purse she hesitated a bit
then she placed them in his hand The cyclist put
them in his pocket and left again The woman
saw him calmly vanish at the end of the road
and felt so abandoned and unprotected as if being happy
Exactly at that moment the first raindrops fell
and the wet road shined up to the edge of the world

Athens, 20-4-71

Relocations

Mothers were dying early How we grew like that
in foster homes Winter mornings with a piece of
moist bread and a bit of sugar The alarm clocks
cut our sleep in half We used to go out to the street unwashed
We moved from house to house so often We'd always
leave something – a chest with a few books a broken mandolin
We said – we would go by – one Sunday and take them
But we never did And that suitcase made of cloth
in the middle of the room ripped
with its straps spread on the floor Inside we had
left an old talisman with a black string and
those thousands-of-times-seen indecent pictures
exclusively of naked women of old times with a wide
pelvis slender waist and big breasts
                                    One of them
was lying face down as though crying And truly she
was crying in front of the wall with the rusted nails
from where a pair of open scissors and suspenders were hanging

Athens, 21-4-71

Old Expiation

Down there in the low-lying houses with the hungry cats
the evenings fell silently in the courtyards They lit the lanterns
The women slept in their clothes Men
returned home late – they had eaten in the tavern

There was nothing left for us at night Through
darkness we stared at the old oil lamp in the kitchen
with the supper leftovers We gazed at it intensely so that
it could change into a cage with a thin canary or into
a moon in a bird's shape
                          We conversed with it secretly
so that it wouldn't chirp and wake up the bad old men
who could see the four young punished girls
standing white and stony in the four corners
lifting high on their foreheads like baskets
our innocent sins and our great dreams

                                    Athens, 22-4-71

Advise

Don't talk so loud I cannot stand loud voices
Everyone yells – what do they gain? – He said – If
you talk in a low voice I may believe you
                              I have hidden
my clock in the chest – it was cutting my year
crumb by crumb as if to feed the winter sparrows
Though I am not a bird – I want my year whole
without yelling and bangs like that slow train
in the afternoon on the far road toward Liosion[1] Street
with plenty of wagons one behind the other
loaded with coal and on top of the heap the shovels

Athens, 22-4-71

Urgency

In this cafe no one spoke or even if one did
it was done in an unfamiliar language Toward the evening
a young limping girl with a basket by her elbow would enter
to place a small bouquet of flowers on each table then she would
leave without coming back to collect money or the flowers

And we wouldn't touch them at all as though she would
        come back
later on when the cafe would be empty to collect them
with certain compassion we thought of that basket
empty now and leaning on the old chair
next to the kite of her youngest dead brother

Athens, 23-4-71

---

[1] *Athens Street leading to the north part of the city*

Decay

Deep in the interior space without any trees
though meaning the trees that became chairs
stools tables crates On the chest a woman
sits silently she covers her legs
looks at the caterpillar crawling on the floor –
a green fat caterpillar that strayed
the one that ate the forest and came to eat the house
the picture frames on the wall and the rope on the ceiling

Athens, 24-4-71

One Sunday

One honey bee sits on the glass and a sudden recollection
that it is Sunday with deep-sealed calmness
of a white kitchen after washing the plates
and the dead sitting silently in the inner rooms
with their old slippers without any demand
perhaps a bit annoyed by the lack of
one specific interest and by the commotion
of the first cicadas outside the window shutters

Athens, 25-4-71

Possible Deformities

They placed the mirror inside the box
They covered the box with a blanket
Now they could move around freely
they could cough gesture kneel
pour water convincingly in the vase
with large paper flowers However they stayed silent
weak-willed sorrowful motionless from fear that perhaps the
mirror spied on them intensely from depths presenting
their idols as gigantic disproportional upside down
with gigantic feet and without any heads

Athens, 25-4-71

Inconsistencies

The presence of witnesses – he says – always unbearable The same
with the lack of witnesses One of them hangs from the lamp
The second bites his shoe The ugly woman
walks with her head on the floor Down in the street
the produce sellers yell From the seventh floor
they throw bottles in the light shaft "Myrcine Myrcine"
"Myrcine" someone called And suddenly it turned dark
At the intersection the tall traffic controller raised his right arm
under the lights The traffic stopped At that point
the hearse carrying the dead woman turned back toward the house

Athens, 26-4-71

Uncompromised

Streets buses signs names doors
dust smoke one tree self-interests I threw
the ring on the plate The beer pubs open
every night and close with calculated noise The windows
are clouded by golden letters In the washroom
waiters smoke Someone who is tired looks
at the floor or the wall avoids seeing
avoids having to show to name Every word
is a treason On the billiard table
the chubby woman lies naked hiding
her ravaged face with her thin hair while
big flies with clipped wings walk on her breasts

Athens, 27-4-71

Evening Headache

One vanished behind the corner Three were asleep
The woman with the umbrella on the bench
It wasn't raining The others made love
behind the stone wall Every day turned dark
They wrapped the bones with flags
What do you carry? – We asked They didn't answer
They climbed up the hill They didn't look back
The bones The flags One lizard on the rock
I tell you this is nothing It has already passed
And this yellow dress suits you so well
If you just put on a gold belt

Athens, 1-5-71

Flow

You found the lumberjack's son under the trees
He wasn't injured You took off his shoes
You cleaned the ants from his armpits He let you
You leaned your cheek on his belly He let you
You heard behind the cane fields on the opposite
bank that they were throwing their axes in the river

Athens, 4-5-71

Private Productions

He took the binoculars and his undershirt from the chest
He had closed the windows already The fly
sat on the glass He didn't scare it away
He spread the starch paper on the floor He took the scissors
He cut off the hat the sword the belt
He attached them firmly with a few more pins
than necessary They stood upright
He put the binoculars on the side and waited
When they rang the doorbell he didn't open
He had the binoculars so he could see afar

Athens, 4-5-71

Fictitious Murders

This woman – I don't even know her name – Katina? Euridice? –
she beats me she pushes the knife in my neck I know it
the knife is made of paper I pretend I'm dead I half
open one of my eyes I see better this way At night I get up
I go down to the blacksmith's shop with all the mice
I light the fire I blow with the big bellows of the church
I prepare the four horseshoes the tall water cup I sharpen
the big illegal two-edged knife and I give it to her
hand in hand secretly erotically under the pillow

Athens, 4-5-71

The Other Health

When the water pump stopped by the hospital right at noon
    during the summer
pumping water up to the second floor
    we woke up
we slowly gazed on the snow white metal beds outside
we heard the hot cicadas and the young keeper's footsteps
and we were certain that the two nurses lowered from the roof
the dry starched bed sheets and at any time
they would yell from the middle of the stairs when a tiny
bug would crawl up the knee of the youngest
                      And as if suddenly
the Director would enter our quarters he'd find us all
calm smiling toward the wall And he would get angry
But we were innocent with no fever not sick Only that
that tiny bug was in cahoots with us from the beginning

Athens, 4-5-71

Mistakes

The man was sitting on the couch he was speaking
he was listening to his voice he corrected its tone The woman
fixed up her hair before the mirror

Her hair was dyed
The man's voice was dyed They knew it

The lights went out They kneeled opposite each other and cried
After that they made love on the floor And outside the old
woman
knocked the latch of the metal door

Athens, 5-5-71

Dance of a Woman not so Young

Don't tell me Let me guess – he says I guess
I jump from one balcony to the other moving
only the fingers of one of my hands I unhook
the white curtain I place it on my shoulder
I remember that I am shoeless This gives me
the sense of dance I dance in the air Look
My left leg is lighter The right
more skillful – I follow myself look and I am
Every rope at its end right at its edge always
has a tight knot so it doesn't unravel
Isn't the unforeseeable the same way? – always at the end

I wish I could teach this dance to someone

Athens, 5-5-71

Limits of Drunkenness

The endless and the unfinished – he said – at any time
You turn a coffee cup upside down You look in it
Time has turned upside down on its own The baby
holds the old man on his knee and feeds him
The dining room tree is full of buds
made of small mirrors Moments objects landscapes go
through the mirrors and the face of the young
servant girl with her long braids
who just came from the baker's shop and has
lost the change and she cries some glassy perfectly round tears
and the foreigner under the table smiles because he
is the one who found the money and he gives it to her

Athens, 5-5-71

Buildings

Did you hang the yellow blanket on the balcony?
Did you make the sign of a cross on the bread?
It was me behind the wall I saw the shadow
of your left hand on the door I didn't see
the knife at all
                    We omitted the rest –
how the word is formed how the forest warden
walks alone on the hill before dusk
and the rocks rumble down – dogs bite them
carry them to the river next to the caldron
where the women wash garments of the dead
                                    Later the dogs
stand motionless with gaping mouths with bare teeth
as if holding the same rocks and stare upward –
at the rocks we used to build the vacant house with no roof

Athens, 6-5-71

Difficult Confession

I took the nails and the planks Don't expose me
I could have kept it to myself I cannot When the others
naked in the sun pounded the hammers He climbed up
well dressed and with his tie He unfolded the drawing
        quite large
he pointed with his finger He froze me The hammers didn't pound

Now after all I know the difference between paper and steel
        The world
divided in two Whether you admit it or not – it doesn't unite

Athens, 6-5-71

Transformations

I coaxed her – he says the black bear I tamed her
first I threw my bread at her then my head
Now I am the bear and I am the mirror
I sit on the chair I take care of my nails
I paint them red or yellow I see them I like them
I cannot touch anything I'm afraid of death
I turn the chain of my neck into a crown and
I place it on my forehead Now what could I do?
I must keep my head high and always
gaze upward However at midnight
in my new sleeplessness in whichever way I walk
I hear my footsteps echoing down through the trapdoor
where the other chains hang from the walls

Athens, 6-5-71

Link

You denied the lonely old woman her ravaged chin
her gummy eyes her black teeth
Now she roams the garbage dumps with the dogs
Her arms longer more bony enclosed
by a refined kindness She looks at your window
You throw at her the towel she left behind She
lets it fall on the ground takes it folds it
puts it under her arm climbs the stairs
and leaves the towel before your door – she doesn't come in

Athens, 6-5-71

Secret

When we looked back the city
lights were lit – the big factory
the patisserie in the central plaza
the gardens of the houses The three youngest men
had already taken off their shoes
The old man wasn't pounding his cane anymore
The first one urinated by the tree The woman
"Why did I want to be with you?" she said
However she had taken along threads thimble
needle in a white plastic round little box
George stayed for last He was cutting his buttons
one by one I was the only one who saw him
I didn't say anything to anyone I walked first
so that my smile wasn't visible anymore

Athens, 6-5-71

Prisms of the Hour

You cursed again you said those bad words
when the coffin stumbled on the door – they almost
dropped all the flowers and the icon on the ground
And the horse limped through the street in the heat
so that you felt like begging his pardon However
you didn't feel like taking back the curses
knowing that now inside the house foreign women
started bizarre behavior in the kitchen   hitting
the odd glasses the coffee cups   they emptied
the largest room and placed the chairs
one next to the other by the wall

Athens, 7-5-71

A Gesture

This again is something you like unexpectedly
something insignificant like the gesture of the woman
who picks the dry flowers off the vase arrangement –
she doesn't throw them away she stays thinks
a hovering gesture regretted from the start –
if you talk to her she won't listen – a gesture
completely deaf like the word you place in a poem
then you turn and ask "did you say something?"
And you don't care that war was declared
that the big airplanes shred the dusk
with two-edged black shadows amid the red

Athens, 7-5-71

Honesty

In May when the sun returns it hits the house
from the west The dusks get longer One band
of sun almost golden cuts the wall vertically Then the
people stand by the edge of a deep revelation
The patisserie tables are placed on the sidewalk
The red lilies are discerned from behind the glass Opposite
in the tall building they opened the windows The emptiness
of the vacant room is obvious
                          And yet – who knows –
perhaps it was you who give the order before nightfall
to light the green lamps in the church's foreground
because it is the days of difficult inversions
                                        Yes you
the appointed (by whom?) you who evidently place wooden
horses in the poem and the keys from old lost suitcases
and this rubber imitation of three or more frogs
jumping softly in the non-existent water garden

Athens, 7-5-71

You and the Crab

Thus you finish everything always ingloriously disproving
so many expectations and demands even
of the well-initiated
                    A red crab
sauntered by the rock that afternoon
by the dock and you said "He walks sideways
let me see him" You may even have believed it You added
"To observe means to be in power"
                                    Then
the crab jumped in the water And of course
you didn't order that and the lights weren't turned on
for the ship loading up fresh wood products

Athens, 8-5-71

Devout Comparison

Next to each other the cafe the pharmacy the patisserie
and closer by the small flower shop People don't stop
The women look at themselves in the windows before dusk Behind
the half-built stone fence in the stadium with the mallows
everyone throws their own – paper trays
little medication bottles broken cups glasses
rotten flowers
        The old women and the dogs gather there
searching in the pile carefully absentmindedly – they don't look
at the golden sundown they search like poets for their poem
the most bitter old women the abandoned so happy
with a dry orange peel with a piece of a mirror
with a blue pharmacy tube that has on top of it
the white trace of the homeless slug
and in its empty space the sound of the Larissa train

Athens, 8-5-71

Holy Communion

Thus with sweaty hair silent lonely
The whitewash of the stone wall blinds him
The birds fall on the scorched rocks
And he there on the road in the sweltering heat
walks full of dust calm holding
a small package under arm –
that doormat where so many
had wiped their shoes one moment before
they entered the house straight to the kitchen
to drink a glass of cold water

Athens, 9-5-71

The Other Exactness

Measure well register accurately
the borders the distances stooping laying
the meter right on the ground and so seriously
dedicated to the number – perhaps – you may forget the borders
perhaps you may discover the great exactness
            alone and self-sufficient
because your fingers by chance may touch the clasp of Helen's belt
on the ground – the one she wore one evening
on top of the walls above the quarrels of Acheans and Trojans
while behind her like fate ecstatically following her
with eyes half closed the black she-dog almost ready to give birth

Athens, 10-5-71

The Karlovasi Wharf

We didn't know when how or from where
they carried those huge rafters to the wharf
from trunks of beautiful trees Next to the steel
tar barrels we walked alone we sniffed
the wood's aroma with an emotion of lost health
with a general feeling of a secret treason When night came
before the lights on the poles were lit and all the harbor
was lit from lamps of moored ships then
we clearly felt that it was unjust to think that
all this wood would become crosses The next day
the wharf was empty – neither wood nor barrels –
and it all glittered washed from the night rain

Athens, 10-5-71

Encounter

Nothing of course comes on its own
You have to search so you may find it In the mornings
the sun enters from the eastern window it discolors
the two purple chairs it stays a while retreats
leaving behind an impression of gentleness – that
serene extinguishing
                        And the carpet flowers
stepped on from before are right they have
their ears glued to the floor they listen
to the rhythmic galloping of underworld horses Then
the silent woman enters and you see it
that she tries not to step on those flowers

Perhaps two together can endure the inconceivable
although it always appears to just one

Athens, 11-5-71

Equal Pieces

Then all of a sudden the wind ceased
Someone shut off the bathroom faucet
The secret agreement was consummated
The man with a finger on his lips
nodded "yes" The short woman
made the sign of cross with her hand
on the forehead of the sleeping child
I saw the shadow of her hand on the wall
between an Apollo lithograph
and the Crucifix embroidered in satin cloth

Athens, 11-5-71

Heavenly Fondness

These houses where we spend our lives
the same houses that we search every day
in the basements the wall closets the lamps
behind the mirrors or under the beds
for a hairpin a pencil case a broken clock
for a box of ancient matches – they don't even light anymore –
for things known to us that suddenly became
so unknown and farfetched or totally opposite
in these houses under the tables
for a slice of hardened bread (from which dinner I question?)
not to eat it of course (no one is hungry anymore)
but only to discover it
                    And if someone
enters the room at that moment we
bite on the bread at once – although afraid
of breaking our last teeth – there
inside the calm evening dimly lit room
in the deep most sweet empathy of time in our
own same empathy for us for everything for everyone

Athens, 12-5-71

Relevance of the Irrelevant

What to say now? – he says – what use do the many
        explanations have?
when as you walk hurriedly to catch up
with your friends waiting for you for something
very important having to do with you and others and others
you suddenly stop in the middle of the street to look
at that bird walking on the asphalt calmly
with his head raised ecstatically more informed
with a bus ticket in his long beak

Athens, 12-5-71

A Familiar Dog

This dog we have known for years – always the same
always with a big bone in his teeth that he doesn't even eat
his teeth don't let it go (and how is he to bark?)
unless every night when we sleep while hiding
he gnaws it secretly and digging somewhere – who knows –
he finds a new bone for the next day or unless
he has learned that barking is useless
that he doesn't protect anybody neither garden nor house
neither fountain nor himself from the moon from time
        from the thieves

Athens, 12-5-71

Upward

This was all and all From the window
they threw down gold coins
The others in the street didn't collect them they stayed
motionless silent looking up
perhaps at the contracted hungry hand
perhaps at the cloud or at the earthen statue
or that big nail from where
Anna   some years ago hung herself
Then they fell down finally and collected the coins You
stayed again alone in the dust
hiding the severed arm in your shirt

Athens, 12-5-71

Today

Today you stood just like that in the middle of day
like a small nickel spoon with vanilla
in a glass filled with cold water on top
of the green table of the seashore patisserie
one secluded table
                The one who was suppose to
eat the vanilla delays in the washroom

No then the water wasn't cold enough

Athens, 13-5-71

Direction

Financial planning maps compasses dividers –
we understood nothing of all that The preliminary
study was always doomed to fail
                                We
holding on the rope descended further down
in the ancient water well feeling on our soles
the dark coolness of depth
                                Up on the opening
a faint light (perhaps the glowing end of our cigarette)
and the stones rumbling to the bottom
pointing to our position in the hung world

Athens, 13-5-71

We Continue

Every time he says "I'm finished" he never finishes
Sometimes it is the window with the long flowing curtain
sometimes the fourth leg of the chair sometime the glass
left under the bed next to the shoes
especially the inside part of the fridge – so artificially white –
with the bitten red apple still preserved
showing clearly traces of the same teeth

Athens, 14-5-71

On Two Levels

This beautiful climbing rosebush leaning
on the iron frame – a transformed deep red color
(who knows from what secret mixing) a hue
gracefully rosy yet closer to silver – shines
these spring days lights the marble stairs
the outside walls even inside the small kitchen pots

only that this wasteful wealth brings to mind
those old (and future) autumns when
the yard tiles the storage room the cistern
even the upstairs rooms the library the beds
fill with dry petals stems thorns leaves
and you need to sweep them so often
                                    For this reason
when we express our admiration to the lady of the house
for her beautiful rosebush – what a color what a shine –
she just smiles in a certain sorrowful and remote way
as if she would prefer that it was
a very delicate ring on her pinkie finger

Athens, 15-5-71

After One Pause

After some months when he sat again to write something
he suddenly felt unkempt unwashed abandoned
like the unmarried woman devoted to the house
chores all day and when evening approaches she unintentionally
passes in front of the mirror and her glance falls
on her neglected idol suddenly she remembers
that all day she didn't look at her in the mirror not even once

Has she then aged so much? Has she already died? Why
would she comb her hair now? – The day is over Nobody
is going to see her – not anymore She takes the black comb
and starts combing her long hair to the end
like she combs her dead friend her beloved one
the one suddenly so alien with closed eyes and a wart
      on her nose

Athens, 15-5-71

A Street in Athens

The blind musician the blind lotto-vendor
the blind day the blind dog Niki street
guitar violin accordion the guitar more blind

you shifted them you designated their song
the lotto-vendor: the violin the dog: the lotto-tickets
the old woman: the accordion   the guitar: alone

At dusk the music echoes so nicely on Niki street
outside the pharmacy where they throw in the street
the brown little bottles with sleeping pills
and the cut-off fingers of the last customer:
the beautiful piano player of night restaurants

And the gauzes and substitutions have been used up

Athens, 17-5-71

Saving Fall

You'll carry on with the conversation – you who so often
stopped at the meaning of pause or pauses carrying on
the old dilapidated pushcart (with the dignity of a responsible
day laborer of course)
the furniture of the poor student (who honored you with his
      choice)
from one basement to the other or the loft on Periandros Street
being careful as you carried down the narrow rotten stairs
the two unmatched chairs so that they wouldn't scratch the wall

because the stony merciless landlady stood at the top
behind the railing with crossed arms observing you
when you tumbled down the stairs and landing on the ground you
simply sat on one chair having the other chair on your head
upside down like a strange impenetrable helmet
with four antennae or four legs raised in the sun

Athens, 17-5-71

The Ropewalker and the Spectators

Handsome amazing ropewalker high up in the air –
what supple soles and the tips of his toes – marvel
stylish steady with his yellow umbrella – like
a halo supposedly – with two three chairs
held by his teeth with many balls and rings
up and down in his hands Handsome truly
high up there above the spectator's chairs above
the rose bushes trees lamps of the Garden
then amid the clapping when he collected
his tools with such a strange calm while at
the same time he bowed indifferently – the balls
in their cases same with the rings Silent Lastly
he closed his yellow umbrella Now the rope is around
his neck he's not stepping on it anymore but directly in the air

And while smoking we waited a bit longer for usually
the continuation of the program mostly
that piece with thousands of women's legs in
black nylons and high heels whirling up in the air

Athens, 17-5-71

Rough Plan

Perhaps the houses grow bigger Opposite to that
people steadily become smaller In the elevator
three naked laughing women lift the huge
picture of some old bearded man
while in the elevator mirror sandwiched
shine the two buttocks and breasts of the third one
and the fogged-up spine of the picture with its small
cobwebs and the pulled triangular fly-spat string

Athens, 19-5-71

Like Poetry

Bad woman you say this beautifully and somehow sad
this one like the dedicated blind vigilante At night
when you go to bed she stands above you observing
lurking for your breath You pretend to be asleep
She is not convinced She waits still A bit later
you hear her searching your coat pocket after pocket
(you placed it on purpose on the back of the chair)
she searches the pants your vest Then barefoot
she searches your overcoat in the hallway And strange as it is
she will always find something of value in your clothes
that you didn't know you had Then at once you open
one of your eyes and you take it from her On the floor
your two slippers have become larger occupying half of the room

Athens, 21-5-71

Miracle

It is a miracle – he says – even more than a miracle
where everything is exhausted (and first of all me) I discover
amid the pebbles at the seashore the holy skull
of one of Achille's horses – perhaps that of Xanthos
amid the chamomiles I discover the Patriarch's crutch
I lift it reverently I climb up the marble stairs
I don't pound the steps with it scores of people gather
I stand before the podium I feel my hair becoming motionless
flowing on my shoulders scores of people can't wait they jostle
I open my mouth to speak and suddenly I understand
that I am deaf and they hear me

Athens, 10-5-71

Short Admission

1978

The sea – he said –
I don't have birds in my hair
I hurl a stone
I become light blue
a golden thread
hangs from my ear
I hear clearly
the sleeping turtle
and my awkward silence

Kalamos, 7-5-78

In the afternoon the boys
took to the streets
they killed the old men
I am the only survivor
I buy chocolates for them
I wash their hands
I spank their rear ends
in the evening they sing
a long song
mine

Kalamos, 7-5-78

Yellow color
on the wall
behind the washrooms
nettles
you were bitter
Saturday night
with the little soldiers
with the dulcimer
as when the grasses sigh
and the words wonder

Kalamos, 7-5-78

Sunday night
the buses are gone –
oh how pleasant mourning
(he said so)
the complete
calm goodbye
as over the sea
in the olive grove
the voice of an owl crosses over
the voice of the nightingale

Kalamos, 7-5-78

I don't know where this starts
where it ends
Tuesday Friday
musical instruments are heard from the inn
soldiers come out
look at the sky
they vanish
faint touch of flesh
remains in the air
with two or three fingers
and the dark music
all across the wall

Athens, 9-5-78

They were rocks
boys wore
colorful shirts
I'll go down – said the youngest –
the water well was deep
then nothing
only the sea
on the other side
endless
and a ship farther away

Athens, 9-5-78

He made a hole in the void
put his head through
now he is staring
at us
someone should
apologize –
should it be him or should we?

Athens, 9-5-78

Since there was light
and voices of vendors
and fishes in the aquarium
and flowers on the balcony
he made a big hat
out of newspaper
he flew
over the temple

Athens, 9-5-78

She saw the beautiful thief
as he was jumping
out of the window
Since then
she leaves her door
wide open
The rest of her jewels
in an approachable place
He never came back

Athens, 9-5-78

You make fun of us – they told him –
yes – he says –
but I don't know
who I make fun of the most
you? myself?
the red light bulb?
the guilty mirror?
or our double death?

Athens, 9-5-78

No
at the last moment
he shouldn't have kneeled
he shouldn't have given up
his empty suitcase –
at least here we resisted
with hammers we pounded
thousands of nails
thousands of drums

Athens, 10-5-78

He stepped out of the train
he wasn't returning from the front
on his blanket
signs of lonely nights
in his temples
two rusted nails –
silent pride
of no submission
of no confession
in the desolate city

Athens, 10-5-78

White vertical levels –
upward?
downward?
white
Greek
at the far end the blond archer
and the number 7

Athens, 10-5-78

He walks toward the suburb
air flutters through his shirt –
pottery shops carpenters' shops
four bicycle riders –
impoverished things
how they get enlarged
before these statues
that pretend to stare elsewhere
like you do

Athens, 10-5-78

Newspapers radios
clapping appearances
and you're searching
among so many faces
so many words
for a word of your own
humbly uttered
in front of the common cafe
while it rains on the tin awning
and on the black umbrella
where the music mixes with
the rain quite vaguely

Athens, 10-5-78

Leave I say to you
this color is not red
when I clap my hands
there is no sound
when I say *water*
a bird flies away
for this
leave I say to you
all the pale color
is pinned on the wall
with tiny pins
from new shirts of
wild boys
one Sunday after
the neighborhood football game

Athens, 10-5-78

A sharper tone
more intense
sunshine on the flagstones
urchins against the white
and a totally naked statue
on the green hill –
is what I try to dress
is what I miss

Athens, 10-5-78

Pieces of black
at the street corners –
ah tired insistence
after the song
between two thieves
and two church candles

Athens, 11-5-78

The disapprovals
commence again
who is he?
and that one?
and this scepter?
and this hat?
though on the other
side clapping
be careful

Athens, 11-5-78

No I don't want – he says –
it is half
less than half
for this reason I knock at the door
pretending I don't know
that the house is vacant

Athens, 11-5-78

These people died
and also the others
a pair of scissors on the table
rags in the corner
fluff of blankets –
however we knew
they had died for a while
we don't need to
pretend anymore

Athens, 11-5-78

Words
names of places
names of bodies
bodies
naked or dressed
disguises transformations
of the o n e

Athens, 11-5-78

At the train station
exactly there
nothing happened
it was raining
the attendant was sleeping
under the brim of his cap
his black mustache

Athens, 11-5-78

Cheap coffins
made of planks
iron handles
when you left at night
in the drizzle
the old woman turned on the faucet
the towel on the floor
the old man changed his shoes
put on Electra's wig
Maria
couldn't find a way to cry
she entered the hair salon
in vigil

Athens, 12-5-78

Let it spread farther
to include the mountain ridge
the five trees
the three statues
and the small hammer
you used to crack almonds
last night in the moonlight

Athens, 12-5-78

This man
how strange
turns the zero upside down
it is still zero
then
he puts his hand in the hole
pulls out a bird
then a house
then a blackboard
the chalk on the floor

Athens, 12-5-78

Flags and dead
flags and alive
again flags
comrades
only flags

Athens, 15-5-78

We left that city
with its many rats
with police wagons
with dogs' teeth
with the dead bull –
there
a table made of tin
green
under the only tree
in the plaza with the statues

Athens, 18-5-78

Because of the light
and the hill line
the deep rows of olive trees
white rock
them in the river
and their clothes among the wild bushes
there was neither hesitation
nor question

Athens, 18-5-78

I saw the mountain
then the cloud
closer yet the bird
I took an oath
I stayed here
without shoes
without a shirt
without the watch
of my wrist

Athens, 18-5-78

Limpidity
you travel distances
the secretive urchin
the proud turtle
the snow white horse
snow white snow white
with pitch black testicles

Athens, 18-5-78

To say the name
your mouth fills
I aimed at
a feather
the wind blew it away
now I pretend
that I don't know this place
that I am not myself

Athens, 18-5-78

Sunshine by the window –
he was paralyzed
and walked
(perhaps he wasn't?)
the apples on the table
the shovel in the yard
and him speechless

Athens, 18-5-78

Old woman with the mortar
the dog with the bones
old man shrunk
he shrunk within himself
one bite of bread
crumb-warm bread
kneaded in his fingers
within him
(how else?)
he smiles at the wolves

Athens, 18-5-78

Let death be our protector – he said –
revenge – he said –
they stole my nails
they nailed on the wall
my most naked picture
I only managed to disguise
just my knee
and my mouth

Athens, 18-5-78

How did you create
this beautiful mosaic
with just a few wheels
from broken watches
and with cigarette butts?

Athens, 18-5-78

He drew no conclusion
fruits cigarettes poems
blood pressure pills –
he sits down
he eats the soil
he created within himself
from saliva and soil
his statue
and yours
he got very heavy
he flies

Athens, 19-5-78

The nail hiding
behind the picture
holding the picture up
in the picture there are
no nails
only
the naked body
flooded by the light
red
over the red blanket
red body
turned toward the wall –
perhaps staring at
the nails

Athens, 19-5-78

What you offered
what you lost
what they deny you
belongs to you
Lift your bed
take off your wings
walk

Athens, 19-5-78

Replacements
1978

Unexpected

Half a glass of water remains on the table The newspapers
don't adapt to the space at all Here I am – he said –
amid the leaves and the stones I can open the door
I can live without words   The stony woman
supported her chin with her fist Suddenly
wind blew the leaves fell covering him

Karlovasi, 10-8-78

Farm Scene

The hunter under the tree A bird
flutters opposite him In his beak
he has one bullet – the one that almost
killed him For this the bullet shines
for this his beak shines and the whole forest

Karlovasi, 12-8-78

Pointless Solemnity

He remembers nothing Not even why
the napkin is lying on the floor Yet he insists
to give order to things completely lost
to find a word with less death – one word
that could save him from the lottery vendors

Karlovasi, 12-8-78

Intentional Ignorance

Sculptured stones painted stones – the woman
with long free-flowing hair the handsome boy
how nicely he leans his forehead the elegant prince
lost one of his sandals among the lilies the old woman
still smiles at her children who have departed   I don't
know what I miss – something vaguely certain –
thus I don't know when or to what direction to smile

Karlovasi, 12-8-78

Holidays

You find again the indifferently useful time
you cut a sheet with certain meaning you throw a word
in the dark water well and you don't know at all
whether it will float or will go through to the other side People
cross the roads in a hurry they buy meat
shirts fruit paper and envelopes matches Women
try on summer hats in front of mirrors
they often have a headache they eat big grapes
one grape falls on the floor – don't step on it the poem

Karlovasi, 12-8-78

Mortality

Don't talk anymore There is no continuance You search
the shapes the colors You pretend to choose
Motorcycles are noisy Windowpanes break Paul
believed in people They killed him A lot gets forgotten
a lot remains half-done Solemn women
wash the glass tubes they leave them in the sun
children sleep in their clothes at night The compass
has been left on the table for years I'll go out – he said –
I'll buy a watermelon as big as the whole world
I'll slice it in two to stare at its dark red color
firmly nailed with black nails And I shall eat it

Karlovasi, 14-8-78

Farewells

Large rooms of old stately homes in rural areas
filled by whistles of faraway ships filled
with vanished bell chiming and deep sounds
of ancient clocks Nobody lives in here
other than shadows and a violin hanging on the wall
and the useless currency bills scattered on the armchairs
and on the large bed with the yellow blanket At night
the moon descends passes by the breathless mirrors
and with the slowest gestures places in order farewell
whistles of sunken ships behind the windowpanes

Karlovasi, 15-8-78

Equations

In that glyph a naked ephebe like a stele
his left arm below his puberty holding
a piece of cloth like a bath towel his right arm
softly attached to his hip the head leaning
with graceful loneliness Above him two women
(perhaps his mother and sister) with solemn expressions One
of them with a long peplos the other naked no signature of
the creator anywhere And thus with cleverly incised letters
I engrave my name at the bottom – not like a usurper
but like a Greek with his rights and not that I am the sculptor
but the handsome naked ephebe with the towel

Karlovasi, 15-8-78

Neutral Area

Afternoon radios chairs cafes
One holds a large fish The other is angry
At night it turns a bit cold The pregnant women
eat boiled wheat The ship whistles
Suddenly they turn on the lights Part of the street
with a bicycle in the middle shines out of embarrassment
And suddenly I discover the poem alone beyond the words

Karlovasi, 14-8-67

Nevertheless

Place a boulder in the spot of the one who left
a boulder is a good sign in this foreign place perhaps
it will become a stool pillow or a street signpost Because
you know slowly things vanish lose their weight
almost vaporize Outside the National Chemistry Lab
the war amputees pass by in their wheelchairs
and they cough persistently The statues turn silent and look
with a stony glance of general futility Nevertheless
as soon as the last visitor moves away they carefully
adjust on their shoulders the pleat of their chitons

Karlovasi, 16-8-78

Thus

The high mountain with a church
two whitewashed houses with three plane
trees and a bull hide behind a few leaves
Thus behind the words hides the poem

Karlovasi, 16-8-78

Conjunction

The hand resting on the table – it doesn't beg it doesn't give
beautiful suntanned arm Next to it the cup
and the copper turtle Just these Once upon a time
we kept silent almost out of stubbornness and all those
unconnected
had a common root From time to time a large moon
hit the walls with its finger gold and silver coins
fell and later on the three metal keys of dead Ariadne

Karlovasi, 16-8-78

Emptiness

They were paralyzed and walked were blind and saw
the hospital was emptied – other times so full of action
so full of glasses bed sheets bowls ringing of bells
yearning despair anger Completely empty Now
the white beds lined up The silent hallways
as though the general manager was killed In the operating room
emptiness lies motionless with closed eyes pretending to be
the last injured who was left behind While the five black wet
umbrellas remain in the change rooms alone and austere

Karlovasi, 17-8-78

The Transparent Assets

You should invest these transparent assets Who knows –
they may get developed by someone in the future Repetitions
don't negate the originality experiences don't obstruct
A pile of cartons of common patisserie trays
get moist warp in the basement Perhaps the dominating
faces of theater were created from them? And the others
out of a different substance almost invisible in strange sorrowful
shapes of tall glass or crystal naked statues
don't they still live in the beautiful transparent city
where poets and those concerted to moonlight keep their vigil?

Karlovasi, 17-8-78

Of the Province

On Saturday nights soldiers on relief are in the taverns
small shops close in the autumn sundowns
carrion crows on the branches large solemn colors
the lonely one-horse carriage passes the seashore road
next to the lamppost the moon – two hanged people
and the island fool is dead they found him in the raisin storage
and the old woman insisted on ringing bells all night
Under each word lies a lethargic small lizard

Karlovasi, 17-8-78

Gradually

It is always difficult to draw the first line The intent of
the artist is discerned his hesitation the uncertain end Further
your step becomes lighter as though you tread on pine needles
on the hill
you discern someone limping with a basket full of grapes
the pregnant woman holds in her arms a fat yellow chicken
you may go sidelong toward the sea knowing by now
the smell of salt and of chopped wood knowing still
that the good lion the one having many wounds the one staring
like a mother is tied in the hold of the docked ship

Karlovasi, 18-8-78

The Error

He spoke eloquently using simple words slightly abstract
as it suits a master of speeches However at one point
an unforgivable mistake – that word
it should had been left out so that the deep loss the absence
would be more obvious Then of course we forgot
whether that word was the word *cape* or the word *hammer*

Karlovasi, 21-8-78

Bright Light

The trees enter through the windows leaves fill the tables
the two armchairs the bed No space is left for
your movement or action Everything is foreign You should
be attached to the sounds of the sea to the voices
of the grape pickers the fruit vendor the swimmers The rhetors
stepped down from the stage The musicians scattered There is
nothing left but a gold sword piercing the drum

Karlovasi, 21-8-78

The Personal Element

As soon as he lay down they got him up from his poor bed
they dressed him in a shining uniform – golden epaulets braids –
a crown in his hair – of olive branches? ivy? or laurel? –
He didn't know they didn't give him time to have a quick
          look in the mirror
they stood him on the stage before the cheering crowd
among the clapping And him hanging in the air
beyond himself almost comfortable he stepped on the planks
just on the tiptoes of his right foot – because on this foot
in their haste they let him wear his sock with a hole and being
pleasantly stretched out of shape And this still allowed him to
think
this still allowed him to be an unknown man among the
populace

Karlovasi, 21-8-78

The Unknown Essentials

He often goes back to the same subject Repetition
is already a change Besides words follow
their own direction toward secret erotic springs
beyond our wish And that sweet old man
using his little finger made a hole in the blank sheet of paper
he placed it under the lamp and smiling he whispered
I know to cough and listen to my coughing

Karlovasi, 21-8-78

Glory

You don't have to undress anymore to close your eyes for a while
The most bitter substitution for life is glory

Karlovasi, 21-8-78

Protection

He reversed a lot He changed a lot of values
Many are in his hands still If only the merciless Guard
wouldn't find out that in the basket
he hid the snake the bird the bitten apple

Karlovasi, 22-8-78

Still

Since you became a statue why do you need
this valise and this disguise?

Karlovasi, 22-8-78

That Bird and You

You believe that what time takes from you you get back
perhaps you do yes – but they are not the same And perhaps
these are better – but they are not the same Now the beautiful
    wings
of that bird decorate your hat they evoke respect
the old women salute you humbly even the traffic controller
but what about that bird? – and you of course aren't going to fly

Karlovasi, 22-8-78

Sometime

Sometime even the poem kneels before its white paper
or hides behind it staring at the world

Karlovasi, 22-8-78

Suddenly

Summer days – the light the rocks sea grapes
Erased events The horizon same to its end On the wall
of the hostel the map faded from the sunlight
The newspapers arrive late – you don't read them
In the midst of the valley the hat of a grape picker shines
The blind man plays the accordion Tourists go by with
        sleeping bags
And suddenly at midnight the absolute word reaches you
like a ship whistle in your sleep and you cannot wake up

Karlovasi. 22-8-78

Unavoidable

The delegates are downstairs Discreet music is heard from upstairs
These talk about the murder The others about the apple crop
Secretly under the official table with candleholders
follows the rhythm of music with his foot trying to retain
some of his share of independence while he already knows
that his name is first in both lists of the pre-convicted

Karlovasi, 22-8-78

Disorientation

In the summer the trees won us Some people went down to the sea
others climbed up the mountains During the day the thorns
            shine golden
amid the marbles The young waiters with blond mustaches
who work for the two seashore restaurants wear red armbands
During the night the ambulance arrives very late
The crowd gathers around it as though to discover someone
they know among the injured The youngest wears
a snow white shirt and a gold buckle on his belt And as soon as
the stretchers by the lampposts disappear music recommences

Karlovasi, 22-8-78

Memory of One Night

The one-horse carriage was crossing the bridge The solemn
    woman
was holding something like a watering can or bouquet The man
seemed to be angry he yelled something On top of the hill
thick smoke and fires rose The arsonists entered
our houses slept in our own beds
and outside in the garden we the innocent listened to their snoring

Karlovasi, 23-8-78

July's Blind

Beautiful blind man under the lamppost in July's scorching sun
selling paper hats to tourists He is true Hellene
on his waist a belt made of rope scattered mauve osier flowers
on his blond beard He knows how in the night under
the bright moonlight the seabirds sleep inside
the sandals of ephebes or young gods borrow them
to climb the rope ladders and at the rosy dawn
still warm from their exquisite feet are left noiselessly
next to the sleeping youngsters Perhaps he is not truly blind?

Karlovasi, 23-8-78

Artist's Foresight

They dismounted their horses they took off the great winds
and entered their houses got fat and died You luckily
managed to create them naked just with their spurs
on their white ankles Thus these days none will
understand while staring at their great
cenotaph in the sunlight of July that we are all tired

Karlovasi, 23-8-78

Contradictions

Strange man His face changes so often
His words change And a little while ago he was
stooping to nail the wooden crate with the glassware suddenly
you see him run to the garden and strike a tree with his cane

Karlovasi, 23-8-78

In the Harbor

Tobacco merchants porters seamen noise winches
Ship whistles they arrive they depart One anchor shines
Soldiers in the washrooms One woman with a yellow umbrella
People mingle they part – mostly they part At dusk the
        lighthouse
keeper went down to the dock He unfolds a big kerchief
he folds it back and puts it in his pocket with
that deep lonely gesture of non-confession

Karlovasi, 24-8-78

Eleusinean [1]

There was neither a reveille nor a last post at the army base
They bound the trumpeter hand and foot No one
ever learned the reason Only that in the grounds the dark small
pines appeared as if there were more and darker One night
the youngest soldier with the scar on his chin suddenly
threw off his clothes walked out to the middle of the street naked
climbed up to the roof and lowered the flag half-mast
The same night they unbounded the trumpeter bounded the
        soldier
and the last post was heard again as sad as ever

Karlovasi, 24-8-78

---

[1] *Eleusis, a city to the west of Athens; center of the ancient
Eleusinian Mysteries*

Avoiding to Answer

How the beautiful lines of hills the voices from vineyards
remained so meaningless in the quiet afternoon
the two buses on the opposite street behind the heliotropes
the olive trees half lit half dark the church clock
and the one who saws quite unseen – a tree perhaps
or the stool of the deaf old woman or the big table
of the old burnt-up hostel And even the horse
that appeared amid the yellow corn fields – I don't know
what to answer I don't know why And the light turns red
and the violet slowly steams up the mountains and my papers

Karlovasi, 24-8-78

Then and Now

So long as they had him muzzled he had so much to say ˙
Now that they took the muzzle off   he looks all around
he cannot find any word not even for those things Thus at night
in front of the mirror under dim light he tries alone
to tie around his mouth a white handkerchief

Karlovasi, 25-8-78

Ritual

The ritual had started The procession climbed up the hill
In their hands they held wooden statues wearing peplos Korae
in diaphanous chitons threw their spears Under the poplars
the nine thieves rolled the dice Farther down by the river
the strict supervisors counted the ephebes' phalluses
most accurately Eumolpos always lazy
was eating out of a can under the arch Then the Blind One
with a white band on his forehead and a basket of grapes
passed by before me and placed the lyre on my knees

Karlovasi, 25-8-78

Sharp End

What you replaced with those and those with others
repeated circle or better rising helix
swirling motionlessly and turning into marble – glorious a column
sculpted spiral exclusive column of an invisible temple and
       at its apex
not the thorny Corinthian capital but the stylite
upright speechless with a bandage around its eyes

Karlovasi, 25-8-78

The World is One
1978

for Nicola Crocetti

First Night in Mondello

The sea was like a flash lightly ironed by the hand
of a new moon And it was a nice antithesis to the hairy
huge arms of the player who moved the puppets
of the outdoor theater
                              The night was fragrant
by girly sweat and urchin They offered us fried
eggplant and beer on the large balcony A verse by Dante
shined for just one moment held by the sound of two
friendly glasses clinking in the air
                                    The same night
in the mopped closed fish market under the lamppost we saw
a carton crate filled with empty bottles We didn't disclose it
      However
the music coming from the windows of the all-night restaurant
already declared it in front of the balcony doors of the sleeping
      newlyweds

Mondello, 15-9-78

Unclear Encounters

Those who met by chance on the road were strangers they didn't
     speak
they didn't beckon with their hands or a glance Although
they looked as if they agreed with the moonlight entering through
the blinds in a closed villa as though in agreement with the
     whimper
of a shirt falling on the floor – Perhaps Hellenes They had
a scar on their foreheads – an intimate mark – sometime ago red
had turned whitish lighting their faces They didn't speak

Only during the nights of September they look absentmindedly
at the gardens of old houses the gas stations the kiosks
a light blue lamp under the trees the clock of the
     Customs Building
and bit by bit their arms become longer they turned into fishes
those who learned the deep underwater voices and now stay silent

Mondello, 15-9-78

Freedom of Travel

One whole day we traveled in desolate seashores
Boats swimmers a red landmark a naked woman
the excavator wrapped in a large snow white nylon
a hotel with a colonnade under the trees The yellow bird
looked elsewhere it vanished its shadow nailed on the road Then
drops of fish blood appeared on the marble staircase The woman
was frightened The children shouted by the sea Even making
    love is tiring
Until evening comes with faint lights to windows and ships
amid a deep somehow sad lightness contented by the blue void

Palermo, 16-9-78

Morning in Salerno, I

Sunlit day houses trees cables the endless sea
shining everywhere in a carefree friendliness In the piazza
fish vendors oarsmen lovers The handsome portiere –
gold ring on his forth finger gold watch
gold cross amid his chest hairs and the buckle
of his belt gleaming reflecting a piece of sea
                          Oh immense
Italian Sunday with wide words and tall masts
fragrance of salt and morning coffee Many things that these
    people dreamed of
remained behind got forgotten and the others that they did
    commit
they also forgot – heretical memory non-resentful
start and end of the endless start in the indocile body

Salerno, 17-9-78

Morning in Salerno, II

What provocation hides behind the supposedly meek light?
    Only men
and boys go out to the streets The beautiful women
still asleep in ship cabins tired from
swimming and lovemaking The morning sea dampness
moistens their unraveled hair catching on their eyelashes
    and their lips
while behind the steamed up windowpanes of the large cafe
the unemployed poetry observes with some imperceptible
    sadness
writing on my cigarette pack some small numbers –
the price of coffee of ice-cream of pistachios of gasoline
and the price of delayed unspoken words

Salerno, 17-9-78

Morning in Salerno, III

A large explicit earthen pitcher
(nevertheless always amorous) painted with
fleshy light blue and red flowers stood
in the middle of the street among the busy people
So that is the answer we had sought in debates
in museums in postponements and silences?

I retain this joy attached to my flesh like a handbook to discover
a speechless affirmation amid the awkwardness of words and deeds
    I held up
this pitcher with my arms I brought it to my lips It was empty
An azure and a red flower fell in my two pockets They
    didn't wilt

Salerno, 17-9-78

Morning in Salerno, IV

In spite of Sunday's idleness selling and buying kept going on
at the wooden sheds Big motionless fishes shone
in wide baskets Dried salt sparkling on their
gray-rose scales
                              One of them
for a moment winked his eye at me He opened it again it looked
at me completely round
I was enjoying the cunning of dead their obvious choice
especially for me – perhaps a secret kinship
perhaps they expected their resurrection from me
                                                    The Customs officer
stood officially by the door I pretended not to see him
The hands of course are rapacious animals – they speak more
     truthfully than lips

Salerno, 17-9-78

Repossession of Rights

The motorcycle in lightning speed passed by It was love
Fluttering of hair Radiance of the sea At the agora
loads of cactus pears sunbathed in insolence
in baskets made of cane – primeval testicles
light strikes like a spark in their blond hairs
                                    The girls laugh
before the doors They slit open the thick rind of
the cactus pears with small knives Their laughter
conceals a secret erotic murder Perhaps for that reason
the slightest snow white cloud shadows one yard of the opposite
blue mountain at the far end of the horizon
                                    What a beautiful day
beautiful more beautiful protecting again
somewhat late a certain right of ours in admiration
a certain right of ours in the eternal youth of the world

Kostiera Amalfitana, 17-9-78

Immediate Reproduction

And suddenly we heard him saying: I want to become a
photographer yes
        a photographer
ah what exquisite color pictures I
have nothing else to add Over here everything
is said by the landscape itself with a big green leaf
with a drop of water with a glittering insect
with a white yacht going away in love with its reflection

This landscape embodies your entire naked body
with a wide wreath of purple peppers hanging from
your neck drawing on your chest and belly
large shadows of erect penises leaving
the disparate speech in its covert immenseness

                                        Pozitano, 17-9-78

New Simplicity

Lots of grapevines stroll down toward the sea –
grapevine-domes of temples grapevine-multilevel villas
grapevine-music schools factories brothels Boats go by
overloaded with grapes
                              What we called inconceivable
while pressing our nails in our palm is the autonomous
that crosses through the pointless – we didn't know anymore
we didn't ask now the measure of value is lost I don't care –
      John said –
was it this? wasn't it? what was it then?
                                          The body
simply with a few syllables: I like it – he says And further on
the light blue island Iskia – I'll place this as a sapphire
on the ring I prepare to put again on the pinky finger
on the left hand of poetry as an engagement ring

Pozitano, 17-9-78

The Poem – Pozitano

Ocher rust-colored white amid abundant green of the foliage
amid the light blue of sky and sea Beautiful analogies
and that joy of friendly participation as though we also
had contributed in the selection and arrangement of colors and
    shapes
maintaining a graceful anonymity
                      Nevertheless
these five domed windows where five girls
pulled the curtains to one side to look at the sea –
one of them holding a grape picking one by one
the purple grapes the other combing her black hair
the third holding a handkerchief – and perhaps waved at the
    white boat
the other two made their lips round as though they
were getting ready to whistle a short erotic song
                      Therefore
I wished that I signed my whole name under these five windows
and quite calligraphically yet resembling a five verse poem

Pozitano, 17-9-78

Immobilizing the Boundless

Nicola – he would yell – drive slower I like to see
this face this body that rock
this half-naked girl with water dripping from her breasts
this street peddler with a basket of golden lemons
and this fully bloomed lyrical tree Take your foot off the gas Stop

Take a picture of me not with this old tourist woman
made up like a harlequin with her colorful swimsuit no no
but with this statue – I'll lean on his shoulder erotically
handsome self-sufficient Hellene and behind my back
the wholesome twinkling sea – my azure mother
boundless and borderless – this azure mother who embraces
    but never confines

Pozitano, 17-9-78

Encounters

Handsome sea-born youths on cobblestone roads
opposite the sparkling sea they sell hazelnuts
pistachios walnuts lemons and large braids of red peppers
to the tourists
        This red more than any other complements
their cleverness and black hair We wrapped the peppers
in two morning newspapers where it was written in large letters
the five brutal murders and the three unexplainable suicides

Sorrento, 17-9-78

Pompey – Red

Ah pain stricken erotic Pompey deep-shadowed Mansion of
    Mysteries
circular group baths for music for sperm and roses
exquisite pornographic sketches on the brothel walls
altars columns dreams drainpipes gardens
this exquisite red of the frescoes – that taught
the ascetic craftsmen of Byzantium and Renaissance
the vital red –
            five o'clock brilliant afternoon of a fiery September
and we here with insatiable eyes glued on the keyhole
    of History
dignified voyeurs in full erection we watch the endless
lovemaking of upstanding naked Hellenes and Romans

Pompey, 17-9-78

Pompey – Death and Love

To call it punishment? To call it repayment? – It was death
The two charred bodies in their glass boxes
petrified ash – we didn't get scared at all Outside in the street
a child collected stones from Pompey in his light blue bucket
the guards – one an old man his eyes sparkling under his
blue cap looking toward the pretty tourist girls the other
young with a pitch black mustache touched the mural with his
pointer exactly on top of the naked woman's belly button
as if showing to us the center of earth (And of course
love more powerful than death)
                         We came out through
the second archway inside the glorious gold-purple sundown
holding tight in our fingers the admission ticket like we held tight
an obscene erotic note although we wanted to announce it to
        the whole world

                                Pompey, 17-9-78

Pompey – Carnal Delight

Pompey-museum Pompey-life galloping lust
Pompey with Pans having large penises beautifully stamped
on September's full moon Pompey
naked lascivious – tattooed by a fiery needle
in arms and breasts of sailors

      By the exit
I found two rusted razors on its sun-scorched soil –
Oh surely the jubilant and willing harlots shaved
their underarms their vulvae with these – the harlots who now are
painted on top of the stony beds looking at us
with a shadowless smile from within their death
adding an unknown lust to the lust we still enjoy

Pompey, 17-9-78

Farewell to Pompey

Hello Pompey goodbye Pompey thank you Pompey
for the poems you gave me thank you
for this silver key that you hung on my bosom
to unlock the borders all over again to enter again
the world of beauty and love Yes the world is always one

Yes and the dead remember   They stand by the windows at night
they gaze at the starlight they breathe timidly they smile
toward the thermometer on the wall On their left hand
they hold a large yellow lemon every so often they smell it
(perhaps in order to defuse the drowsiness from the foliage's
        movement)
and after that they throw it in the street The lemons roll
up to the white court shoes of the juvenile forever virgin Kore
standing under the lamppost Yes the world is always one

Pompey, 17-9-78

Rome at Night

Beautiful night tired eleven o'clock Blackened statues
Truly even statues get blackened under the shadows and
        the lights –
Piazza di Spania Trinita dei Mondï On the marble staircase
young tourists embrace each other sleep smoke A Spaniard
hastily draws a sketch of me – one of my eyes completely shut
one-eyed man (half hidden and half given) – as though
        he knew –
and the other eye gaping in the September night of immense Rome
that in her flesh a myriad thrills of erotic stars swarm like ants

Rome, 17-9-78

The Everlasting Trip

This night doesn't want to end Smells from closed restaurants
from underarms from turned off lights on staircases of cheap hotels
from bloomed trees and cigarette butts thrown in the streets Big
buses parked still maintaining inside them a thickened
yet silenced hum of day momentary touch of bodies In front
    of their windshields
steamed up by the breath of night the wild boys stop for
    a while
re-arrange their hair locks they leave In the telephone booths
some make phone calls from darkness to darkness nothing is
    heard –
    perhaps they are
the new dead refusing to die at such a young age perhaps they claim
    their share
of love and that of the street lights – starlit streets
from the deep cigarette inhaling of lovers in an anxious hunt No no
sleep won't deprive us again a bit more of our lives Goodnight
    strange bed
let the dreams wear the white sheets and let the old hotel manager
    wait
with his head leaning on the thick guest book Ai Fontana
    di Trevi
here we are with the waters and the statues I'll jump dressed up
    into the fountain
to touch this exquisite marble leg And then
wet soaking wet I'll stand shivering by the thrill
    of stars
tossing all my coins in the water so that I'll remain penniless
    not having
even a small contribution for the Shadowy Ferryman so that
    he may leave me in the World Above
to travel endlessly from Athens to Rome and from Rome
    to Athens

Rome, 17-9-78

In Piazza Navona

Looking outside you look deeper inside – he was saying Oh night
Italian night concealed and dressed Piazza Navona
tall lampposts dampened benches water fountains big doors
arched multi-engraved – like those the old card-reader woman
    mentioned
you will pass a big door I see a crown don't throw away
the ring of keys   keep them under your arm

    Oh night
a girl pitch black from the sun with her white lacy headscarf
a boy-girl with blond hair from a Pasolini film
wooden barracks with colorful lights impenitent night people
    two drunks
cheap ice cream cones kisses if by chance and this
    bare-breasted handsome
youth his forehead leaning on the thigh of a statue getting totally
    wet by
the undying water fountain as though all the nights of Rome cry
    on him

Rome, 17-9-78

Vatican Museum

da Vinci Raphael Michelangelo – how they incised
the greatest skies in the human face in the human body
toenails and fingernails leaves and stars nipples dreams lips –
to red and the light blue the tangible and the inconceivable
     Perhaps from
touching of these two fingers the world was reborn The space
between these two fingers still measures accurately
the earth's pull and duration

                      I can't bear it – he said –
so much beauty and so much sinful sanctity I'll go out to the white
balcony and smoke fifteen cigarettes in a row marveling at the
view of Rome from high above looking at the big buses below
unloading bunches of tourists at the Museum's front
breaking with my two fingers in my pants pocket
a bunch of stolen toothpicks as if I would break all
the wooden crosses where all human desires were crucified

                        Rome, 18-9-78

The Street That Was Not Named "Pasolini Street"

Wide morning in Rome that widens the consonant *l*
amid the vendors yelling the tires of buses
and the statues' silence
                        Ocher shadowed in the eastern facades
of stores and buildings Doors and doors uphold
the semicircles of shadows *at one time* Strange –
      he said –
in an ancient city with red and dark yellow colors
to find children held by their mother's hand
in these very busy streets under the countless windows
      here
where Pasolini saunter in the night – Termini Station here
in an outdoor wooden kiosk a contemporary fat Nero was
selling colorful scarves to tourists I bought a red one
and tied it around my neck and in the midst of the street I whistled
C o m e o n a l l t h e e a r t h's s i n f u l C o m e o n a l l t h e
      e a r t h's s i n f u l

Rome, 18-9-78

Regained Unity

Fountains obelisks balconies churches – Romani Forum
Temple of Aphrodite Colosseum Basilica of Maccentio –
    how they get forgotten
wars animosities crow-winged little generals
with black boots and jaws of sharks
                            Nevertheless
the works of art are always here present amputated intact
silent and polyglot And they all have something to
confide to us so that we speak of it so that it will be heard again
under the innocence of the united sky among
the unblemished gleam of the Mediterranean sun something
that annuls differences and death and leaves only
on doors on balconies in the train stations
the first love and the deep companionship of all peoples
who as they go to their work hastily chewing on a sandwich
you would think that they chew on a slice of light and the streets
    shine by an invincible health

Rome, 18-9-78

Horseshoe of Siena

Quiet Siena as though of a bygone Monday Kids with roller
scooters rattle the cobbled street This place with so many
windows green gray brown we have known for
a long time elsewhere gazing down the hill
to the precipice with bloomed trees
                                        Yesterday Sunday
here in the piazza next to the fountain with the statues of beautiful
        virgins
here where the gray pigeons bathe non-stop
the gladiator's dance unfolds its pleats
with their black and red horses
                                And also by the kiosk
unfurl multicolored silk flags
with animal images – beetle deer frog turtle wolf –
        they flap
as though the whole animal kingdom were winged I found
        a horseshoe
under one table of the outdoor patisserie –
the one I hanged on the door of this book – good luck
        for me
good luck for those who read think act fall in
        love and sing

                                        Siena, 18-9-78

Opening of Vault

Bustling Rome solemn Siena pale Florence
circular Bologna proletariat Milan – day trip
with wide open eyes out of breath because of the beauty
                                                    I retain
Arno's bridge with lights tambourines flame-eaters
the knee of a young moon dipped in the river a plaza
in the shape and smoothness of a conch – there
handsome dark skin waiters come and go as though dancing
among a thousand tables with nickel trays
overloaded with coffees ice creams sweets on spoons
                                                    I retain
a balcony decorated by washed up undergarments of women
and sports undershirts Monday afternoon
                                        I retain
the shadow of a bronze statue in the ancient flagstone street –
the hand of this shadow holds a glass vessel filled
by a floodlit green fluid lighting deep under the arch
two youths kissing
                        And all these airy I load up
on the shoulders of words to saunter out in the world with
        the new moon
and ah that way youths will kiss each other louder and the
        blind men
        will regain their sight at the bridges
and the ones who died early will come back to the train stations
        to look at
the big posters of Che and will smile

                                        Milan, 18-9-78

Furnished Rooms

1978-1979

Memory of Velies

At dusk women went down to the spring –
barrels pitchers next to the river The boys
came for the horses the mules the eels
Women yelled horses neighed However a deep
silence steamed up the air like you needed
to separate things in two and choose
between only a horse and a pitcher

Athens, 5-7-78

Migration

One by one they left no one knows where They never came back
The lone village remained under its three mulberry trees
to contemplate up to the river – not further The birds
became totally tame at dusk they saunter in the plaza
as if they're the only inhabitants there having
learned by now that statues have to be naked and sad
and the long and narrow outdoor table of the old meat market
is meant for the long nights of the dead and the émigrés

Athens, 6-12-78

Couplet

Two sailors sweating profusely in the hold Outside the door
their four boots stretch out completely open to the world

Athens, 11-12-78

Dejection

The blind man saw deeper I sat on the chair
They brought me some flowers I pulled off their petals A man
was locked up in the dark blacksmith's shop
The beating of the sea on the rocks was heard from afar
And the bitch old woman threw our bread to the crows

Athens, 11-12-78

Peeling

Call the elevator Take out the garbage bags
The door is glass This is more interesting to me
The trains go by silently The lights of the lampposts are turned on
Blind men pound the sidewalk with their white canes One
by one all the glasses crack at night For this reason
I want to play a short song on the back of the casserole
so that it doesn't show that we get smaller as we age

Athens, 11-12-78

Entrance – Exit

To open the door to open the tree
to get deep into it and grow leaves
This impenitent thing is yours
The night erases your shadow Now they play
the piano in the opposite house Yes and also for you

Athens, 11-12-78

After the Dream

It was smoke – it vanished – gray smoke light blue
The naked body remained all alone on the red blanket

Athens, 12-12-78

Noticeable Difference

He broke the stone with a stone
After that neither mass nor sound
This is not empty it's being emptied

Athens, 12-12-78

Aimless Gesture

The same house the bed the mirror
scent of smoke and dissolved soap
the overcoats hang in the hallway like visitors
Extend one of your arms outside the window –
perhaps that will lend some meaning to the disparate city

Athens, 13-12-78

Morning for Poetry

The sun enters through the window
The woman is still asleep
Names of islands shiver on the walls —
small hills one horse one tree
a chair tied by a string

Athens, 15-12-78

Secret

When the girl grows up she will wear a black dress and
    red shoes
from the opposite window they throw orange peels in the street
the lottery vendor mimics the voice of the blind quite successfully
and I am the only one who knows it and I don't betray him
So just like that a bit later the miracle spreads among the words

Athens, 15-12-78

Classification

In the middle of the night there was a second beggar Barefoot
foreigners with obscene masks went down the stairs
carrying carpets and blankets underarm
moon with its two turtles sauntered in the garden
I closed the crack with planks I knew where to step

Athens, 15-12-78

Third Representation

You look at the quiet street through the window
I peel an apple I don't eat it
I show it to the handsome guard who is asleep
No the apple had no worm I had taken it out

Kalamos, 16-12-78

Old Age

Old women come they fill the house they hold
umbrellas fans small or big black hats
purses with hand-mirrors handkerchiefs lipsticks compacts
they unravel big balls of string they shut the doors
most of them are deaf or dumb One of them shouts
and sock-needles pills and pins fall on the floor
he pounds fragrant cloves and chickpeas in the mortar
he deafens the old women he throws their keys in the well
and I am young Sunday morning with the strong winds

Kalamos, 16-12-78

Copying

The babies in strollers the women on trees
at night the bear on the bench of the money changer
we had some differences not any understanding   keep quiet
the coal vendor the contractor the barber the mailman
the elevator is a deep ascending well
the unemployed mirror copies with severe impartiality
convulsive movements of wound-up wooden hands

Kalamos, 17-12-78

Process

You talked about the wheel the curtain the wheat
the dead tiger had blocked the door
what you didn't say turned into ants
they sauntered under the earth they carried seeds
they had incised your crown on a corn seed

Athens, 18-12-78

Way of Life

I have the light – he says He doesn't seek other allies
Monday to Saturday is a slow process The trains leave
He passes by in front of the cafe he looks inside
legs and legs under the tables glasses
on the tables and cups and a lemon
big bronze buttons from ripped coats
roll down the bare slope he hears them
each of them stops in a different spot They don't reach the sea

Athens, 18-12-78

Associations

The proper space the light and hour are necessary
a piece of furniture here the candleholder the mirror
you take the pins you pin them to the apple
the three lampposts are visible through the window
the sidewalk is white the old woman black
wraps the slaughtered chicken in two newspapers

Athens, 18-12-78

Nightly Chronicle

Large dark rooms darkness multiplied
in the cheerless mirrors Endless hallways
above the world and rows of closed doors
and at the far end a statue in a raincoat Suddenly
sound of excavators red lights flashing down the street
the traffic controller was running the wood worker threw his
    mask away
I had nothing to be afraid of – not even myself
I put on my child's shoes and I limp along the wall

Athens, 19-12-78

Breakout

Where they walk barefoot and flat soled
where they cook red fishes on charcoal
where they crucify big octopi in the sunlight –
trees in boats wind in chest hair
naked forgetfulness and sea myth of birth
month of July Monday gleaming on the seagull eggs

Athens, 2-12-78

Disinterment

Threads from clothes of the dead on the thorns of prickly pear trees
Shutters pounding in the pelagos Windowpanes break
Whistles of ships are heard Saturday nights in the taverns
A fist that hits the table The glasses tip off
Account books calculations the sleepy boys the sad words
Women with brooms come and sweep the glass fragments
 they leave
Immense uninhabited harbor lemons floating the closed up
 customs office
and the water's bubbling on a stove in the vacant sailor's dormitory
How with an eyelid's flutter with nothing the world is
reconstructed

Athens, 20-12-78

Vague Preparation

Loud echoes from large empty rooms They must nail something
perhaps the ancestors' pictures Two horses gallop in the field
The garden has corn and heliotropes Pregnant women
go out to the doorstep look at the mountain they come back in
Children carry dusty laurels I
have to tie the rope from one tree to the other
so that the fool may walk with my yellow umbrella

Athens, 20-12-78

Suburban

They wore wide green red face masks
long mustaches hung savage locks of hair hid their eyes
his thick shoes showed under the calico skirts
they didn't have a monkey – she had died two months ago
one afternoon Petros took the train the girls read
the dates and window displays got mix up however always
a tiny fire flickered in a corner of the children's bedrooms
that had been sealed by the old men who smoked on the balcony

Kalamos, 23-12-78

Viewing

The sea forgotten in the cloudy weather Olive trees to the top
    of the hill
The strange invisible bird went *Clou clou* *Clou clou* in the field
Small carton boxes in the locked house
A man had a dream he had taken his glasses off
Soldiers on relief sauntered in the agora Two by two they took
the elevator to the fifth floor they vanished in the hallways
I pretended that I believed the man was blind I undressed
took off my shoes my socks I stand by the window
looking at the three men in black dresses gluing posters
and the short traffic controller with his wet solemn shadow

Kalamos, 23-12-78

Consequences

He got wet in the rain he wiped himself with my towel
he wore my blazer And then this awkwardness:
that I exist twice though being absent Steam and smell of fat
and vinegar reached us from the kitchen
Then I pinned the picture of the naked woman on the wall
I opened the fridge and put in the big fishes

Kalamos, 23-12-78

Kalamos

The rain never stopped all night it brought down soil
and turned the sea into mud Helen held the grater
looking outside the window Vangelis pretended he was deaf
The others seemed busy trying to start
a bus stopped by the river in
an unknown setting by the frontier The driver
wore a brown leather jacket with a pair of pliers in his belt
And it was a Sunday morning with droplets falling
and time escaped grayish from the overflowing gutters

Kalamos, 24-12-78

Pointing Out

We got sick and tired of the crippled the dead the deaf
hanging on this colorless spot on the walls
undefined pictures and they fall whether they break or not
there is no sound And since when do the three white-attired sailors
appear in the courtyard of the neoclassic house? One
of them holds a big mirror in his arms like an icon
and the two others look in and comb their hair with red combs

Kalamos, 24-12-78

Double Disguise

The insufficient the endless the reoccurring
the one starting all over half-hearted what ends without end –
once he himself had named it inexhaustible now
he keeps a lot of nails in his teeth (pointy side outward)
in a wild and funny grimace I don't look at him I extend
my two arms spread on the long steel table

Kalamos, 24-12-78

Over Strain

Bit by bit the space takes shape The words
don't resist the inexpressible You sit
on the cement floor you break walnuts
you look at the clouds on the balcony door However
don't forget that you are a Hellene – he said –
Ion naked by the front step holds a pair of scissors
clips his toenails waiting for
his two provincial friends from Sparta

Kalamos, 25-12-78

Without Explanations

Suddenly the sun came up Euboea[1] appeared across the water
A big dog walked in the field
The boys from Corinth came they unfolded
a huge red fluffy blanket they covered
the headless statue Alex went to the kitchen
to brew coffees He lit a cigarette I had
learned to knit undershirts I pretended not to stare

Kalamos, 25-12-78

Aftermath of the Feast

The youth choir had left Only the music stands remained behind
The one with the Band-Aid on his forehead stood next to the door
then he went close to the piano unbuttoned himself   hit a
        few keys
of the deep notes with his penis Inside the other room
the old woman fried potatoes talking to the parrot

Kalamos, 25-12-78

---

[1]*Area north of Athens and south of Lamia*

Sightseeing Bus

The barber shops are closed the umbrella shops shirt shops
Four-day holiday Short sightseeing excursions to the suburbs
The coach broke down One window looks to the sea
There are still some sparrows A certain reflection on the hill
Unexplained diamonds under the trees My God what words –
aimless words – they don't serve they confuse – what can you do?
Better that way Tuesday afternoon A train ticket
Where to? – I ask Where to? Manolis comes down
with a cloth suitcase he doesn't wear a scarf He approaches me and
in a conspiratorial way shows me his wristwatch

Kalamos, 26-12-78

Leftovers

After they moved the slaughtered from the hospital
coins for the phone a handkerchief a blond hairpiece
were left on the marble floor

Kalamos, 26-12-78

Converging Depictions

George gets off the trolley-bus he wears a tie Euridice
bought a dozen glasses – each of different color
Alex moved to a different neighborhood Sunday morning
Big room even nails on the wall are whitewashed
View to the street the small cleaner's shop is visible At the far end
the dark workshop of the old artist In the window display
naked gypsum statues – imitations of classical models –
perhaps he had molds And suddenly we had the impression
that he used Telis as his model who had disappeared
from our company for two months For this reason at night
on Saturdays or sometimes on Mondays we stopped at the
    Old Bridge
gaping at the bare-breasted Italian pyro-juggler for hours on end
and we threw pieces of afternoon newspapers in the river

Kalamos, 26-12-78

Resemblance

He got tired from trip to trip Keys suitcases
hotels shirts statues one umbrella
the time that shops close down and the lights go out
and Helen's bracelets are in the pawn shop
and juvenile heroes with loose belts are forgotten
ruffians verse-masters prostitutes and police informers He
    got tired
he shuts his eyes tight looking at the moon in the open field
calm shadow walking covering the rabbit the violin the river

Kalamos, 26-12-78

In the Rain

Chattering strange stories – he said Soldiers saunter
in the Thession station It drizzles George
volunteered in the navy Sorrowful words
forgotten in old gardens The trees turn yellow
Vlassis' bicycle rusted What we called glory
was the chord's breaking that was heard in the basement
from Anna's left-behind guitar After that
the empty cage of the parrot was left on the uncovered
table next to Argyri's worn-out wool gloves
and under the bed Ajax with his butchered ram

Athens, 27-12-78

Participation

In the dark stumbling on knees and sometimes
on a certain soft hat The slightest gleam
from the white vertical cloth and the small flashlight
of the usherette The two robbers wane away
one of them holds my suitcase the other my overcoat
(despite the distance I discern them clearly)
and suddenly they throw at my lap somehow hastily
first my overcoat then my suitcase I open it
and there I see pictures of my childhood
pinned one by one with rusted thumbtacks

Athens, 28-12-78

Inventions

They sauntered from one room to the other with open umbrellas
running faucets were heard then they stopped He
called out number eighteen and covered my unwritten poem

Athens, 30-12-78

House with One Bed

Where are you going? – he asked – this house is yours
A second person of course doesn't fit in it The whole world
    fits in it
One broom one large mirror There are
no chairs anymore Only the bed
no one knows where – everywhere – naked energetic flat down
it scratches your knees whether you try to go inside
or to go out to the street with the butcher shops

Athens, 31-12-78

On the Same Subject

They left They sat on rocks They looked at the sea
Young deserters shaved hair curly mustaches
With a certain sadness they get one of their feet wet in the water
like she did in old forgotten and forbidden folksongs
when down in the yard the mother yelled the chicken laid an egg
and the white of the egg is confused like I am in the middle of
the hot day

Athens, 31-12-78

Suspicion

How did you enclose all these in one stone? –
bare breasts foreheads eyes mouths nostrils
sadness of presence sadness of the great absence
and in the other room the spiteful woman irons
double bed sheets underwear shirts handkerchiefs
and a gray blazer with drops of wax on the right lapel

Athens, 31-12-78

Unconvinced

Winter sunshine on the hills A small house –
we see it from the balcony door The baskets
of the young vendors in a row at the train station
here is the jasmine vendor with the old black dress
soldiers with broad palms smoking by the bridge
and him gazing at the mountain with an unexplained persistence
biting one end of the string without knowing
where its other end is dipped or tied

Athens, 1-1-79

Conclusion

He read the biography of the blind lotto vendor
He saw the bicycle riders passing by under the trees
The heroes stayed behind wrapped in old newspapers
In the evening they turn the lights on in the jeweler
    display windows
The student's accordion is heard in the suburb with the acacias
Then Christmas arrives The carpentry shops shut down
The coal vendor with wet hair looks at the women
The old woman scares the mice by hitting boiling coffeepots
Then the fool got his opportunity he wore his mother's dress
climbed up to the roof and sang just for me

Athens, 1-1-79

Insinuations

Suitcases thrown on the floor empty
I remember the coal miners Saturday night
tall beer glasses smoke cursing
Two women with uncombed hair yelled by the door
The child died The entrance light bulb burned out
Trains go by loaded with river fishes
Your hair is full of charcoal dust George
entered the other room He wore a shirt
completely yellow as though dipped in the moon
and everything was sad even more so the bed

Athens, 2-1-79

Bodies

Naked bodies breathing deeply under their clothes
The hand touches the back of the chair
stays motionless on the knee or turns on the light
takes the big glass in pausing motion dreams of –
the young naked bodies in any position in their
random tiny movements making love while
in the baths all the faucets are running
and buzz from the steam with flashes with mirrors
concealing expressively the great exclamation

Athens, 2-1-79

Interchanges

Don't leave the bicycle there it may be stolen
Nights come that I am absent to find myself at the wide
colonnade at dawn holding in my right hand
the big basket with my wise tamed snakes
trained for beautiful exhibitions at the Agora the Stadium
as they coil around my waist my arms my neck
and sometimes around my eyes to conceal my fear

Athens, 2-1-79

Performance

We didn't like at all the way they made the sets
on Stadiou Street – cheap planks cartons and papers
roughly painted as though they were columns at Apollo's temple
and Ion with a broom made of nylon laurel branches
sweeping the floor with assumed piety Nevertheless
the legs of the young actor were exquisite And as
the July sun went down suddenly two purple
seals shone on his ankles and the bloodied
night fell on the buses of Attica returning
from Eleusis with the boxing winners

Athens, 4-1-79

Sequence

The word *ether* didn't mean anything to us
From all our readings we selected just
two words *seaman* and *customs officer*
later on *windowpanes* and *afternoon* as
the train loaded with wires went away
and the dog went by the smoke along the wall
while a string tied on his tail chimed
a child's bell over the apple trees
over the graves of young heroes and the old woman
ripped with her teeth a white cloth in the night

Athens, 5-1-79

Illegal Act

Lucas Lucas – they yelled The railings shone at dusk
They threw pop bottles in the light-well The hallway
was unfinished with rotten planks Saturday night I remember
his belt and his comb on the table When he entered
the wholesale drugstore the bat flew from the statue's shoulder
and hid behind the green glass bowl Ah Lucas – he said –
what days we spent And suddenly the lights came on in the park
and the policemen pushed the small vendors into the
        holding tanks
We just had enough time to hide our hand-writings in the wall

Athens, 5-1-79

Shoeshine

Various people go to the shoeshine of the neighborhood –
local kids drivers soldiers traffic controllers The arms
of the shoeshine men are painted up to the elbows Even this
        disabled
man just twenty-four years old always insists that
I paint his crutches red But I am
an islander and I have only light blue colors
and the only thing I know how to paint is my face

Athens, 6-1-79

Connections

Strange relations develop between things –
the empty birdcage the curtain two eggs in the fruit bowl
retired train workers spend their day at the cafe
smoke and whistles of trains cover the newspapers
I'm called to settle intricate foreign matters
a skillful amateur only that first I have to cover
the two opposite mirrors and then the tin washbowl

Athens, 6-1-79

Sicilian Recollection

These people who saunter around the fish-market were not
there to buy fish The sea was visible behind
the wooden sheds Bare-chested seamen
played backgammon in moored boats They
demolished the old army barracks on the hill Large rocks
rolled down the shore When night came
soldiers sauntered in the harbor with young whores
under the lights of the tavern "Red Prawn"
There exactly the circle got complete leaving out
the piece of marble with a silver conch

Athens, 6-1-79

Abandonment

Dead night-flies on the floor You go
to the two bedrooms same thing The others
went up the hill to the lime kilns they started up fires
we waited for them three nights The moon leaned
then the city was deserted the lights went out
the empty stores remained and the discolored clowns

Athens, 7-1-79

Unanswered

Messengers came they brought news
baskets flowerpots bouquets boxes
a large silver candleholder The wind
pushed down the yard trees The cool
servant accepted the gifts he bowed
The receiving hall was closed Nothing
was heard from inside the house – footsteps coughing talk
nor clink of knives and glasses However
I saw through the glass the host lying down
on a marble table and a boy was
combing his long black beard slowly

Athens, 7-1-79

Wonders

Time flies – Philimon said – we grow old we forget The strange
    thing
is that we remember other things forgotten – places people
dead poets' verses or wise sayings of ancient philosophers
and that fat servant with the huge ceiling duster
wiping the big hairy spiders off the ceiling
then vanishing in the hallway wearing the mask of a swordsman

Athens, 7-1-79

Nightly Saunter

He dressed the big bear with his clothes Now
naked hanging under her belly he saunters
night after night among the deaf houses
up to the ancient Vegetable Market where
handsome sweaty charioteers sleep next to the one-eyed moon

Athens, 8-1-79

Confusion

Diaphanous – he said – diaphanous and perhaps he meant
    himself·
Indeed the mountains were diaphanous Down in the basements
the fugitives lit oil lamps in barrels
Further inside the sound of a sewing machine was heard Out in
    the street
with the well-lit patisseries seventeen-year-old boys
glued yellow posters on the walls with faces of outlaws

Athens, 8-1-79

A Different Night

This one with the guitar that one with the accordion Late hour
Music by itself And how to undress? It was cold
Wooden staircase some small lamps the white basin
Inside the closed restaurant the violin on the chair
On the second floor footsteps of barefoot dancers
mixing up bottles red ribbons black hats
Then we saw how glory covers her eyes with one of her feathers

Athens, 8-1-79

By the Sea

He was interested – he said – in the psychology of fish when
their shadows are displayed on the deck of a sunken ship
and on the pier young girls with sailors
start big fires and then sit on anchors and cry

Athens, 8-1-79

Reversal of Roles

I met the jester in the park He pretended he didn't see me
Then I put on my shoes in reverse I dipped in the river
I held myself from the one finger of my statue
and walked out on the opposite bank with a crown of daisies
The jester dried me with his towel he took my crown

Athens, 8-1-79

Passage

He stopped short in front of window displays of small shops He
    didn't
want to buy anything only this way the sea was
heard better behind his back Then he saw
the three cursing longshoremen with black
caps come carrying on a glass stretcher
a huge thick-haired fish with completely yellow eyes

Athens, 9-1-79

Gesture

Suddenly two sparrows entered the room
All went silent Alkistis took one of her earrings off
and placed it quietly on the table

Athens, 9-1-79

Untransmitted

One cigarette in the tight lips of the lighthouse keeper
One abandoned poem without its reader
I'll read it out loud in the empty room
with the audience of only the fish in the fishbowl
Then I'll throw the glass into the sea and I'll really cough

Athens, 9-1-79

Theater

There was a lake a woman a pitcher The scene of
duelists unfolded farther on in the forest opening The two
others wore long beards and high boots
The role of the youngest was to throw a glass sphere in the
    staircase
And the blind man put his chewed gum in the mouth of the
    coachman

Athens, 10-1-79

At the Goula Castle

Displacements inconsistencies re-attachments Top of the castle
prickly pears ruins and crows Lizards run through
they push rusted keys with their bellies The guard
became part of the huge rock Sea birds roost
in his hair on his shoulders Coarse salt
drips from his sleeves returns to the sea dissolves
Ah the glass law the un-shattered law of all the shattered

Athens, 11-1-79

Old Cafe

That old cafe with the marble tables –
what strange encounters quarrels silences newspapers
retired athletes the backgammon the suburb ice vendor
two old unsuccessful actors with deep wrinkles
the gypsum statue the dark-skinned knife sharpener the flower
    vendors
and suddenly beginning July toward dusk Phedros came in
pulling a peacock on a golden chain he stood
before the glass door and drank a pop from the bottle
while drops dripped from his lips onto his yellow shirt

Athens, 11-1-79

Dark Contact

He lurks behind things words – an owl on the cover
of the magazine the title of a book the photographer's shadow
darkening the picture at the feet of the diver or that
nasal sound under the bed – it isn't the sleeping dog –
Ah everything – he says – without giving and without
                retribution and always
this awkwardness when meeting by the narrow stone staircase –
the lighthouse keeper climbing up and me still descending

Athens, 11-1-79

Certainty?

Every word is a miracle – Alexander said I lift
a small stone I find two ants – one of them limps
I stand by the window I throw the almonds in the street I see
the handsome runner vanishing under the trees The doorbell
is heard Before I open Urania enters
holding a platter covered with my lost keys

Athens, 11-1-79

Reoccurring Matter

To the right as we climb the circular wooden stairs
there was a domed alcove where a statue sat at some time
perhaps it still does the space is not well lit during the day
at night the ceiling lamp is burned out – they never replaced it
however even in our most covert benign passing that statue
(perhaps totally naked) will make a slight movement
it will say something for the used-up matches in the closed
        bedrooms
or for that naked leg stepping on a small piece of calendar paper
where my telephone number is written then
when we descend going out the double glass door
a bicycle goes by loaded with red balloons

Athens, 11-1-79

Since Then

The leaning candle drips on the table made of planks
Old hat boxes get dusty on top of the closet
There is a moon outside the windows It is cold You
have a high fever I remember the stairs at Gytheon
The high-school boys descended them Calliope had left
Zelinda played the piano in the afternoon One discolored car
parked in front of the small shop Cinnamon candies
in glass jars I didn't like Agis' poem I write
something else more mine – perhaps with a bit of sea at the far end
something with five yellow lemons on a straw chair

Athens, 12-1-79

Illegible Omens

He had tied around his neck the sleeves of his pullover
It was chilly Put it on Those were pardoned The cart's wheels
got stuck in the mud The travelers held tamed birds
Their feathers were rain-drenched When we arrived at the
      inn
we saw the horses gathered in the yard The innkeeper yelled
The blacksmith had a horseshoe in his teeth And no one
imagined
that this child with the wet hair was already the angel
    of glory

Athens, 12-1-79

Like Exodus

The first wall was yellow the second light blue
the third red The other six we never found out
what color they were When we went out of
the gate the sea appeared sparkling down the shore A huge fish
was hanging from the mast of a ship Laypeople
without impediment of thought tobacco vendors fishermen
came out of the mystery timidly they didn't wear hats
they put their hands in their pockets walked up and down
among the pitchers wire ropes bird cages barrels –
but perhaps it was we who thought of them

Athens, 12-1-79

Why?

He placed his hand in the water inside the white bowl
he took out an ancient silver coin
he wiped his fingers slowly with his handkerchief
he lights a cigarette He smokes That star
on top of the hill we saw it almost simultaneously
I cannot claim precedence Why then
does he cover the glass with his right palm?

Kalamos, 13-1-79

Approaching Noon

Large whitewashed room stuffy from the breaths
of the sleeping people Opposite on the wall the mirror
reflected only on their naked soles Outside
in the garden the lonely bird chirped *no no no*
and in the kitchen silent women were already boiling vegetables

Kalamos, 14-1-79

Guilt

They allowed us – he said – enough freedom in small doses
enough so that we forget the dead the burnt up houses trees
and truly we completely forgot them The chickens went wild
they laid their eggs amid the nettles And the statues
slowly turn their backs and stare at the evening
pretending that they don't know anything of our guilt

Athens, 15-1-79

Different Meaning

Late at night when they put the kids to bed
he went down the inside staircase hastily barefoot
and brought the bird cages to the three candle-makers Upstairs
on the second floor the beautiful woman sorrowfully
plucked feathers from the shoulders of the stuffed stork
and put together a smaller bird without feet or eyes

Athens, 15-12-79

Static

One limps so that he doesn't show pride at all
you climb supported by an invisible arm
a completely naked woman hiding her femininity with a newspaper
and the sponge dipped in vinegar on the marble table next to my
    papers

Athens, 15-1-79

Morning

Opposite the window a huge winch lifts
a big wooden crate with clothes of the slaughtered
Four of them on their backs slept on the grass The fifth one
sleeps also naked with his face to the ground

Athens, 16-1-79

Night Music

A hand that so often throws wheat in the fire
a one-eyed fish crossing the room
the secret animals of the night behind the houses
and he's sitting on the bed with a pair of pliers
Peter entered the bathroom to wash his hands
I look as though uninvolved I hold the folded umbrella

Athens, 17-1-79

Touch of Loneliness

Just this Nothing else Time dismembered
Windmills gape on ancient exile hills
The sponge divers didn't return An undershirt unfurls on the
    clothesline
I light my lamp and work alone
in the night on the same nude statue without a model

Athens, 17-1-79

Absences

Fish bones on the outdoor plank table
Urchins move on the flagstones A ladder on the tree
Three young men emigrated On the ancient dock
old fishermen repair the huge net
ripped by nails of the last Siren
Shadows come down the mountains Doors close
I just in time manage to hide behind the bull

Athens, 18-1-79

Concentration

The old Paissios sits here motionless
He listens to the roots under the soil He sees
the bird's shadow the shadow of the cloud on the hill
Ah fingers dipped in the big river
old coins hidden under the rocks
the ones cashing in the deaths of tomorrow

Athens, 18-1-79

Perhaps Poetry

How two chairs float on this void –
on one of them a hammer on the other a rose
The beautiful naked woman comes she wears only
long black nylons I ask for an explanation She
stares the other way she smiles she feeds her dog
with miniscule square pieces of chocolate The silver wrapper
hangs like a mirror in the faint breeze reflecting
my youngish though deformed face

Athens, 19-1-79

The Departed

They put their hands in their pockets They wane away –
as if indifferent – and perhaps scared They never turned back Each
wore two or three curtains In the afternoon you could
listen to Nina's flute above the carpenter shop Water
from the broken pipes constantly flows on the sidewalk
coloring the prostitute's shoes and my handkerchief red

Athens, 19-1-79

Persistent Idea

To name one by one each member with their exact name
with touch with taste with speech – every line and color
every niche protuberance corner contour and the sum total
incalculable when the others on the big table
eat with voracity napkins fall on the floor The plates
are so apathetically round that the Thirteenth one
slips under the table crawls barks
biting the ankles of the fellow diners

Athens, 20-1-79

Unexplored

Unexplored – he said I went through underground stoas
I met icy waters and deformed statues I saw
the large storage jars empty along the length of time It became
      night
A lot of stars fell on rocky crevasses Now I return
The street is empty Pale dawn By my front door I find
the covered basket with the snake and the pearl

Athens, 21-1-79

They Left
1979-1980

Three

They open the windows Winter sunshine
The three women with mirrors They put makeup on
They have a lot of jewelry in small boxes
They have gold crosses and cats They go
from one room to the other always careful
not to look lonely And suddenly
the trumpet is heard from the army camp on the hill –
one of them puts on her heavy coat the other breaks her comb
the third one steps in the shower and turns the water on

Kalamos, 1-12-79

Misunderstandings

They didn't return they didn't leave on time The chair
of the crippled woman and her knitting left on the top step
The fruit vendors cried out in the street The dishwasher
clamored in the kitchen The tired son of the supervisor
went up the stairs dragging behind him a big
dead shark tied with a rope
he laid it down in the middle of the room he got totally undressed
stood before the mirror and observed in detail
in almost sexual desire the large red mark
that was drawn on his belly at that exact moment

Kalamos, 2-12-79

Bitter Time

Old men and old men with the big waning full-moon
with the tall lampposts next to the sea It wouldn't
have been hard for them to leave if one asked them
if one helped them put on their heavy coat if
a child stood next to them for a while to look
at the ship with its serene lights waning away But
the young men frequent other places noisy places
under dimmed red lights they don't know
the charisma of their own youth when the beautiful woman
falls off the seventh floor to the garden dressed in only
her white nightgown embroidered with purple pansies

Kalamos, 2-12-79

Delusions

Go – he said So that the phone won't ring anymore
so I can be alone with my body to pick up
the socks the shirts from the floor to wash
the coffee cups the glasses Late at night
I'll dress the statue with my clothes I'll put on his head
my cap with the gold bells – they won't ring anymore
amid its definite motionlessness And then
totally naked I'll start a fire I'll throw in all my papers
thus burning the great absence while the red chair
and the boots of the slaughtered man will reflect in the mirror

Kalamos, 2-12-79

Man with the Black Hat

They gather the dead The place emptied The houses
stayed shut all around And who could live there?
Would the spread blankets be in the backyard?
And that man forgotten in the mirror
wore a black hat covering his eyes Later on
we met him on top of the high mountain gathering
among the snowed up shrubs horseshoes whistles
and empty cartridges The following evening he disappeared
Perhaps he walked into the storm or returned
and with his black hat crawled back into the mirror

Athens, 4-12-79

As He Grows Old

As this man grows old he turns more alien to the old men
alien to the children He doesn't like to wear slippers
he prefers to be barefoot inside the house What
we once called fulfillment was the emptying Down in
the cellars empty barrels empty storage jars And the piano without keys
        However in the evenings
with the calm moon spread on his table he becomes the same
as before – a stopped sound from the old ringing of the doorbell
stopped time inexistent time and the big white bath towel
still dripping has retained the upright shape
of his curly neck of the youthful knees and strong shoulders

Athens, 6-12-79

Distance

Perhaps they travel perhaps they have died Their shoes
warp under the bed or at sometime during the night
you hear them walking alone in a contour space
stumbling on dried up orange seeds or on
dismembered dolls of wild boys who now
serve in the army Under their boots nettles and
mud remain glued At night with a faint moon at the guard post
they whistle in a low voice the discordant songs of those who left
The kicked dogs gather there five meters further
and with bowed heads gaze at them urinating in haste

Athens, 6-12-79

Afternoon Relationship

In the afternoons pregnant women saunter in the gardens
They are very sad due to their thick unknown Every so often
stop a while before a frog or a flower
searching for a distant indeterminable relation to something
dead or unborn and yet existing – something calming
the secret unachievable like when you engrave your name on the tree
with your jackknife and the tree's white fluid drips
with the generally consoling white The other women
delay in the bedrooms with a lot of clothes piled
on the beds or the couch while from the feathery duster
a green fluff falls slowly on the bronze ashtray

Athens, 7-12-79

Secret Looting

Everything had quieted down in the twilight only down the road
the infrequent footsteps of passers-by were heard with the fish's
walk in the fishbowl and the few raindrops left on the trees Buy
     – he said –
a loaf of bread and three candles perhaps we may need them at night
at the time that we think of the lighthouse keeper at a distance always
     alone
with woolen underwear without mermaids in the darkness of the sea
and drown people start strange friendships with small-size dolphins
creating with them a soft music for Sunday mornings when
     the boys
still sleep on their woolen blankets not knowing that glory
is an old woman made up thousands of times over with a golden
     hair piece
an old toothless woman who drinks their blood and sperm but
     never gives birth

Kalamos, 8-12-79

The Borderless

These sudden summer days in the middle of winter –
great unfettered limpidity it turns the grass of the fields green
the naked fig trees become white the olive trees shine freshly washed
a second ship went by the dog looks at something that belongs to him
a hiding bird chirps the hunters have distanced themselves.
the three women take their pans to the public oven The ones who went
left no absence behind them only a tall glass
with some clear water And the mountains at the far end
are cut by a light blue tissue paper Behind them the other mountains
and more can be seen up to the borderless place where Michael
sits at the sunny front step peeling potatoes with his jackknife

Kalamos, 8-12-79

The Unshared

When the stores close on Saturday evenings or even Monday
and the lights dim in the streets and the gardens the still-lit
display windows of stores start their secret life
related to scenes of the moon or to ancient fires on the hills –
white bath accessories dolls with beautiful gowns jewelry shops
music stores with albums with big pianos cellos
with a huge *sol* key on the glass door Further down
the slipper shop and the bicycle shop The wheels shine At night
there is something that yearns to be shared yet it stays unshared
although condensed and thin and at the same time constantly
        enlarging
it occupies the space pushes you to the wall and you don't have
        anything
else but to pierce it with your old nails Then a deep music
is heard that only you can hear up to the primeval mourning

Kalamos, 8-12-79

Morning Dejection

Beautiful morning And him still dejected Where to go?
what to do with the glittering cables amid this sky-blue? He
puts his coat on his back   buttons it on his chest without
        wearing it
as if he had no arms   as though he doesn't want to take or give anything
with empty sleeves loose hanging they display (to whom I wonder)
an indifference neither proud nor sorrowful while in his pockets
he keeps buttons cigarettes marbles nail-clippers and small mirrors

Kalamos, 8-12-79

Two Different Ceremonies

Behind the glass mountains at the edge of the forest there is
a large kitchen made of marble like a temple In there
women and men dressed in white with wooden ladles
with graters with skewers with double-edged knives prepare
in ancient copper cauldrons in roasting tins on grills
or pots the foods the sweets the pies
for the holiday of Saint Asomatoi But him
a heretic strips naked at night when the moon goes down
he covertly lights a tall candle double his height and reverently goes
down one after the other the made of tough-stone steps of life and death
to the lower level of the chapel of Saint Asomatoi there where
slavery and freedom meet in their first and last love affair

Kalamos, 8-12-79

Sunday at Kalamos

Wavering day a bit cloudy a bit sunny dampened landscape
trees and ships The old men cough cough again Two fishermen
in the cafe wearing their Sunday outfits The blind man and his daughter
pass by slowly toward the olive grove Solemn women
behind the windows hear the hunters shooting Everything we
had denied has remained a bit behind – they don't leave Further down
a big boat moors villagers take out to the dock crated boxes
with fat yellow chickens the chickens quack And no one knows anymore
if these holes are from the moths the cigarettes or the bullets

Kalamos, 9-12-79

Neutral Time

There are books of small size with drops of wax on their covers
as though a woman cried in the next room There are people
much glorified in their lives forgotten after their deaths And while
no one paid attention to us anymore we managed to look
quite freely opposite at the temple pediment the three marble riders
        naked most ever handsome
without spears and shields golden from the sunset light
to walk with silent understanding toward our guesthouse
where we had left a whole mountain of folded blankets
and big clocks of sunken ships stopped for a long time

Kalamos, 9-12-79

Listening

The doors closed one by one Solemn soldiers with
dark glances saunter in the streets They look at
the citizens only from the knees down Dice clink in
their pockets sometimes – and this increases
the circle of silence all around them However at night
at some point high in the air a sound trembles
as though an invisible pulley lifts the weight of the world
and inside the deep dormitory the tired poor patrons
tense their ears with elation and awe like in the ancient years when
the distant lions in the forest listened to the recluse's flute for the
    first time

Kalamos, 9-12-79

Storing

Pillars of emptiness in the rooms from the passing of those who left
steam rises over the empty beds stays in the air for a while
as if trying to remember something and then dissolve A box
falls off the shelf it doesn't break it creates a self-propelled circle on
      the floor
rocks back and forth ambivalent and stays still surprised in its movement
curved earthen with its painted flowers somehow blown up Then
a woman with long hair enters she lifts it in her hands
brings it to her breast tenderly like a tearless baby
to whom she has entrusted her deep secret knowing
it doesn't know yet how to reveal however
a quiet sunset when she is out will say it with precise accuracy

Athens, 10-12-79

Transparent Things

Transparent things – they exist they don't exist among them
other things are discerned windows glasses flower vases
the inside the outside the in-between the farther away – like when
    you wear
a glass mask and you see the sea floor Next to you the naked divers
given to the water slide along the fish they don't pay attention to you
they don't belong to anything given with all their bodies
to their lightness And when they go out to the shore they hold a broken
triune or a cross or a pitcher their glance with a bit more sky blue
they place them on the rocks take off their masks they look
    round as though blind
wipe themselves with a small towel get dressed and suddenly they
throw their findings again to the bottom of the sea and get on their
    bicycles

Athens, 10-12-79

In Search of a Poem

The boy delays in coming back today Perhaps he lost himself
in the neighborhood flower shop staring at the flowers
in the cooler Perhaps he has delayed
in the elevator talking to that sweet spinster
with the thin dyed hair Usually she holds in her hand
a yellow net with dandelions or some fruits She always has
a solemn face as though she has caused all this ugliness (or
perhaps this is a patient change that all have worked against her?)
because as she holds the net her right arm bit by bit grows longer
hesitantly like an unsaid *forgive me* and her kind profile
in the elevator mirror that she doesn't look into
assumes this gentle light like of saints so that you the arrogant man
want like a hair dresser to raise her hair in a bun

Athens, 11-12-79

Hellenic Duration

The end of this story as well The end The light clamor
of serenity is already heard from under the door Again you can
stand by the window gazing farther on at the green hills
each of them with a white chapel on its side or looking at
the drops of whitewash in the black hair of young construction workers
at the opposite construction site This Hellenic gentle friendship
that re-ties the cut off thread and the knot remains soft –
memory of duration not of suspension And as you again turn
inward from the window the room is a transparent
fully lit fish bowl where naked young girls
saunter in the water with a silent erotic delight
riding gold purple rosy and green fishes

Athens, 12-12-79

Motionless Fluctuations

Repetitions events cost of living processions sludge tankers
in front of the doors garbage bags lottery vendors
blind people with accordions at the escalator on the subway
    dusty small lamps
dusty voices and furniture that gets old with patience
but the others too distant on rainy autumn evenings
behind the hospital cypresses trumpeting in dark army barracks
and the helpless woman patching the shirt of the gambler
    under the lamp One night
people ran to the streets gathered the injured wrapped them
    with blankets
the old man with the wet beard appeared in the middle of the plaza
stretched his thin finger pointing away to a certain spot
perhaps known to them but forgotten and they all sat
    around him on the ground
with the flashlights between their knees And suddenly
a black purple shadowy sun rose so that all of them women
    and men
while smiling felt an unbearable guilt for some
certain and yet unrecognizable sin of theirs or that of somebody else

Athens, 13-12-79

Like This Forever

Despite all these the next day it dawned again The houses
were completely square with clear diagonal shadows Large roofs
spread graded up to the far end Colorful clothes waved
over the headache of the lower rooms with the dark colored
mirrors self-praising in front of vacant armchairs
and the ashtrays cleaned up already Outside on the balcony
the two parrots in their cages stubbornly silent
as if you had to acknowledge that it was them who had
purged a trap set for you At exactly that time the beautiful woman
entered barefoot holding a tray with red apples Among
        the apples
a broken doll opened and closed her light blue eyes cunningly

Athens, 14-12-79

Final Affirmation

How everything got tangled up suicides heroes émigrés buses
ships from the orient trains from the west lottery vendors flags
university upheavals statues huge billboards
gas stations stamp collectors the football the plugged pipes
burglaries of Banks of jewelry stores pedophiles informers –
man is prey of another man my child –this he said – and how
        can you hide
the poem in a crack of death? – because you see even death
has its cracks and its omissions at the time
that the woman comes out of the bath fresh and fired up
and with utmost attention she polishes her husband's shoes
on the balcony having forgotten her comb in a piece of
        her damp hair

Athens, 15-12-79

Birds and Glasses

Many pigeons too many – you don't know whose they are
        where they roost –
they occupy the winter mornings the roofs
they nibble bread crumbs stand on the railings stare at the city
between the TV antennae or from time to time
they saunter on the roofs with their own expression next to small
        sparrows
without any communication between them When women
come out from glass patio doors to feed them they fly away
with a loud noise pushing the air with their breasts
leaving behind some light contours from where later on
gray white or rose-green feathers fall off   These feathers
hover for a while and then they slide and breath between the breasts
of young girls washing some big crystal glasses in the kitchen

Athens, 15-12-79

From Pictures

Protests objections demonstrations Then things calmed down
Most of them pulled back silenced Shadows of swallows
imprinted on the white curtains Lefteris and Paul
exchanged girlfriends again On Sundays Vangelis
goes fishing – alone he says He has bought
a red motorcycle His helmet is sky blue He resembles Cyclops –
And what stories – Nausica Antinoos the Circe pig farm –
and Maria insisted: the bending of the football players'
legs is esthetic In addition – she says – the esthetic in our days
        and always
equates sensuous After that we separated They left
We found some curly hairs in the bed sheets And Che Guevara's
        poster
discolored from the glare in the university student's room which
had remained vacant for months and with lots of nails on the walls

Athens, 16-12-79

Fog

Lights of ships criss-crossed in the fog Vague signals
from one bridge to the other And perhaps those
were the ones we went to meet and them us The houses
    closed shut
and the keys rusting year after year in the pockets
of ancient fashion black overcoats Oh what discreet absence
    like then when
we brought a snow white seabird in the bedroom
with his long yellow legs and red beak We lighted the lamps
we placed the bird before the mirror – it didn't even recognize itself
it only turned its head to pluck one of its feathers and held it high
    in its beak
the exact resemblance of a cross At once the young girls
undressed hastily and went to bed For the first time they didn't laugh

Kalamos, 16-12-79

Unnoticed Deaths

Fragile beautiful objects – crystals porcelains some gold
    or silver
gifts from friends or honorary awards – trophies of decorous athletic
    games
that we never expected recognition for We enjoyed them so much
    back then
we paid much attention to them and we placed them (with some
    hesitation really)
in appropriate positions – not that conspicuous Sometimes at night
when the lights came on in the opposite bar we showed them
    to two-three friends
the most trustworthy (if such truly exist) As the years went by
they multiplied – a true headache – where can one put them how
    can one secure them
and the dust the smoke the dampness the habit They got forgotten
in carton boxes in the attic in burlap sacks wrapped in
old heroic newspapers Nevertheless at night from time to time
you hear a din and again a din as they nudge each other
like glass bells on the deaths of young forgotten girls

Athens, 16-12-79

Like a Myth

Old women with mouse traps over the trap doors they snort grunt
greasy with uncombed hair with black nails not clipped
they have long tongs around them from long-snuffed fireplaces
fake rings and bracelets and panties sequins and beads
they are up to something they prepare some revenge In vigil
        for nights and nights
they tune their ears to the congealed waters flowing in sewers
they slice the green soap in small pieces throw it in the copper
        bowl
they secretly enter the vacant corridors of city hall after the ceremony
they pluck dead chickens shake off the feathers fill the tables and shelves
they go down the stairs laughing spitefully as though no eagle
is left in this world But the next day the young supervisor
gathers the feathers joyfully he places them in his pillow –
the one he puts under the waist of his beloved –
and in the window the white eagle of the moon flaps his
        big wings

                        Athens, 17-12-79

Long Journey

The two ropewalkers who sleep with the same girl
the old woman with three canaries and a flowerpot with the geranium
the photographer with his darkroom and the paper women
swimming in the smallest river the traffic controller
when he goes off work and lights his cigarette in front of
        fully lit window displays
full of electric fridges and vacuums the disabled seamstress
who again forgot to buy a toothbrush and will go to bed with
        not brushed teeth
he who while naked in another place hugs the neck of the white
        horse
secrets from books and moonlit nights and closed up cafes
and Helen after the return pounding with a stone a bigger stone
saying her name intermittently between the bangs
as though building again a new world with big windows and
        small trees –
my first childish kite is caught in one of its branches

Athens, 18-12-79

A Mouse

All night long drums voices drunken songs
fires in the plazas the landscape went red the closed
rooms turned red Perhaps they butchered the statues again
perhaps they burn effigies of gods or tyrants One mouse
stood under the cross and stared with red eyes
wondering whether the alarm clock of the miner would strike on time
whether this night fire would turn into music

Athens, 20-12-79

Identification

He always searched for something he didn't know and perhaps this
would explain to him someday what he sought An insect stayed
motionless on the window glass for a long time His black wings
folded And yet this had no relation
with the clock on the wall   Its fingers turned
with premeditated accuracy almost spitefully
as if to remind us of one of our own insecurities and even so
one of our unexplainable delays – to what?
to an encounter? to a discovery? to a debt? When
the twelve loud persistent clock-strikes one by one
were heard in the drums or the walls or the door, he
responded in synchronized intervals as though he was
the creator of the sounds from inside him Thus
he put his cigarette out closed his eyes and was relieved

Athens, 21-12-79

Mutual Dependencies

Wayward things – he says – covers silences disguises
big masks of frozen grimaces over the clatter
colorful lights billboards glories looted graves
yesterday's heroes playing the tambourine for carnival monkeys
and that statue (how pretty it was) with its pointer finger severed
     (perhaps it was pointing to you) –
oh paranoid reality – he said That man with the thick mustache
plucked off his wife's hair and made a hair piece
which he wears at night in bed And that woman
plucked his penis and ate it In five months
she gave birth to two dogs and a chicken My god what hatred – he said –
from a person to a person To spit on the ground to spit
so it will sprout a serene tree in peacetime
and an orange balloon without a thread going up in the air alone

Athens, 22-12-79

His House

Hey what can I do – he says – what can I do with these stones
that they used to stone me I have built my house Now
I sit inside and snuggle I see the world through
the small skylight It is a silent beautiful song
I hear it What can I do? – he says – I still smile

Athens, 22-12-79

In Two Levels

The circus with the animals and dancers the fish-tank with rosy fishes
the city with flags political parties civil servants museums
the coal vendor with his smudged face as if on purpose for me
so that I retain an image of purity Alex looked at
the opposite hills the clouds the space above – as he called it –
and perhaps he meant the one above the city or above death
    there
where the unspoken words are educated and the uncured time
melts calmly Then the children take their hands from under the blankets
and play with the morning rays in their fingers while on the nightstand
a cup of warm milk's fragrance steams up the world over again

Athens, 23-12-79

The Big Door

You met the coffee bar woman the card reader the chicken seer
you also saw the shadows of birds sliding on the ground
you saw fire's tongue licking the feet of night and its
usual oracles – persistent knocks on the big door
though no one knew what was inside – the blacksmith? the lute player?
or perhaps the woman kneading bread? However in the deepest corner
would have been that big bellows like an old church organ
where one stormy night totally unexpectedly
you had played Jason's song and in the mirror
the same naked purple body had turned his back on you

Athens, 24-12-79

The Farthest Point

Newspapers hand writings statues ashtrays
and others dead (from natural or violent death) – the space is filled
you don't know where to place your hand or a thought The worst is:
these pictures thousands – how did they pile up here? –
they are all his yes in various times and places in various poses
others rhetorical or distant underside lighting or vertical
some in dim mornings or evenings with a dog by the shore
or with a candleholder on the stairs or on the platform with all his medals
Poseidon? Apollo? Christ? demagogue? actor? or perhaps
     recluse?
with a grasshopper on his shoulder a butterfly in his hair
with yellow thorns in his temples and feet Who is he
the eulogized and the stoned? Where is he to hide his glance?
at what distance? how can he respond? to whom? And as he sinks
among so many faces who have given to him who have taken from him
     I see him
with his right hand perforated alone over the deluge
     waving
a whitewashed undershirt hung from the tree on the hill

Athens, 25-12-79

The Inside and Outside Woman

The woman with crossed arms was pacing on the tiled dining room
pale tightened lips – perhaps she was praying
her eye discreetly avoids the chandelier the two flower vases
the night watchman's boots under the table The five masks
still hanging on the wall: the tiger's the horse's
the lion's the deer's and the black cow's You don't know whether
they are there to remind you of the forest fire or to urge you to
a selection and a certain way of life Outside in the garden
the other woman resembling the first one stoops and gathers
some small light blue lily and the broken glass from last night's
     explosions

Athens, 26-12-79

Vaguely Familiar Space

The night smelled of woolen blankets The three large
elephants went by this way farther back the tired camels
the ones kneeling on the ground letting off the naked boys
so they could swim with the moon in the river Then their hair
dripped all the way to the ivy-covered cave The walkers leave
dry fruit there bottles of myrrh silver flagstones
and gold plated knives At the opening of the entrance
the solemn guard stands he clips the parrots' wings with a pair of scissors
he teaches them bad words numbers with double meaning curses
he lights a fire with dry tree branches he burns snake skins feathers nails
pubic hair wooden crosses Then totally drunk from the smoke he
     goes in
takes his boots off rubs his strong feet looks at them and sings

Athens, 27-12-79

Friday Night

In the dark smoke shop three soldiers are fired up
from the scent of their bodies The woman with the makeup
no – she said – another time in the same place Her front teeth
were missing Behind the stairs a demijohn with oil full
of sediments was left   The old men are sleepy
before it even turns dark They look at the lights from the windows
They forget to turn the calendar date Where did it go that
which defined time in speed and slow motion?
that which counted everything on the scale of the pharmacy? The
        sounds of
the two big clocks are heard quite clearly still
over the roofs or inside the houses and then they fall
like dead fishes in small side-streets without lampposts
there where the dogs lick the sperm of the ephebes off the walls

                                    Athens, 28-12-79

The Perfect Staging

Heavy dark curtains purple or olive green Behind them
big three-legged pianos copper statues gold-tiled mirrors
the quick passing of a woman's bra and the woman is absent
Then a glass ball rolled with a strange sound as if made of cloth
The secret yearning to be expressed remained an even bigger secret
Subterranean voices of servants in a deeper space was heard –
perhaps they were skinning rabbits or plucking bird feathers because so
    often
some feathers fell shining like gold over his body
that stayed lying down on the red carpet handsome with open arms
like being crucified on the floor however always waiting
(and this was discerned in the cunning trembling of his closed eyelids)
the start of the music in the inside rooms that he can stand up and dance

Athens, 30-12-79

At the Inn

In time the discoveries lessen same with the inventions
The ancient logos has nothing more to reveal
as it has nothing to hide Women with uncombed hair
sit at the steps of the inn talk about their periods
or their husbands' penises wink their eyes guffaw there
always around the pole like horses on the threshing floor The straw
is blown by the wind shines in the sunshine entangles in their hair
then they come out of the windows shake off the blankets
        the large bed sheets
where at night the hunters and the cart-drivers slept Suddenly
        they stop
and panicky they listen to the heavy pounding of hammers in the
basement
where the laconic hairy blacksmith for days now has been preparing a
huge metal cage for an unknown beast or for these same women

Athens, 30-12-79

Hellenic Line

On this pediment how nicely the people entangle with the horses –
naked limbs corners contours the exquisite leg positions the manes
the marble breathes steam in the sun One horse bolts
jumps over the fence canters Behind it young provincial men coming
out of common baths run The horse reaches the shore
raises his neck looks at the sea the horizon sparkles
a small craft with vacationers passes edge to edge guitars are played
they toss glasses in the water they wave handkerchiefs Death
inexistent in his diaphaneity here where the absolute white reigns
and a horse observes the immenseness while on
its left hind leg the severed rope shines like a bracelet

Athens, 30-12-79

The Fundamental

Obstinate sun unconvinced inside and out of houses all day long
the white of whitewash the black of iron the few sparrows
the mirrors are like vertical flashes they don't contain any armchairs
      bottles
not even hangers and old men I – he says – shall buy
a new shirt new shoes I'm still handsome in the sunset
the girls look at me I place my hands in my pockets – you saw that? –
It is the sun it stings my eyes I enter the elevator I go up
I didn't buy a newspaper My mother had her hands always in flour
she never stopped she would leave two five-finger marks on your lapel
for a moment I remembered it I don't know No no I go out to the roof
among the washed white sheets colorful bras underwear undershirts
like sails flapping I sail away I leave to enter a body

Athens, 31-12-79

Morning Qualities

In the morning with the sun the houses open again From windows
steam of the room vapors smells of warmed up clothes come
from shoes arrayed in the hallway from folded umbrellas
from dried raincoats Downstairs in the cellars lots of rusted
music stands remain movable bed tripods suitcases
of those who left (for two-three months, they had said – have never
    come back)
half melted spermaceti candles in big candleholders crystal jugs –
Ah what strange nights passed with red divans red curtains
naked women opened the fridges and took out ice cubes until all the
    alarm
clocks of the neighborhood workers rang at the same time the train
        whistled
young girls with flower baskets stopped the workers at the station
they gracefully pinned on their lapel a slightest plastic dove
for the collection of Saint Nicolas And yesterday's murderer disguised
ran to light a match for me as I brought the cigarette to my lips

Athens, 31-12-79

Just Division

The old women mumble amid their jaws The old men
hit their canes on the floor softly The younger women
go back and forth without any reason Men are absent The gold coin
is placed in the bread – its position marked They all
know the sign They are angry Until grandmother Urania comes in
with her old purple dress She smiles offers a coin of double value
to each of us Then all together they throw themselves to the table
and start crying like cheated crooks now relaxed in
the community of this last parity in equation

Athens, 1-1-80

On the Same Subject

The glass jar in front of the window
light shines through it its shadow is outlined on the wall
limpid glassy as well And so many deserted
things although often visited and so much
corrosive disbelief amid their supposedly credulous
limpidity The traces of nails are discernable
even if they have closed the holes carefully The poems – you know –
in their solemn arrogance are absolutely lonely
while in the courtyard the sharpener sharpens a second knife

Athens, 2-1-80

Part of the Unsaid

Images words windowpanes shadows – pretences pretences
perhaps that the unsaid will be said at some moment in such a way
that it doesn't seem said For this reason Telis likes
to sit at the cafe in the afternoon observing
the backs of the backgammon players Behind the glass partition
pass the beautiful neighborhood girls who have suddenly grown up
the football players go by and those very smart young boys
the small vendors with their baskets full of combs marbles
plastic airplanes and statuettes of black men Often close to the evening
policemen throw them in holding cells The next day
the copper disc thrower of the plaza is wet although it hadn't rained

Athens, 2-1-80

Night of the Downpour

Peter left in the downpour with a storm lamp The others
went down the mountains soaking wet to the bone haunted
by the luminous lightning bolts They took off their boots in the
    hallway
wrapped themselves in a blanket and at once laid down with their
    ears glued on the cement
listening to the rivers in the streets and the overflowing sludge tanks
    The five old men
sat by the fire They tried to recall a heroic story
They couldn't remember any They stared at their nails Even George
idol of the neighborhood children handsome athletic (for a moon
he played the bouzouki he sang folk songs) in just a few years
he had also aged And you knew that it rained for him
as much as it did for us Kontradillas with the rough beard
stood up grabbed a coal with the tongs and gave to all
to light their cigarettes He lighted last Then with a calm gesture
even calmer because of the clamor of the downpour
he placed the tongs with the coal near the fuse of the dynamite

Athens, 3-1-80

After the Trumpeters' Escape

To gather things – he says – to gather what? – burnt up matches
buttons from vests of dead people broken combs
worn-out words and the others those vague and anonymous
        Nevertheless
for two months now the trumpeters have vanished behind the hills
or behind the high mountains You never hear them in the afternoon
anymore not even at midnight or sometimes with the moon eclipse
Certainly the next day women went out to the nearby forest to gather
escargot in their old baskets They had left the unwashed glasses
and pieces of smoked up glass in the sink However I
neither had anything nor knew anything I had only kept
the word *mountain* And I truly ascended and indeed with confidence
knew that I would see to the opposite side the Red Tower And I saw it

Athens, 4-1-80

Neighborhood Events

Black river at the edge of the suburb where the beggars
paint their feet black where speechless black-cloaked women
toss the shoes and the mattresses of the slaughtered Unwashed boys
search in the black mud for metal boxes for bottles One evening
they found a big turtle they brought it to the plaza
gathered some coins from the spectators they went to the movies
together with the turtle The movie goers screamed A black man
appeared on the screen swimming in the river After that he came out
and hid in the cane field From the other side
a white girl appeared also naked riding a deer
Then the screen became dark as though dipped in the black river
But the boys knew it (and suddenly their pants felt tight)
that the white girl and the black man made love at this spot
because all darkness shivered and the canes whistled like flutes
and when the lights came back on the turtle had vanished

Athens, 5-1-80

Wintery

Collected now – perhaps from some avenged passion
or from some tired pride Their high foreheads
smooth almost without any wrinkles Wise men indeed We never
     saw them
wearing any glasses or giving speeches on podiums Nevertheless
particularly at dusk a subterranean suspicion from ripped bed sheets
ripped mosquito nets and socks floated in the rooms
and behind the doors there were inscriptions made by knife or nails
Suddenly we felt that the flies had died they didn't buzz around
     the glasses
     At daybreak
the workers' footsteps were heard from the street   And in the fridge
some cartons with sweets were left (most likely spoiled)
from a child's forgotten celebration with covered mirrors

                              Athens, 6-1-80

Changes

In the evenings the statuary apprentice hung around the display windows
The other sauntered around the small restaurants with a basket of
    artichokes
and he neither sold them nor ate them until they dried up
and thus they turned into a thorn crown The pale woman
had her umbrella in her closet folded Down in the basement
the Saints were silent along with the mice and the bats
But as it was natural at some point the lamp glass broke
The smoke smudged their faces Now they could go out to the street
without any fear They'd say good evening to the porters
they'd buy peanuts at the station they'd eat them with thriftiness
    one by one
the taste of the roasted salt remained on their mustaches The city
always grew larger The taxi drivers more handsome
Last year's children polished their shoes at the shoe-shines And
    the poem
passed through the shadow of the roses by the delicatessens at the
    Hauteia Plaza

Athens, 7-1-80

Unexpected Outing

Intermarriages conformity negotiations intersections
sacks of cement on the sidewalk huge excavator
a pail with whitewash The boys went by They cursed
The old man lit a cigarette in front of the butcher shop The woman
looked on from behind the curtain If they knew – she said –
an evening with dim lights when the Larissa train whistles
what a profound forgetfulness – perhaps they didn't like to remember
Gunshots were heard again in the circus Five dancers with short
     rosy skirts
run through Liosion Street The spotlight was turned on
     It went out They vanished
But there was an opening in the back of the garden fragrant dampness
deep loud silence from sealed water wells and the serene long worms
When suddenly the unexpected speech and the fully lit wide-open house
The staircase covered by a red carpet with its spread daisies

Athens, 8-1-80

A Summer Picture

Beautiful bodies naked lying down on the sand one next to the other
in a worry-free line their eyes closed
perhaps because of the strong sunlight or to help our perusal
or even our choice It must have been summer – more than likely July
the sea's reflection shone on their toenails
their nostrils quiver from the smell of salt On the upper part
right corner of the picture the whistle of a ship was
steamed up still and exactly below it a basket of grapes sat
Ai summer – he said – wide mouth fleshy only for the kiss and the
     cigarette
all the useless words melt in your saliva

Athens, 9-1-80

The Base of Music

He knew it almost all along He never said anything to anyone Under
    the purple carpet
there was a secret trapdoor In there at night
they threw gloves with holes condoms small fluffy pillows
broken dolls slippers broken glasses And perhaps for that reason
when they played the piano at midnight or even later the echoes
were longer and perhaps deeper The music was heard
more beautiful and even more innocent The young piano player's
    big hands
didn't hit the keys they floated elsewhere they caressed
a naked body from the lower lip to the feet a body
lying erotically not on the purple carpet but on the white tiles

Athens, 10-1-80

Uneasy Times

Traps set for you (or perhaps by you for the others?)
The white cloth pinned on the door with twelve nails
A black feather wedged in the crack of the wood
A strong wind was blowing The escapees went down the hill
they fell in the ravine into the muddy river They held
big branches When the airplanes flew over them
they sat on the ground resembling the trees And with them
were two actors and the wood carver with the nice mustache
Soon after the snowstorm started nothing was visible anymore
Only late at night we learned that the train was blown up
And the key holder returned like a snowman with a big flashlight

Athens, 11-1-80

Understanding

He spoke of other things – perhaps avoiding to think of these
Insects burn in the candle's flame they fell on the table
He gathered them carefully he placed them in a cigarette pack
with a gesture of unexplained evasion In the other room
the footsteps of the woman were heard who most likely carried
ironed bed sheets from the chairs to the closet In a while
she went to the kitchen in such a way as though she had forgotten
something important and at the same time unexpected The sound of
        the fridge was heard Him
torturing a cigarette in his fingers without lighting it
and he pretended he didn't hear anything Then we understood
that indeed these who perhaps for the first time in their lives
had learned how to fly had finally forgotten how to walk

Athens, 11-1-80

Until When?

At the hour when he tried for the third time to say thank you
a third slap disfigured his mouth

Athens, 11-1-80

Punishment

One day time takes its revenge on behalf of all
    the embittered
one day the beautiful braggarts with the curly hair and black
    mustaches are punished
with the muscular bodies the big hands the leather bracelets on
    their left wrists
these in the ships' holds or the gas stations with their long pipes
these on Saturday nights with the sad zembeikikos dance with the
    heavy eyelids and with the knives
these with the gold watches who never check the time They get punished
Lard hangs from their bellies Bit by bit their hair falls
off their thighs and calves The ships that don't take them go away
    One night
with a washed out crossed-eyed glance in the fully lit central
    plaza they see Him passing
He who still retains the beautiful truthful smile of the most bitter
    life and the song
that song they have all forgotten and which only he whistles The worst
    of all is
that they don't understand their severe punishment and for this reason
they age faster and more severely in their unwashed houses with
    the old spiders

Athens, 12-1-80

Vague Fears

Lying down their breaths are heavy Their mothers don't know anything
Their arms out of the blankets strong Farther down
the train goes by In the stations there are baskets with eggs and peanuts
or chestnuts from Crete What images – he said – I remember the
    station master
wore his cap crooked and he had a lot of canaries
In the afternoon at the end of celebration the three drummers
    passed by the plaza
the walkers pull to the side with obvious fear in their faces
that suddenly the drummers will play a rough marching song
    for them

Athens, 12-1-80

Nothing

They came they smoked they left On the chairs
bit by bit the warmth of their bodies evaporated
and a memory from a Saturday night on the old bridge
that under it the gypsy with his bear and his tin plate
    passed by –
that exact moment on the hill the full moon struck and in
    the army camp
they moved on stretchers the two soldiers who killed one another

Athens, 13-1-80

The Antidotes

So many so many deaths wrapped in multi-paged Sunday newspapers
and others in dailies with large or small letters –
tossed-out clothes the unstitched curtain the hand's hold from
        the foreign overcoat
faces painted with chalk with soot with ash with pounded clay
there on a line-up in front of the big hallway doors but also
the memory from the broken reflection of a swan in the lake and more so
the sudden blow that pushed your hair to the side and then
the water in the bathroom was heard like an antidote Don't search
anymore
        – he said –
people were descending ascending the upper floors with lit candles
and the blacksmith down in the basement among his tools What do
        you think?
        – he said –
me who you see in a black shirt like this
I can take off my underwear my socks and remain
with my two black arms equally balanced on my waist And he made
        a gesture
as though dismounting a horse The horse's nostrils steamed up his neck

Athens, 13-1-80

Marks

Darkness had thickened Some scattered flashlights
bore holes in the night From these holes
the Magus' snakes stuck out their heads Three of them
squeezed between their teeth Euridice's bracelets
The fourth one held the golden denture of Helen The fifth
was dead – it was hanging limp – limp like the penis
of the dead Cyclop Exactly at that moment from the narrow cobblestone
sidewalk we heard nails from the boots of soldiers on relief returning
to the camp on the hill with a certain delay having marks on their
necks from the blush of that very cunning toothless old prostitute

Athens, 14-1-80

Observing

The young child cried next to the bombed train
The old man tried to start a fire The seven slaughtered soldiers
lay on the snow One of them face down And a motorcycle
Women with black shawls on their heads And rocks Not a single cry
      was heard
Broken iron things and windows Neither houses nor chickens not
      even stairs
The second old man carried in one of his arms a violin on his other
      a chair
I believe we had met him some forty or two hundred years ago
always haunted and always running – and of course he had forgotten how
to play the violin But at least he must have found some space
to place his chair and sit? So
what are you mumbling now between your teeth? what discoveries
      do you mean?
      what naked words?
Leave me here after the conflagration on the snow next to the firefighters
me without a helmet with only a small screwdriver to take care of things
before the new fire starts to pull out this nail from the heel of
young Iphigenia that hurts her so much and makes her limp
(and she doesn't like this at all – she is very proud) as she walks
      to the gallows

Athens, 15-1-80

Bad Omen

Distant lights flicker and a red one Big spotlights nail the walls
deftly pitch dark things made of steel cross the city
and there are ships with coiled ropes and anchors and smokestacks
Others stare from behind the blinds some from their sleep others
      are naked
The stretcher-bearers wear white outfits to be discerned in the night
However the voices come from the opposite side Two pharmacies
must stay open all night in the suburb because a smell of camphor
and cinnamon oil comes from further down Nevertheless
a person quite old – perhaps a retired customs officer –
wants to commit a calm act of his own besides the general fear
beyond the coming clamor that is already heard He stops
in front of a man selling chestnuts in the underground station
      he buys chestnuts he peels them he eats them
then he lights a cigarette from the man's burner He smokes calmly
      in the dark
on the third drag of the smoke a bullet cuts off the glowing end

Athens, 16-1-80

At the Tobacco Shop

In the tobacco shop there are two wooden high stools On one of
    them sits
the son of the proprietor On the other the bitter mother – how
    uncomfortable
    On the wall
a small slant mirror is hanging It is obvious that she avoids seeing
part of the opposite shelf in the mirror She waits patiently for
a twenty drachma bill from her son She doesn't ask for it
A soldier buys some cigarettes in bulk A very solemn girl
pays for a spool of black thread vanishes in the sundown
    The son
is angry He feels on his back the eye of the old woman
    counting like pennies
one by one his vertebrae under his shirt Alright then
    mother
it's dark now one can't even scratch his balls Suddenly
a strong rain started In front of the tobacco shop door
twelve umbrellas open at the same time The thirteenth
pale like a crucified man stays closed in that oblong
    slant mirror

                                  Athens, 17-1-80

Parting

Friendship with the ships or the clouds it is the same – he says He
stood for a while at the doorstep Don't forget the garden – he said to her
Just a few roses – you know Oh inhospitable evening
when the barbershops close the bakeries the butcher shops Only
    the florists
although closed as well stay fully lit
like luxurious halls for a ceremony of the absent Nevertheless
flowers and lights and two-minded perfumes cannot overpower
the tall and skinny Invisible And even the childish harmonica behind
    the wall
they left they left they left – is the only thing it says though in a tone
of stillness staying in the same place for the secret homecoming

Athens, 18-1-80

Evening

Deep slow passing of day behind the stained glass
contemplative colors deserted scenes luminous landscapes
large fruits and wings of angels And all these mixed with
the outside tax collectors tobacco merchants notary publics And
lumberjacks stayed in the forest with the young shepherds and the birds
    And
that black and hairy roughness was walking almost imperceptibly
behind
    the houses
until we reach the word *twilight* and the darkness arrives
in an eggplant color with yellow spots and a water pitcher But the only
tangible thing I retained in the meantime was none other than
the subtlest layer of wind between your skin and your shirt

Kalamos, 19-1-80

Voiceless Place

The horse grazes on the grass In the horse's eyes
there are two miniature houses and him splitting wood
Farther on the bicycle a cloud a chicken
In the evening they start fires on the hills and the plain
The burnt up wood smells The moon rises
Fortune hunters rent rooms at the inn
The maid and the inn's driver sleep in the stable
Then for their own reasons they call the frogs
And then eight vigorous sailors with black boots
carry an enormous mirror to the middle of the plaza
they leave it there face up and vanish In the mirror
is a blind old man with a white beard and not a single word

Kalamos, 19-1-80

This Continuance

Chatter – he says A carriage went by A small craft goes away
Since morning hunters' gunshots in the cypresses
A pregnant woman looks on from behind the glass
Make sure you buy petrol for the heater New strikes
You don't even feel it is Sunday Vangelis
mailed a letter Euterpe – her arm in a cast
The old men cough more and more Perhaps this way they avenge
someone hidden in the closet or under the table On the other hand
what decreases appears in the corners of rooms with the spiders
and from the negative silence accompanying the click of the lighter

Kalamos, 20-1-80

The Meaning of Cold

They said it as they meant it – rained trees rained sparrows
But the statues retained a different posture Two bikers
passed by the seashore road You found it more natural
that they've forgotten the promise they made to you And even
the fog which was spread (we didn't speak of that) was an assurance
for the upcoming (more than likely soft) The big door
suddenly shut I just managed to look at the camp bed
in the dark hallway and the two huge boots the ones
that soldiers wear in myths A bit later
I saw musicians climbing the stairs They stopped me
they opened their instrument cases and showed me One of them
had inside a red slaughtered hare The other flour The third one
two killed crows – one of them wrapped in golden paper
        the other in newspapers

Kalamos, 20-1-80

Sunday

So is it the same cold inside and outside the poem?

Kalamos, 20-1-80

For This Reason

We reached the bombed city at the time of twilight
A handsome tired unshaven soldier
entered the destroyed house sat and played the piano
For this I tell you For this reason we never refused to the bitter end

Kalamos, 20-1-80

On Gray Color

Soft hills half-vanished in the fog
Houses behind the trees The new grass One dog
with the sea as a background looking afar
underscoring the loneliness of a third one It is time – he said –
for recollection and waiting – gray weather
We went to the Old Folks Home Christmas Eve
Ms Mary died two months ago
We gave the cologne to the Director The sweets
to the three nurses Time for recollection – he said –
but also for waiting Because under those blankets
gray and blind there is a naked red body
that as it breathes unquestionably the whole house
stirs and the apples roll from the top of the table to under the bed

Kalamos, 20-1-80

Failure

The naked trees were nothing but an excuse One closed door
a second a third door – how many others? He had counted them
almost with composure He escorted the limping woman at night
he pretended to limp as well In front of the all night pharmacy
he showed her the green fish-tank with the calm gold fishes Death
        – he said –
is irrelevant whether the red light is on or the green
No no – she said – go I prefer to limp on my own

Athens, 21-1-80

Process

Those who work with steel have hands of steel
Those who keep silent – nothing Don't do wrong to them
Day before yesterday the strong wind broke the flowerpots
He took a broom out to the big rooftop
at night midnight so that the neighbors wouldn't see him He swept
roots dry branches worms soil He threw the refuse
to the street with the moon's complicity
The next morning the shop owners shouted From the window
he stared at them as if innocent and surprised The secret he knew
he kept amid the calm words and he couldn't get angry anymore

Athens, 21-1-80

The Agreement

The coal vendor and the fish seller of the neighborhood Very light
smoke in light blue color in the winter sunshine One sparrow
saunters here and there on the roof – funny Why leave?
     – he said –
These shout these gesticulate The same and the same The tailor
passes a thread through the needle constantly – he has lots of
     unstitched clothes
one of them is pale the other gray another green The old woman
     looks on
with a hollow smile She has forgotten the colors I placed her calmly
on the armchair I peeled the egg for her I brought milk to her
and four paper napkins I want to be nice so that I can rediscover
how the colors agree among themselves but also with the fish and
with the door handle and with the smoke and more so with me –
a preexisting agreement that you forget and rediscover
     every so often –
a gentle friendly agreement without any rules terms and clauses

Athens, 21-1-80

Unproven Exercise

Birds arrive from the south they come near they grow
they rest a bit on coiled wet ship ropes
then they leave unknown to where Women with makeup
climb the exterior wooden stairs Laconic men
with vigorous hair and beards smoke big cigarettes
over the long discolored couches The parrot
is very solemn Gouu and gouu – he quacks in his cage
Oh what voyages that changed direction – kitchens of restaurants
mirrors in dark entrances sounds of big clocks
one terrified elephant among the traffic lights –
And he who we waited on for hours at the station
was sitting on the made bed all dressed and with his cap
and a naked woman leaned her head on his knees

Athens, 22-1-80

Expanse

The good weather is enough Not a single grudge Nevertheless
the poet still lurks The young lumberjack
leaves his ax on the rock He looks at a cloud
He has no friendships with birds and leaves In the hair of his chest
the large hand of the wind passes very sensually

Athens, 23-1-80

The Asleep and the Other

They sleep One blanket under one blanket over They are young
Shadows go by They look at them The asleep ones don't see them Eyes
    closed
open mouth Perhaps they too are expecting something In the stable
the horse hair falls with a hollow sound The moon
strikes one-by-one its matches on the walls They don't hear a thing
He asks for the simplest tone for what went silent or are silent
    Then
he wraps himself in a blanket He also lies down next to the others
    He pretends that he is asleep

Athens, 24-1-80

Then

It was a quiet night from those back then with sheep and stars
A table in the yard one water pitcher the watered daisies
Down at the lake the frogs croaked A woman in a white dress
walked softly on the grass Every so often she stopped
    She listened
In the inside room the three mountaineers slept in the same big bed
There was a mirror someplace behind the red curtain
There was a distant ignorance And when they asked Him
he had indeed forgotten the city the street and number and his name –
because the poem is a world in the world and a person
walks by slanting his left shoulder under the weight of the wind

Athens, 25-1-80

Sovereign Emotion

From the window we saw the young circus dancers leaving
riding the elephants The same night the women
pulled into the bedrooms alone Perhaps they tried
their old dresses perhaps their bridal gowns The children
pretended to read They didn't read They listened to the footsteps
of a very sad animal in the garden – this was known
from the way it delayed in front of the Antinoos statue
or before the big yellow rose hiding the whole
observatory building Then they all closed their eyes
waiting from moment to moment for the long distance phone call
      with the news about a death

Athens, 26-1-80

Unknown Debts

We sat under the trees to remember something important
We didn't know what To think of something after all At a distance the sea
elongated silent with two columns of smoke and a cloud On the hill
a yellow house with an open window There are some
secret relations between disparate things They all mesh Manolis
I cannot come to any conclusion – he said – and I won't try
But the mailman when he goes by the poplars
as though no one sees him he lifts a stone he examines it
and he puts it in his pocket Certainly he is the one who opens our mail
and although we are disgusted with this we always need him
for our own protection as if we apply a general leniency for the others

Athens, 27-1-80

Deaths

They also died naturally and unexpectedly And they had left
some little bags with stale legumes and some others
with lead balls or with moths of flowers and vegetables
No one has opened them since No one learned what they thought
about the duration in general or their personal duration
To me – said Maria – it is impressive that each little bag
is tied with a string of different color – yellow purple
olive green silver There is no red Maria said this
and all of a sudden her face turned red inexplicably We
bowed our heads as though being sorrowful we agreed Later on
the strings discolored – it wouldn't show that the red was missing

Athens, 28-1-80

Instinctive Reactions

They are thoughtful people with lots of experience They are silent
        There are others
holding in their hands a childish plastic toy or a flower
or a broken guitar or the old wall clock Then others
hold a pair of pliers in such a way as though they want to pull out
your strongest teeth But these as well as those every so often
look at the thermometer to see what clothes to put on And they all
know that they should defrost the fridge a bit more often
        to properly preserve
the fresh butter the fruits and the three golden swallows

Athens, 28-1-80

Elsewhere

They leave their bundles on the ground They stare at the mountains And
        of course words
become hard to pronounce when the eyes deepen Once upon a time
there were some laws some rules The mirrors showed
those cloudless mornings along with the shadowy face
a piece of the sky and the upper corner of the closet
The idea of an encounter stirred the white curtain But this
was postponed a number of times Later on other frictions appeared
Women got old faster They painted their nails a rose color
However they never pin any flowers in their hair You by the window
were looking through the same sailor's binoculars The bell tower
        was visible

Athens, 29-1-80

Ambush

Who abandoned these three baskets on the dock?
one of them with eggs the second with apples and the third with flowers
Perhaps behind the lamppost their owner lurks
to see who will snatch them You turn your glance around
in the evening twilight to discover and to unmask
his simple-minded stupid ambushes And suddenly
the lights of the seashore taverns are turned on And you see him
coming straight toward you The two baskets
are in your hands The third one hangs from your teeth You
        cannot speak

Athens, 30-1-80

Betrayal

The travelers left But what was felt more in the evening
was that the sailors had left The women closed themselves in the houses
they counted some wrinkled money They took the comb
and by chance they combed their hair In the yard there were
tires of trucks piled This pain is gone as well – Jason said –
and the upcoming one Nevertheless on the side in the harbor
a large barge was rocking with an ambivalent meaning totally covered
with a white ship sailcloth and surrounded by a black band

Athens, 30-1-80

Radiations

He saw the deserters behind the fence wall He didn't give them up He
     gazed at the tree
with two sparrows – each held a long yellow thread
in his beak Finally evening came And he was curious for the
continuance
of an unknown event very much his and the foreigner's For this
he stooped under the small door he took matches and struck them one
     by one
inviting the night insects and the small brother mouse
for a common joyful decoding of the great Enclosed
while behind the glass the handsome blond servant
with self-assured almost dance-like movements threw sawdust
in the gold-trimmed hall for the dinner parties At one moment
he stood in front of the mirror he smiled and fixed a piece of his hair
as if he was the one who would always say the last word

Athens, 31-1-80 and 2-2-80

Degradation

So many things gathered – flower vases ashtrays paintings
porcelain masks small statues crystals – one covering
    the other –
they hide they get choked the house got flooded the doors
are blocked the windows to the middle and the view is obstructed
they hinder the movement the sleep – mirrors closets chests
    suitcases –
the most important keys are lost along with the desire to look for
    them again
to re-examine them to choose one and place it on the table
in a prominent place to study or for recollection Only
a sorrowful leniency for everything and for all that is left with you
especially in the afternoons when it rains and a white long
smooth worm without eyes and mouth saunters along the gray wall
and you don't discern which is its head and which its tail
    Nevertheless
from this worm's passing when the lights go out a long silver line
phosphorescence on the roof peak continuing beyond
    the house
further from the huge garages further from the city perhaps
    further from death

Kalamos, 3-2-80

Return

Nonetheless a bit later a strong desire returned
for a price increase and for classification From the window
the telegraph poles were visible the olive trees part of the sea
the three old women gathering dandelions in the grassy field
in a humble seemly and tender way stooping on the ground as if praying
    And this
wasn't an allegory at all We had learned through the years
to stay clear of the symbols and fanciful versions of things
    Vangelis
lit the heater gathered the used matches from the floor
then he put his two hands in the sack with the flour as though
he'd knead some bread for us or he was to dust with flour a big
invisible fish with intended gestures for the supper of some
      suddenly-expected visitors

Kalamos, 3-2-80

Acquittal

Big dump trucks went by the shoreline road they created dust
Then two horse riders and a man on foot Then the fishermen came out
A soldier under the wild pear tree shakes off his blanket
    The other
in order to avoid answering the vague signals that didn't concern him
pulled his hat up to his eyebrows and climbed up the hill
to see when night came the lights turn on down in the harbor
This way he acquits himself without disclosing any of his mistakes

Athens, 4-2-80

Incident in the Harbor

Longshoremen tobacco merchants porters boxes hoists
jostling shouts And him asleep on the flagstones
His shirt off his waist – his belly is visible
Dead? Wounded? Drunk? Has he come out of a brothel?
Under his ear are some red marks Where is the knife?
And this light edge to edge on his lips It shines Then he
rose up a bit searched himself and lighted a cigarette At that moment
two women came out of the ship holding hatboxes
and two more with bouquets They lean down one by one
and kiss him then all five vanish While a big hoist
lifted an angel – on his shoulders he holds a small dolphin

Athens, 5-2-80

Motionlessness of the Top

Tamed acceptance of the inexplicable as night falls a woman
stands by the window looks at the muddy street of the suburb
she stares at those self-taught lights of the common restaurants
The blind lotto vendor is outside the florist The dead
child's bicycle rusts in the yard Remember – he said
Whoever remembers knows well The thread is wrapped
around the motionless top – wooden old worn-out top
the one containing so many dead and unborn whirls And
        for this
our deepest human movements are imposed on us by the
        stillness of the statues
We lighted a cigarette We looked at our hands We were not
        the statues

Athens, 6-2-80

The Sin

They left they left – he said They stayed – he said in a while They stayed
    They are
Gullible days lost And there were a few trees
The roofs leaned more impressively on their shoulders George
on top of the ladder was fixing the plaster festoon
of the neoclassical house Further down in the harbor
the longshoremen were creating havoc They carried
large wooden boxes tied with ropes Two dogs
walked edge to edge in the street Those days
we enclosed in parentheses the most important things Him
with the black patch over his right eye gaping at the shabby
display-windows he collected (perhaps on our behalf) a few objects
match boxes words images and some other nameless and
    invisible things –
always clumsy with his muddy shoes and completely innocent
The absolute – he said – is our profound sin And as the lights
    were turned on
on the ships in the bars in the patisseries they underscored exactly that

Athens, 7-2-80

Inhalings
1980

Poetry
present of the future
two grains of wheat
one apple
the snake red
and golden

Athens, 27-2-80

Breakfast
under the trees
two cups
a lot of birds
I look at the statue
he has a hole
in his right rib –
ah my poor mother

Athens, 28-2-80

The bird looks at him
from the window
he leaves the pliers
on the table
the word *p l i e r s*
has its jaws open
it pulls the nail
the mirror falls

Athens, 29-2-80

I talked to you
about this miracle
when someone leaves
and his shirt remains
on the back of the chair
and the curtain waves
for the second time *y e s*
for both of us

Athens, 29-2-80

I tossed a stone
in the water well
the sound I had heard
from before
fit perfectly
with the new sound
therefore
my fingers count correctly
before the lit windows

                              Athens, 29-2-80

Low ceiling shacks
smoke
a water pitcher
come out
I have to show you
an insect
on a leaf
the bird's shadow
incised in the marble
the tree has
no crutches

                              Athens, 29-2-80

For so long
with barely enough bread
with cheap cigarettes
comrade
how the world grows bigger
from a glance to a glance
from a hand to a hand
in one word comrade

Athens, 29-2-80

The wet wood
creaks
in the afternoon we saw
we didn't ask
the woman with the fish
the voyage is for us
as well –
which oath you spoke of?

Athens, 29-2-80

I found a bone
stuck in the ground
I wiped it on my knee
it is white
I'll make a flute –
white songs
and sometimes red
come out this way
listen

Athens, 29-2-80

An island
a dome
one chair
sit –
ah that I breathe you beauty
the stars will kill me

Athens, 29-2-80

Didn't you hear me?
I said hello to you
nothing else –
was it hello?
goodbye?
Yes yes
it will rain any time now
hello to you

Athens, 29-2-80

I saw the table
in the mirror
not in the room
you were
in the room
I sit there
at the inside table
I pretend that I read
under the newspaper
are the salt cellar
and the knife

Athens, 29-2-80

Smelling
a rose
you grew taller by half a meter
now you cannot fit
under the door
night came
it became cold
the stars appeared
wolves came down

Athens, 29-2-80

Rust and more rust
on the balcony railings
the kitchen air vent
the bed
let it be
what can you repair first?
Be careful with the ants
under the words

Athens, 29-2-80

He saw the salt
spilled on the stairs
the woman's clothes
thrown on the floor
he took the trowel
to stucco the holes
he built a house
full of windows

Athens, 29-2-80

Serene landscape
large storage rooms
carpentry shops
cemetery
and the sea everywhere
saunters in hallways
fills the glasses
the mirrors
people turn light blue
light blue poems float
over the drowning

Athens, 29-2-80

Poetry – he said –
poetry again
poetry wasn't speaking –
on the ladder
I prune the tree
I push off the caterpillars –
amid the branches
I smile
the garden is yours
I am the gardener

Athens, 29-2-80

What can grief do for you?
the bowed head?
unless you bang your fist
the door doesn't open
the wind doesn't blow
the statue doesn't rise

Athens, 29-2-80

The plaster of the poor house
the indigo for the wash
the oven smells fragrant
burnt up bulrush
warm bread
the horse's nostrils
dilated
white horse
on a light blue mountain
ai comrades
what riders we were
in the strong wind

Athens, 29-2-80

Moon moonlight
enters from the window
finds her naked in bed
it licks her whole body –
oi oi moon ah moon
I'll sever your tongue
so I can go to sleep

Athens, 29-2-80

Aerobic exercises
with the open window
the windowpanes mirrors
the naked breast
the hair
the muscles
the snow white teeth
you smile
stop like that
if you don't exhale at once
you will grow leaves and birds
and a small hammer
stubbornly pounding
the ancient coin
with your face engraved in it

Athens, 1-3-80

Love – he said –
Loneliness slaughtered
the most great loneliness –
takes a stone
he doesn't toss it to the sea
he doesn't aim at a bird
neither the man nor the cloud
he breaks the black almonds
he cleans and eats them

Athens, 1-3-80

Thank you – he said –
for all I gave you
for all things not reciprocated
for what is preparing
the secret wealth
the saddest pride
the musical silence
with unconquerable words

Athens, 2-3-80

Precipitous time
limpidity
how pretty it is
when you climb
crushing with each step
a small futility

Athens, 2-3-80

What wasn't visible
gave meaning
to the cut-in-pieces nothing
and your socks
thrown on the floor
not on purpose
I shouted at the policeman
through the window
he didn't hear me

Athens, 2-3-80

You carve the cypress bark
the raisin drips
full of fragrance
but don't forget
to hang the map
over our bed –
no no
I didn't mean anything else

Athens, 2-3-80

Islands of the night
a staircase on the wall
a star in the water
darkness spreads
turns your hands golden
but you
become a rower

Athens, 3-3-80

Trains full of soldiers
ships with drown people
he occupies
my seat
I walk around him
nothing
I go to buy
clay cups
the store is closed
I stay in the street
with the street
with the new moon
with the horse of my shadow

Athens, 3-3-80

Losses losses
Ah secret savings
silent joy
before sleep
when the traffic controller
ends his shift
and you hear his steps in the street
stopping
before the closed flower shop

Athens, 3-3-80

He has nothing
to count
he counts his fingers again
graceful silence
perfected
not the first word
the second
was the right one
and the proper sound
from the pounding and nailing
of the wood

Athens, 3-3-80

He stood opposite
his nearest person
to discern himself
again he wore his hat
he left
he wore gloves
however
his fingerprints
were left
on the doorknob

Athens, 3-3-80

Brave we used to say
whole in his blood
we hid
behind the trees
one of us urinating
the other with his newspaper
the other yet chewing on leaves
the fourth alone
behind the only heliotrope
the fifth one
fell asleep on the grass
until evening

Athens, 3-3-80

This nothing – he said –
is synonym to
everything –
he had a towel around
his waist
 – was he coming out of the bathroom?
was he going in? –
he had beautiful hair
calligraphic legs
we didn't believe him

Athens, 3-3-80

Ai romiosini – they said –
they moistened
their dry bread
birds and plane-tree leaves run
George was throwing the sphere
his muscles tightened
ai romiosini – they said –
horses grazed on the plain
one horse
stayed motionless
looked at the statue
the statue raised his arm
to show the mountain
a bird poked my ear
the sky was reassured

Athens, 3-3-80

These fruits
retain the shape
of the hands which cut them
and of those that placed them
in the large baskets
and of those that transported them
to the city
and of those hands that displayed them
in this crystal fruit bowl –
ah how many hands touching
how many hands touch you
you open the window
search in the street
for a stronger confirmation
on the hands and on the lips
of the passers-by

Athens, 4-3-80

Fragrant evenings
outdoor cinemas
boys with open shirts
noise of uncorking
of a second third lemonade
borderless sky
borderless life
as they break the walnuts
with their teeth
here we are
borderless

Athens, 10-3-80

There
always there
around there
voices movements events
and silence
there
doors windows
open close
towards there
soldiers sailors
the knife sharpener the newspaper vendor
a ripped short tunic
chaki
a girl
a rose
fell from her hand
the bicycle went by
ran over it
there

Athens, 14-3-80

He hung his window
by the forest
the window came back
to the house
he left his glass
in the cloud
the glass returned
on the table
he bestowed his body
unto the birds
his body returned
in his body –
oh unrealized refusal
oh immense body
immense disobedience
in endlessness

Athens, 14-3-80

Serene faces
surrendered bodies
came in my sleep
these tough men
with the thick boots
the rough clothes
the laconic men
at daybreak it rained
the three killed hunters
were drenched in the olive grove

Athens, 16-3-80

On top of the hill
two closed up houses
one of them with purple windows
the other with gray
not any inhabitant
horse plow carriage
nothing
only one chicken
climbs up the stairs
goes down
returns to the road
clucks
ruler of everything
laying every day
two white double-yoke eggs
and a smaller one light blue

Sparta, 22-3-80

Frozen sunshine
orange trees between the houses
the high mountain
the white City Hall
the big plaza
here where we met
the small gods
dressed as soldiers
and the young clown
dressed as Persephone
I'll show you – he said –
how the bird flies
he stretched his neck
he stretched his arms
and started crying
he never flew

Sparta, 23-3-80

Glorious ruins
here where history thickens
and forgets itself
in bird chirping
in cypresses
with small lizards
while the snowed mountain
supervises
ah snow – we said –
spotless snow
repeated relation
forgetfulness and reconnection
to gaze down at the plain
the green grass
the gray olive grove
and a young couple
negating the eternal
biting:
once the girl
once the boy
the same apple

Mystras, 23-3-80

They waited for us there – he said –
the great dead
waited for us there
the children who we were
big rocks and salt
women with sky blue kerchiefs
crumbled balconies
a staircase in the front yard
bearded rowers
the twelve very thin fishermen
and they were all angry
and we
at that limit between
memory and forgetfulness
and even the sea
vigorous and irreversible
amid its eternity
also angry

Monovasia, 23-3-80

Klout klout
the clumsy bird
on top of the ruins
and the cactus pear trees perched
on the church domes
and in the rock crevasses
there where
our best dead dwell
and the venerable old man
takes out of his pocket
the big copper watch
hours don't have numbers
the first number a bat
the second a cross
up to the cross of twelve
timeless time opposite the sea
and the deaf man
listener of the endless

Monovasia, 24-3-80

Naked vertical rock
crows and seagulls crisscross
high up high up
they mingle separate
this way the white
that way the black
they vanished –
naked vertical rock
and the huge bell soundless
rounded up from the tension
of the sealed sounds

Monovasia, 24-3-80

The heroes got so tired
that they exhume them so often
to listen to orators on balconies
flags search their ears
bow their heads
yearn
with their three fingers play
with the middle button of their coats
then they turn their backs
vanish behind the cactus pear trees
behind the black rocks
there where the iron gate shuts
and the sea begins again

Monovasia, 25-3-80

The wild pear trees bloomed
I saw a honey bee
I hear the sparrows
the voice of the fisherman over the sea
the photographers come
take pictures of trees and girls
two ships
the third one assumes an erotic pose
click ready
click click again
everything visible and famous
the words get ready
and this young soldier
takes off his boots
lifts his underwear to his knees
and saunters by the shore –
how fresh and diaphanous the water
on our foreheads

Kalamos, 28-3-80

The voice of the plowman
in the neighboring field
let's go ai let's go come on
ancient plow
red horse
fragrance of earth
honeybees buzz
enclosed in the white flowers
bare-breasted longshoremen
carry long planks
in the harbor
ai ai May morning
public and private
how everything
finds its naturalness
and the irrational is nothing
but a holey leaf pierced
on a yellow thread
around the wrist of your arm

Kalamos, 29-3-80

The white of Sunday
and the white
seagull
the water
that almost whispers
a carriage passed by
loaded with whitewash
if I find a white word
I'll let you know

Kalamos, 30-3-80

Large fresh moon
a star even higher
lights scattered on the hill
a fully lit ship
him and his shadow on the road
the possible the impossible
the unaccomplished
he searches his pocket
there are not any
words spoken
or not spoken
nameless silence
road

Kalamos, 30-3-80

Your sleep in pieces
cracks of moon
the night bird
the woman with the ceiling brush
the two opponents
in two opposite armchairs
now gentle
the continuous sound of an
electric vacuum is
heard from the hallway
in a 6/8 rhythm
and suddenly the rose garden
and five large butterflies
snow white
and I cannot remember
further on – further on

Kalamos, 3-3-80

What we loved
and perhaps loved us
houses and trees and horses
the big river
a lamppost a table
the bird on the moon
the moon in the sea
the man on the rock
the *vacancy* of the mirror
closed baby rooms
we leave they leave
and this sweet fragrance
and fortitude
a piece of wood moistened
in the calm water
on the shore of Saint Apostolos

Kalamos, 3-4-80

A lone star
in the whole wide sky
ships leaving at night
invisible
and we are here
and the long bed sheets
hanging on clotheslines
and this secret concentration
to empty the void

Kalamos, 3-4-80

The sea's fragrance
the fragrance of lemon flowers
the fragrance of the dream
cut in four
the satiated hunger
and insubordinate glory
birds chirp over the water well
lone beauty completely alone
not any person

Kalamos, 4-4-80

Wooden body
painted with ocher and ash
sunken in flowers
they spoke sang chanted
carried chairs
lighted candles
drew black crosses
over the doors
the next day
white snow white morning
not any border
not any death
the closed cafes
the big closed pig farm
how calmly the world breaths
so there
the inconceivable exists

Kalamos, 4-4-80

The wild pear tree fully bloomed
behind the white flowers
a piece of sky blue mountain
and a ship
inside this *intact*
almost outlined
by a diaphanous glass front
and five oranges on the table

Kalamos, 5-4-80

It is spring
yet the bird chirps: end –
end of the red roof
end of the quiet sea –
oh unyielding body
under the contraction
of the poem

Kalamos, 5-4-80

You alone different
in the knowledge of your likeness
agreeable and yet persistent
insisting on the uncommitted
the positive
when the pulleys lift
big wooden crates
a metal bed
a headless statue
and the engineer in the sundown
takes off his cap
and lights a cigarette
exactly when some white bird fluff
falls with a bang
in the calm water

Parnitha, 6-4-80

One of the women slices the bread
the other cuts lettuce
the third steps on the stool
grabs an earthen bowl
rain drips on the dog's hair
we do okay with time – she says –
it smells of coal and grease
I ignore
the disproportional exchanges
I hear smell see
with my body I extend
to the mountain with the trees
and further
there where Achilles after his death
on the White Island
feeds his servant seagulls
in the afternoon

Parnitha, 6-4-80

He left the glass on the chair
he climbed up to the attic
the clothes of the dead people are black
a yellow vest
he left the birdcages in the basement
empty
he kept the bird down
hid it in the briefcase
in the smallest drawers
in pillowcases
for this reason
he held on his knees
a big stone
for the rest of the hours

Athens, 7-4-80

Large empty rooms
ripped curtains
one of them kneeling on the floor
red
the mirror ignores it
outside in the garden birds
chirp inexcusably
I'll open the house
I'll wear the gardener's straw hat
I'll cut a few roses
and snails
I've had the young ropewalker
with his purple tricot
locked in the dog's house
since morning
when the moon rises
I'll open it for him

Athens, 8-4-80

Margaret had two German Shepherds
Euridice three cats
Maria one parrot
Helen two canaries
Chryssante held a dusting cloth
Antinoos came in barefoot
his feet indeed touched the floor
light flooded the glass doors
the girls started crying
while I thoughtfully
placed my hands
inside the dead person's shoes
and gained independence

Athens, 9-4-80

The two ropewalkers
their caps
their umbrellas
their baskets
when the lights go out
the horses are heard from the inn
chewing on their hay
the deep breaths of sleeping
hunters are heard
then the ropewalkers
wash their underwear
in the metal tub
they place them on their rope
and a girl sits
by the low window
cheek to cheek with the moon
looking at the white horse grazing
amid the statues of the cemetery

Athens, 9-4-80

Groping the wall
and the other wall
the stone is cold
the guards are large-built
they hold keys and torches
they whistle
long whistles in the hallway
they light matches
the clamor of the sewer is heard
then the train
the big basket with the snakes
hangs from the ceiling
with the nails and bracelets
where the smoke comes from

Athens, 10-4-80

The three girls
open the windows
make the beds
polish the boots
of the hunters
a bird comes in
looks at the glasses
it knows
why we were born

Athens, 11-4-80

He bought lots of mirrors
he wasn't in any of them
only the young ropejuggler walked
on a golden thread
over the table
and outside the motorcycles
and the caterpillars heading
down from the trees
and him covering his hand
with his other hand
looking for justification

Athens, 11-4-80

They do well with the dead
they bring food and clothes to them
beautiful clay pitchers candleholders
they spread large blankets on the shrubs
at night they protect themselves from the cold
they lock up the doors
the dog pees under the lamp stand
before they fall asleep they resort to clemency
they quiet down
they silver plate their old pans
hang them from the walls
they place the plucked chicken in the fridge
water stays completely motionless
the drowning isn't visible

Athens, 12-4-80

Runners go by the suburb
the boy sits at the step of the train
a woman holds two loaves of bread
the worker a shovel
I cannot – he says – undress
the poem is bypassed
two o'clock in the morning
black naked horse-riders
in tall fountains
and a white cloth hovering
in the sleep's smoke

Athens, 12-4-80

The curtain is diaphanous
behind the curtain
TV antennae
red tents
green
the cement factory
the hidden angel
with the crown in his hand
Vangelis didn't look
he scratched his testes
he fell asleep
I covered him with a blanket
coincidence
the blanket was red

Athens, 13-4-80

Two people
in an undefined one
and the one created by itself
and the repentance of perhaps
late at night
in train stations
with unknown émigrés
among the baskets of small vendors
and the train master smokes
while he has a turtle
in his pocket

Athens, 13-4-80

With a stork on the island
with a paper cutter at home
whistles of trains or ships
desires regrets
the aimless bread
the pointless poem
two longshoremen carry
a large couch to the harbor
the woman
closes two windows
wears golden makeup
nothing happens
she opens the windows again
looks at the moon
behind the moon
is the trapdoor

Athens, 15-4-80

Speechless island women
under the moon
they chew gum from Chios
a ship with its lights
goes away quietly
however
he's on the bridge
is he the trumpeter?

Athens, 15-4-80

Sensible morning
windows of the old folks home
gray pajamas on the balcony
thin tree in the courtyard
and a lone bird
the boys have
foreign trademarks
on the backs of their pants
and he's an intruder
among the morning forbearance
he enters the flower shop
buys three roses
asks for forgiveness
and he pulls off the petals

Athens, 16-4-80

They walk barefoot
they have wide feet
raisins on their soles
leaves stick onto them
ants seeds gravel
small pieces of paper
from last night's newspapers
from ripped poems
then
they lie down and go to sleep
noon under the plane trees
strong wind
licks their feet with its tongue
women stand by the windows
more lonely

Athens, 17-4-80

Wild animals of the night
two of them striped
one of them limps
the elephant is sky blue
on its back Euosmos
the one who washed himself in the river
and his hair dripped in the river
and the river rose
and drowned the houses
it drowned the orphanage
and the produce market
now suitcases float
and a small triangular table
and the curly-haired Euosmos
with his third finger
makes a hole in the moon
always riding the elephant

Athens, 17-4-80

Intertwined bodies
smell of raisin
from fallen leaves
and a transistor –
oh numberless night
suckling
with your big fleshy mouth
insects vulvae penises
lamps stairs traffic controllers
sports jerseys
and the small blacksmith shop on the corner
with the two bellows
and Ajax's spear

Athens, 20-4-80

Spectral city
yellow afternoon
yellow houses
black windows
great yellow silence
not any man
in the streets
abandoned motorcycles
bicycles
a truck loaded with apples
an insect-killing pump
the statues
saunter in the yellow avenue
they open the jugglers' suitcases
take their yellow tricots
hand them from the trees
break the patisserie windows
rip pictures of the kings
then they return to their seats
and fall asleep with open eyes

Athens, 22-4-80

They clapped intensely
he
turned to see who they clappped for
he saw himself
in the glass of the opposite door
he wore a black long overcoat
with a big chrysanthemum
on his raised lapel
and a dog by his side –
Unknown man – he said –
My unknown man – he repeated –
how many ashtrays and candleholders
and just one glass
I'll take my underwear to the cleaners
and the blankets
this dog we call World
World World I call it
he wags his tail –
isn't this what you want?
the cow gazed from behind the glass
exactly behind his idol

Athens, 24-4-80

Night is coming
the three old women go down the hills
throw the eggshells in the sea
they see something of theirs far away
they pretend to cough
one of them takes off her shoes
holds them on her knees
the other pounds her cane on the ground
the other is toothless
among her white gums
she bites a silver coin
she spits on it in her palm
wipes it with her apron
places it back between her gums
old woman dirty old woman of the worry
and suddenly the sky
shines like a plain with a thousand daisies
the Victor inhales inhales
with wide open mouth
he has all his teeth
and one more unspoken word

Athens, 26-4-80

BIBLIOGRAPHY

Moonlight Sonata, 1956, Kedros Editions, Athens, Greece (in Greek)

The World's Neighbourhoods, 1957, Kedros Editions, Athens, Greece (in Greek)

Yannis Ritsos – Poems I, 1961, Kedros Editions, Athens, Greece (in Greek) volume consists of:

> *Tractor*
> *Pyramids*
> *Trial*
> *Epitaphios*
> *My Sister's Song*
> *Spring Symphony*
> *The Ocean's March*
> *Notes on the Margins of Time*
> *The Old Mazurka to the Rhythm of Rain*
> *The Last Century*

Yannis Ritsos – Poems II, 1961, Kedros Editions, Athens, Greece (in Greek) volume comprised of:

> *Vigilance*
> *Silent Season*
> *Shift of the Evening Star*
> *Three Chorals*
> *Romiosini*
> *The lady of the Vineyards*
> *Letter to Joliet Curie*
> *We and the River*
> *Skirmish*
> *Goodbye Vladimir Mayiakovsky*
> *Peace*
> *Displacements*
> *The Burial of Orgaz*
> *The Wavering Scales*
> *My Son, My Moon*
> *Old Men and Tranquility*
> *Smoked Earthen Pot*
> *Unsubjugated City*

> *Morning Star*
> *Pitcher*
> *Parentheses I*

Helen, 1972, Kedros Editions, Athens, Greece (in Greek)

Sounder, 1973, Kedros Editions, Athens, Greece (in Greek)

Lady of the Vineyards, 1975, Kedros Editions, Athens, Greece (in Greek)

The Caretaker's Desk, 1976, Kedros Editions, Athens, Greece (in Greek)

Yannis Ritsos – Poems XIV, 2007, Kedros Editions, Athens, Greece (in Greek); volume consists of:

> *Once*
> *Pilos*
> *Short Admission*
> *Replacements*
> *The World is One*
> *Furnished Rooms*
> *Suddenly*
> *They Left*
> *Inhalings*
> *Shadows of Birds*
> *Statue in the Rain*

Repetirions – Testomonies – Parentheses, 1991, Translated by Edmund Keeley, Princeton University Press, Princeton, New Jersey

Yannis Ritsos – Selected Poems 1938-1988, 1989, Edited and Translated by Kimon Friar and Kostas Myrsiades, BOA Editions Limited, Brockport, New York

Remembering Yannis Ritsos – Greek Poet of the Left, 1993, Minas Savvas, Fairleigh Dickinson University

The Cycle of Yannis Ritsos, Mythological Poems, 1980, Chrysa Prokopaki, Theater Review

The Poet Yannis Ritsos, 1980, Ekali, Pantelis Prevelakis, Athens Greece

Mikis Theodorakis, Myths and Politics in Modern Greek Music, 1980, Gail Host

A Salute to Ritsos, 1957, Lettres Francaises, Louis Aragon

BIOGRAPHY

Yannis Ritsos was born in Monemvasia, Greece, on May 1, 1909 to a well-heeled family of land owners. He did his early schooling in the region and finished high school in Gythion, Monemvasia and after graduating in 1925, he moved to Athens where he started working in typing and copying legal documents. A year later he returned to his hometown with the first signs of tuberculosis, where he spent his time writing and drawing, (another form of art that he devoted himself to, though second to writing), for the rest of his life.

In 1927 he went back to Athens and spent the following three years in a tuberculosis sanatorium. During these three years he started publishing poetry and he studied Marxism, committing himself to furthering the ideals of communism.

He spent some time in two different sanatoriums in Crete and finally his disease was brought under control.

Ritsos spent the following six years between 1931 and 1937 in Athens, where he worked as an actor and dancer in theatrical groups. He published his first poetry book *Tractor*, referring to the working class in 1934, and his second book *Pyramids* was released in 1935; a year later his famous *Epitaphios* was published in an edition of ten thousand copies although some of them were publicly burned by the military government of Yannis Metaxas. He had remained close to the communist party of Greece since 1931 and the ideals of the futurism of Vladamir Maïakovski inspired him to try and reach a balance between his faith in the future and his personal despair.

For six months between 1937 and 1938 he stays in the Parnitha sanatorium and during the German occupation he remained in Athens spending his time writing fervidly. Early in 1945 he joined the EAM (National Liberation Front) forces of Greece and contributed theatrical works to the people's Theatre of Macedonia. After the Varkiza agreement of disarmament of various forces, he returned to Athens and he worked as an editor for the publisher Govotsis.

In 1948 the poet is arrested and sent to exile on Limnos and then to Makronissos and later on to Saint Eustratios (Ai Strati). He wrote, undeterred by his imprisonment and kept most of his writing in bottles, while his published work was banned in the whole country. In 1952 he was freed and returned to Athens where he worked for the leftist newspaper Avgi (Dawn).

In 1954 he married Filitsa Georgiadis, a doctor on the island of Samos and their daughter Ery was born in 1955. From this point on, his work began appearing in Greece regularly and his *Moonlight Sonata* won him the National Prize for Poetry.

Three volumes of his poems were released between 1955 and 1967 when he was suddenly arrested by the colonels' junta and sent to exile on Yiaros and then Leros, and his poetry is again banned. In 1968, he is hospitalized in Athens and then sent into exile to his wife's home in Samos where he stays for a year and a half before he goes back to Athens for an operation; after the operation he stays in Athens and publishes various pieces of his poetry in the magazine Nea Keimena although his work is at the time, still officially banned.

In 1972 when the strict restrictions are eased a bit, he publishes seven volumes of poetry written during his time in exile and he is awarded the Grand Prize for Poetry at the Knokke-le-Zout Biennale later that same year. After the dictatorship is dismantled, Ritsos is a free man at last, and can devote all his time to his creative work, getting involved in the publication of everything he'd written up to that time.

In 1975, he was awarded with an honorary doctorate from University of Thessaloniki and the Alfred de Vigny Poetry Prize in France. He published the fourth volume of *Yannis Ritsos – Poems IV* in 1976, and he was awarded the International Poetry Prize of Etna Taormina of Sicily; then in 1977 the Lenin Prize for Poetry, and elected a member of the Mallarme Academy. In following years he was endowed with various awards and honorary positions, while he carried on writing fervidly and produced books regularly, up until to November 1990, when he died in his sleep after a long bout with illness. He was 81 years old.

BOOKS BY YANNIS RITSOS

Tractor, 1934
Pyramids, 1935
Epitaphios, 1936
My Sister's Song, 1937
Spring Symphony, 1938
The Ocean's March, 1940
An Old Mazurka to the Rhythm of Rain, 1943
Trial, 1943
Our Comrade, 1945
The Man with the Carnation, 1952
Vigilance, 1954
Morning Star, 1955
Moonlight Sonata, 1956
Chronicle, 1957
Winter Limpidity, 1957
Petrified Time, 1957
The World's Neighborhoods, 1957
When the Stranger Comes, 1958
Unsubjugated City, 1958
The Architecture of Trees, 1958
Beyond the Shadow of Cypresses (drama), 1959
The Old Women and the Sea, 1959
A Woman Beside the Sea (drama), 1959
The Window, 1960
The Bridge, 1960
The Black Saint, 1961
Poems (Volume I), 1961
Poems (Volume II), 1961
The Dead House, 1962
Under the Mountain's Shadow, 1962
The Prison Tree and the Women, 1963
Twelve Poems for Cavafy, 1963
Testimonies I, 1963
Poems (Volume III), 1964
Games of Sky and Water, 1964
Philoctetes, 1965
Romiosini, 1965

Testimonies II, 1966
Ostrava, 1967
Stones, Repetitions, Barrier, 1972
Helen, 1972
Gestures, 1972
Fourth Dimension, 1972
Iphigenia's Return, 1972
Chrysothemis, 1972
Ismene, 1972
Eighteen Short Songs for the Bitter Motherland, 1973
Hallway and Stairs, 1973
Garganda, 1973
Festivals and Laurels, 1973
The Annihilation of Milos, 1974
Hymn and Lamentation for Cyprus, 1974
Smoked Earthen Pot, 1974
Belltower, 1974
Paper Poems, 1974
The Wall in the Mirror, 1974
Studies (Essays), 1974
The Lady of the Vineyards, 1975
The Last Century Before Man, 1975
The Current, 1975
Poems (Volume IV), 1975
Postscript to Praise, 1975
Exile's Journals, 1975
News Bearers, 1975
The Caretaker's Desk, 1976
The Distant, 1977
Becoming, 1977
Sounder, 1978
Billposter, 1978
Traffic Controller, 1978
The Gate, 1978
Body and Blood, 1978
Women of Monemvasia, 1978
The Monstrous Masterpiece, 1978
Phaedra, 1978
Well?, 1978
The Doorbell, 1978

A Firefly Lights the Night, 1978
Scripture of the Blind, 1979
Midday Summer Dream, 1980
Transparency, 1980
Sidestreet, 1980
Monochords, 1980
Erotica, 1981
Common Songs, 1981
Ariostos the Mindful Narrates Moments of his Life and Sleep (prose), 1982
Hollow, 1982
Italian Triptych, 1982
Monovasia, 1982
Chorale of the Sponge Divers, 1983
Tiresias, 1983
What Strange Things (novel), 1983
With the Nudge of the Elbow, 1984
Tanagra Figurines, 1984
Victory Poems (Volume VIII), 1984
Perhaps it's Also this Way (novel), 1985
The Old Man with the Kites (novel), 1985
Not Only for You (novel), 1985
Sealed with a Smile (novel), 1986
Diminishing Questions (novel), 1986
Ariostos Refuses Sainthood (novel), 1986
Correspondances, 1987
3x111 Tristychs, 1987
Late, Very Late in the Night, 1988
Poems (Volume IX), 1989
Poems (Volume X), 1989
Poems (Volume XI), 1993
Poems (Volume XII), 1997
Poems (Volume XIII), 1999
Ritsos Anthology, 2000
Poems (Volume XIV), 2007

Translation

The Twelve, by Alexander Block, 1957
Anthology of Rumanian Poetry, 1961
Attila Jozsef, Poems, 1963

Vladimir Mayiakofsky Poems, 1964
I, My Mother and the World, by Dora Gabe, poetry, 1965
Nazim Hikmet Poems, 1966
The Tree by Ilya Erenburg, poetry, 1966
The Big Zoo, by Nikolas Guillen, 1966
Anthology of Czech and Slovak Poets, 1966
The Quarrelsome Goat, by Alexis Tolstoy, 1976
Sergey Yesenin Poems, 1981
Dreams With Kites and Doves, by Fereidoun Fariant, 1988

TRANSLATOR'S BIOGRAPHY

Manolis was born in the small village Kolibari west of Chania on the Greek island of Crete in 1947. At a young age his family moved first to Thessaloniki and then to Athens where he was educated, achieving a Bachelor's Degree in Political Science at Panteion Supreme School of Athens. He served in the armed forces for two years, and emigrated to Vancouver in 1973, where he worked in several different jobs over the years. He attended Simon Fraser University for a year, taking English Literature in a non-degree program. He has written three novels, a large number of collections of poetry, which are slowly appearing as published works, various articles and short stories in Greek as well as in English. After working as an iron worker, train labourer, taxi driver, and stock broker, he now lives in White Rock where he spends his time writing, gardening, and traveling. Towards the end of 2006 he founded Libros Libertad, an unorthodox and independent publishing company in Surrey, British Columbia with the goal of publishing literary books.

BOOKS BY MANOLIS

Triptych, poetry, Ekstasis Editions, 2010
Vespers, poetry and paintings, Libros Libertad, 2010
Nuances, poetry, Ekstasis Editions, 2009
Rendition, poetry, Libros Libertad, 2009
Impulses, poetry, Libros Libertad, 2009
Troglodytes, poetry, Libros Libertad, 2008
Petros Spathis, novel, Libros Libertad, 2008
El Greco, poetry, Libros Libertad, 2007
Path of Thorns, poetry, Libros Libertad, 2006
Footprints in Sandstone, poetry, Authorhouse, Bloomington, Indiana, 2006
The Orphans – an Anthology, poetry, Authorhouse, Bloomington,
    Indiana, 2005
Stratis o Roukounas, novel (in Greek), Aristidis Mavridis Publishing,
    Athens, Greece, 1981

Translation

Constantine P. Cafavy – Poems, edited by George Amabile, Libros
    Libertad, 2008